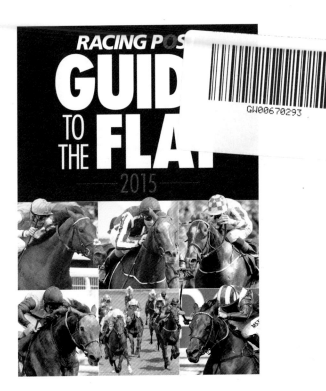

Edited and designed
by David Dew

Contributors

Tom Bull
Scott Burton
Andrew Dietz
Dave Edwards
Katherine Fidler
Nicholas Godfrey
Dylan Hill

James Hill
Ben Hutton
Paul Kealy
Lawrie Kelsey
Andrew King
Kevin Morley
Dave Orton

James Pyman
Mark Storey
Simon Turner
Johnny Ward
Nick Watts

Cover artwork by Jay Vincent
Inside artwork by Nigel Jones and Stefan Searle

Published in 2015 by Racing Post Books, Raceform, 27 Kingfisher Court, Hambridge Road, Newbury, RG14 5SJ

ISBN: 978-1-909471-93-1

LOWDOWN FROM THE TRAINERS

Andrew Balding   **4-7**
Statistical analysis   **8-10**

Marco Botti   **11-14**
Statistical analysis   **15-17**

Richard Fahey   **18-22**
Statistical analysis   **23-25**

Godolphin   **26-29**
Statistical analysis   **30-31**

John Gosden   **32-36**
Statistical analysis   **37-39**

Richard Hannon   **40-43**
Statistical analysis   **44-46**

Mark Johnston   **47-50**
Statistical analysis   **51-53**

David O'Meara   **54-57**
Statistical analysis   **58-60**

Kevin Ryan   **61-64**
Statistical analysis   **65-67**

Roger Varian   **68-70**
Statistical analysis   **71-73**

RACING POST EXPERTS

Johnny Ward View from Ireland **74-77**
Nick Watts Ante-post analysis **78-80**
James Pyman How to make a profit this season **81-90**
Paul Kealy The names to make it pay **92-95**
Katherine Fidler Tapping into potential **96-97**
Dave Orton Dark horses **98-99**
Nicholas Godfrey The international challenge **100-104**
Scott Burton View from France **105-107**

THIS SEASON'S KEY HORSES

Key contenders who can make a mark this season **108-157**
Key contenders listed by trainer **158-159**

STATISTICS

Top Flat trainers 2014 **160**
Top Flat jockeys 2014 **161**
Racing Post Ratings leading Flat performers **162-167**
Topspeed leading Flat performers **168-173**
Index of horses **174-176**

2,000 Guineas the first stop as Elm Park leads charge from Kingsclere

ANDREW BALDING: THIS SEASON'S BRIGHTEST HOPES

LAST year proved to be Andrew Balding's best since taking over the trainer's licence from his father Ian at the historic Park House Stables in Kingsclere, Berkshire, with 119 winners on the board and over £2 million in prize-money.

And Balding is confident the equine squad he has this time round is as strong a team as ever assembled at the yard with one of last season's most prolific juveniles *Elm Park* being readied for the Qipco 2,000 Guineas at Newmarket in May, *writes Andrew King*.

The trainer says of the son of Phoenix Reach: "We're very pleased with the way he's wintered and he'll be going straight to the 2,000 Guineas at Newmarket in May which was always going to be the plan.

"He's really pleased us when stepped up to slightly faster work in recent weeks and is entitled to improve with age like his sire, who was also trained at Kingsclere."

Looking back to last season Balding adds of his potential stable flagbearer: "He was a very progressive two-year-old winning four of his five outings culminating in victory in the Group 1 Racing Post Trophy at Doncaster,

"He's a quality horse who is already a Group 1 winner and has a very high cruising speed but that's not to say he'll have any problem getting longer distances later in the year.

"I couldn't be more delighted with him as he's developed well physically. After the 2,000 Guineas, as long as all is well, the obvious next step will be the Investec Derby at Epsom."

As well as Elm Park, Balding is excited about the prospects of another three-year-old in his care – namely *Rocky Rider* – who also has a Derby entry.

He says: "Rocky Rider is very well-bred and although he's not the biggest he certainly has an engine. He won in spite of the soft ground at Windsor last October.

"Being by Galileo he's bred to stay well and get better with time so we'll start him off in a handicap and take it from there. He's one to stay on the right side of."

Tullius could head to Newbury for another crack at the Lockinge

Master Apprentice is also held in high regard by Balding even though he flopped when sent to contest the Group 1 Criterium International at Saint-Cloud on his final start of last term.

The trainer explains: "He didn't travel to France very well and didn't give his true running. The form of his maiden win at Windsor before his trip to France worked out well enough and I like him a lot."

Punters looking for a darker type among the Balding three-year-olds could do worse than *Dance Of Fire*, who is likely to step up on what he showed last season.

Balding says: "He definitely strikes me as one for the future and is a potential improver when stepped up in distance this spring and summer.

"He disappointed in a Group 3 at Newmarket on his final start last year but missed the break and things just didn't work out for him. He has a workable mark of 81 to start the season."

Since being handed the reins at Kingsclere 12 years ago, Balding has excelled with seasoned horses in the yard and has a formidable array of four- and five-year-olds along with older types ready to pin their colours to the mast in the more prestigious races this term.

The trainer says: "Take *Tullius* for example – he won the Group 2 bet365 Mile at Sandown last April and went on to run some cracking races in Group 1s and Group 2s throughout the summer and autumn.

"He's likely to start off in the Doncaster Mile and then we'd probably think in terms of the Lockinge at Newbury as he was a good second in the race last year.

"He might well be seven years old now but he's rated 118 and remains a really decent horse with some give in the ground. We might try him at a mile and a quarter later on as it will open up a lot more options for him."

Another near veteran performer in Flat terms, *Side Glance*, will also be back in action this term in the hope he can regain the winning thread as he follows a similar globetrotting path to last year

Balding says: "He's still a force to be reckoned with and will be back on his travels to contest Group 1s here, there and everywhere. Although his last success was gained in 2013 – in the Group 1 Mackinnon Stakes at Flemington – he still retains much of his old ability and is obviously a favourite in the yard, when he is actually here!"

Balding has long been a believer in travelling his horses to anywhere he considers they have more than a reasonable chance of making the trip pay off, and the likes of

Elm Park: expected to stay the Derby trip and likely to head to Epsom after 2,000 Guineas

DID YOU KNOW

Andrew Balding won the Oaks in his first year holding a licence. He'd just taken over from his father Ian when his Casual Look struck in the fillies' Classic at Epsom in 2003. Balding hasn't tasted Classic glory since, but his time will surely come again soon.

Havana Beat and *Here Comes When* are perfect examples.

He says: "Havana Beat pleased me with his return to action when fourth at Meydan in February as that was his first run since a fast-finishing third in the American St Leger at Arlington last August

"He's a nice horse who stays well. As he won over two miles at Sandown last summer we might be looking at something like the Yorkshire Cup with him this spring.

"Here Comes When has a mark of 116 going into the new season but has relatively low mileage on the clock and is still going to be a force at seven furlongs and a mile. I think a mile will ultimately be his limit tripwise.

"There was much to like about the way he finished last season in style by winning a Group 2 at Baden-Baden before returning to the domestic front and landing another Group 2 at Newmarket in October. He remains progressive."

The Master of Kingsclere had high hopes for **Scotland** this time 12 months ago after he finished his previous term with a ready success at Epsom, but the son of Monsun failed to live up to expectations

Balding says: "Our positive thoughts about Scotland did not quite materialise despite the horse performing to a very high level in all his races throughout the summer and autumn.

"He's been gelded over the winter and it doesn't appear to have done him any harm as he was always getting a bit worked up and on edge beforehand but that's not the case at present.

"We'll start him off at a mile and a half but I'll definitely not be scared to step him back up to a mile and six furlongs at some stage over the summer."

Absolutely So failed to get the best of passages in the Group 2 Champions Sprint at Ascot at the end of last season but was beaten only just over four lengths and Balding is looking to start him off at Haydock in the John of Gaunt Stakes.

"He's a decent horse on his day but can be a bit hit and miss. I think he's ideally suited by

Here Comes When (front right): could be open to further improvement

a bit of give in the ground over six or seven furlongs, so the Haydock race at the latter trip seems a decent target."

Chesil Beach and *Montaly* both made giant strides up the handicap last year and Balding is preparing the duo to carry on the good work.

Balding says: "Chesil Beach rattled off four wins at the end of last season which saw her rise through the handicap ranks from 65 to a mark of 88.

"I'd like to think there's more to come as she seems progressive and there's no reason why she can't continue to hold her own in decent handicaps throughout the season.

"Montaly also went the right way as he was on a mark of 79 but finished up on 97. Being by Yeats he should improve with age and we'll pick and choose handicaps with him. He wouldn't want the ground too fast, though."

Mymatechris and *Nabatean* are a couple of handicappers going the right way who should earn their keep over the spring and summer months according to the trainer, who says: "Mymatechris has been very pleasing in the way he's progressed this winter on the all-weather and, with that in mind, he could have a crack at the two-mile race at Lingfield on Good Friday.

"Nabatean stays well and seems to like soft ground. He might be on the right side of the handicapper and is on the cusp of squeezing into one of the decent heritage handicaps at some stage."

ANDREW BALDING: ASSESSING THE STATS

Andrew Balding went frustratingly close in 2013 to breaking the century barrier for the first time, clocking 99 winners. He didn't need to wait much longer to achieve that landmark, though, as he sent out 119 winners last term, while a prize-money tally of just over £2 million was also a personal best, *writes Kevin Morley*.

The bias in his yard leans towards three-year-olds, who were profitable to follow to a level stake last term, while the older horses were nowhere near as beneficial to punters. Balding doesn't rush the development of his horses, so it is no surprise to learn two-year-olds make up the least of his overall tally, although he did enjoy a fair campaign with his youngsters last term.

The output in terms of volume was no more than standard with his juveniles but he unleashed a potential star in the shape of Elm Park, who won four of his five starts, culminating with victory in the Group 1 Racing Post Trophy. That contest has produced its fair share of subsequent Derby winners and at this stage Elm Park rates a leading contender for Epsom in June.

Balding strikes at a reasonable rate in handicaps, maidens and Group races but cannot be backed blind in any category.

In terms of distance, older horses do best from a mile to 1m2f, while the layers are often caught out by his stayers in the three-year-old division. There is no specific time of year when Balding excels although he has had a noticeably strong finish to the last two campaigns.

Unusually for a jockey who rides a large portion of the stable's winners, David Probert returns a big level-stake profit for the yard over the past five seasons, which is quite an achievement considering the sample size. Oisin Murphy is a rider going places and Balding is one of many trainers utilising his talent, which has been of benefit to punters judging by his record for the stable. On a smaller scale, the mounts of Andrea Atzeni are worth looking out for as he was three from four for the yard in 2014.

Balding doesn't have an outstanding record at any particular track but performs solidly at the majority with his best figures coming at Chepstow, Chester, Sandown and Windsor. He also sends out plenty of winners on the all-weather but isn't shy on attempts at the various sand tracks so a selective approach is needed when backing his runners on the artificial surfaces.

Andrew Balding's second lot walks through the avenue of trees at Park House Stables after exercise

ANDREW BALDING

KINGSCLERE, HANTS

	No. of Hrs	Races Run	1st	2nd	3rd	Unpl	Per cent	£1 Level Stake
2-y-o	37	96	17	14	13	52	17.7	-6.42
3-y-o	67	340	69	42	57	172	20.3	+15.09
4-y-o+	40	223	33	27	18	144	14.8	-44.28
Totals	144	659	119	83	88	368	18.1	-35.61
2013	153	713	99	93	105	416	13.9	+46.20
2012	161	712	93	96	83	440	13.1	-59.64

BY MONTH

2-y-o	W-R	Per cent	£1 Level Stake	3-y-o	W-R	Per cent	£1 Level Stake
January	0-0	0.0	0.00	January	2-4	50.0	+0.19
February	0-0	0.0	0.00	February	4-10	40.0	-0.40
March	0-0	0.0	0.00	March	9-21	42.9	-0.72
April	0-0	0.0	0.00	April	6-35	17.1	+8.10
May	0-2	0.0	-2.00	May	7-47	14.9	-23.13
June	0-5	0.0	-5.00	June	5-43	11.6	-8.25
July	2-7	28.6	+4.50	July	5-33	15.2	+11.50
August	3-15	20.0	-7.38	August	7-36	19.4	+18.88
September	4-22	18.2	-6.75	September	7-45	15.6	+5.75
October	5-26	19.2	+11.09	October	6-38	15.8	-0.17
November	2-12	16.7	-6.88	November	2-12	16.7	-4.09
December	1-7	14.3	+6.00	December	9-16	56.3	+7.42

4-y-o	W-R	Per cent	£1 Level Stake	Totals	W-R	Per cent	£1 Level Stake
January	0-10	0.0	-10.00	January	2-14	14.3	-9.81
February	0-8	0.0	-8.00	February	4-18	22.2	-8.40
March	2-11	18.2	-4.75	March	11-32	34.4	-5.47
April	4-18	22.2	-4.15	April	10-53	18.9	+3.95
May	8-34	23.5	+1.25	May	15-83	18.1	-23.88
June	3-30	10.0	-17.00	June	8-78	10.3	-30.25
July	4-23	17.4	+8.25	July	11-63	17.5	+24.25
August	2-27	7.4	-9.00	August	12-78	15.4	+2.50
September	1-19	5.3	-16.13	September	12-86	14.0	-17.13
October	5-23	21.7	+19.50	October	16-87	18.4	+30.42
November	2-12	16.7	-2.25	November	6-36	16.7	-6.34
December	2-8	25.0	-2.00	December	12-31	38.7	+5.42

DISTANCE

2-y-o	W-R	Per cent	£1 Level Stake	3-y-o	W-R	Per cent	£1 Level Stake
5f-6f	2-18	11.1	-10.25	5f-6f	8-28	28.6	-3.11
7f-8f	15-74	20.3	+7.83	7f-8f	21-122	17.2	+10.80
9f-13f	0-4	0.0	-4.00	9f-13f	33-169	19.5	-0.80
14f+	0-0	0.0	0.00	14f+	7-21	33.3	+8.19

4-y-o	W-R	Per cent	£1 Level Stake	Totals	W-R	Per cent	£1 Level Stake
5f-6f	10-57	17.5	-5.50	5f-6f	20-103	19.4	-18.86
7f-8f	12-90	13.3	-20.90	7f-8f	48-286	16.8	-2.27
9f-13f	6-47	12.8	-14.25	9f-13f	39-220	17.7	-19.05
14f+	5-29	17.2	-3.63	14f+	12-50	24.0	+4.56

TYPE OF RACE

Non-Handicaps	W-R	Per cent	£1 Level Stake	Handicaps	W-R	Per cent	£1 Level Stake
2-y-o	14-84	16.7	-7.17	2-y-o	3-12	25.0	+0.75
3-y-o	24-133	18.0	-25.64	3-y-o	45-207	21.7	+40.73
4-y-o+	8-62	12.9	+19.00	4-y-o+	25-161	15.5	-30.65

RACE CLASS

	W-R	Per cent	£1 Level Stake
Class 1	9-76	11.8	-27.25
Class 2	19-122	15.6	+10.88
Class 3	14-59	23.7	+22.00
Class 4	25-135	18.5	+3.95
Class 5	39-202	19.3	-35.89
Class 6	13-64	20.3	-8.28
Class 7	0-1	0.0	-1.00

FIRST TIME OUT

	W-R	Per cent	£1 Level Stake
2-y-o	2-37	5.4	-17.00
3-y-o	10-67	14.9	-30.43
4-y-o+	8-40	20.0	-9.90
Totals	20-144	13.9	-57.33

Second lot exercises at Andrew Balding's Park House Stables

Charline and Boistron back to assist in another big campaign for Botti

IN the seven years since Marco Botti began training in Newmarket he has established himself as willing to send horses from Ascot to Arlington and Carlisle to California in search of winners.

His globetrotting style has brought him success, international recognition and the respect of peers and punters alike, *writes Lawrie Kelsey*.

In 2014 Botti saddled 80 winners and amassed his best prize-money tally so far of nearly £1.6 million. Big contributors to that figure were Beverly D Stakes winner Euro Charline and Tac De Boistron, winner of the Group 1 Prix Royal-Oak at Longchamp.

Both stay in training with Botti hoping the eight-year-old *Tac De Boistron* can tick some of the same boxes as last season, starting with the Group 2 Yorkshire Cup, in which he was beaten narrowly last year. He will then head to Royal Ascot for the Gold Cup, as long as the ground isn't too quick.

"Last year we wanted to run him in the Gold Cup but the ground went against us, so we didn't run," says Botti. "He's ground dependent and the softer the better.

"We don't want to jar him up, so if he doesn't run at Ascot we've got other options, one of which is a Group 2 over a mile and six furlongs at Longchamp four days later. If all things go well we could then run him in the Irish St Leger."

After that the itinerary switches to France,

where the Group 1 Prix du Cadran comes in to play – a race in which he was second in 2013, as well as the Group 1 Prix Royal-Oak, which he has won for the last two years.

"He's been an amazing horse for us and looks as good as ever. We've had a mild winter and he's done very well. He's exactly where we want to be," says Botti.

Euro Charline became the first three-year-old filly to win the Beverly D Stakes at Arlington since the race's inception in 1987, earning £257,000 and her trainer's eternal gratitude.

She should have stayed in America to continue racing but suffered a minor fracture in a hind ankle needing arthroscopic surgery, and so was returned to Botti.

The supermare is primed for a crack at the Dubai Turf, formerly the Dubai Duty Free, on World Cup night at Meydan at the end of March.

"It won't be an easy task but she's wintered very well and I couldn't be happier with her," says Botti, who aims to see how she fares in Dubai before mapping out a route through the season that could take in Singapore at the end of May and Royal Ascot.

Naadirr is a tough colt who takes his racing well. He ran six times from April to September last year, starting off with a third in a big sales race at Newmarket and never being out of the first four, including a Group 3 at Newbury, before winning a Listed race at York.

"He was a little weak as a two-year-old but has improved with age. In fact, he improved quite a lot as a three-year-old and has done really well through the winter," says Botti.

"He's developed into a proper sprinter and I'm really looking forward to running him."

He'll start off in a 6f Listed race at Doncaster and if Botti is satisfied with that run, next stop could be the Group 2 Duke of York Stakes over the same distance at the Dante meeting in May.

If Naadirr is still progressing, the Group 1 Diamond Jubilee Stakes at Royal Ascot and Newmarket's July Cup will be considered.

"He's a very exciting horse, possibly the best sprinter I've trained. He's already got some black type but he could be anything," Botti adds.

Unraced at two, *Moohaarib* progressed throughout last season to win three of nine races, ending with a rating of 100. Botti has him primed for a spring campaign, and says: "He's a miler and could be a Listed or Group horse eventually, but he needs good to soft ground so it's doubtful we would run him in the summer. He's more of a spring and autumn horse.

"He's done really well over the winter. He's in fast work, looks great and is ready to run."

Lady Dutch has been a revelation since arriving from Italy in December, adapting to the English weather and a new training regime surprisingly well. She arrived with Botti having finished a close second in the Italian Guineas as well as winning three other races and being placed in a trio of Group and Listed contests.

Those careful form students would have been delighted with odds of 8-1 when she won a six-runner conditions race at Kempton towards the end of February on her British debut.

"That was impressive. We were so pleased because it showed she had adapted well," says Botti. "She was already a black-type filly in Italy and now we'd like her to get some black type over here."

As part of that plan Lady Dutch has been entered for the Listed Snowdrop Stakes at Kempton in April. "We'll see how she goes, then she could go to Epsom for the Group 3 Princess Elizabeth Stakes at the Derby meeting.

"If she performs well we could think about the Group 2 Duke of Cambridge Stakes at Royal Ascot. She's a tough filly."

Pelerin could take a similar path to her stablemate. The Snowdrop Stakes might come a little too soon for her but the Princess Elizabeth and Duke of Cambridge have been pencilled in.

Unlucky in a summer Listed race at Newbury when traffic problems cost her victory, she achieved her trainer's hopes of earning black type by justifying favouritism in a Dundalk Listed race at the end of October.

"She's done very well over the winter and looks stronger than last year. Her target is the Beverly D at Arlington, which we won with Euro Charline."

Alfajer ran twice as a juvenile, running a

well-regarded John Gosden newcomer with a subsequent 1,000 Guineas entry close in a backend Newmarket maiden. She opened her account in style a month later at Lingfield with a strong front-running performance.

"She's a nice filly who has always shown a good attitude at home," says Botti. "She's done very well during the winter physically and looks strong. We have high expectations.

"She's in the Guineas and we'll run her in one of the trials – either the Nell Gwyn or Fred Darling – depending on the ground. She also hold entries in the French Guineas.

"She's training well and looks great. So far we couldn't have asked for any more from her – she's genuine and very straightforward.

"Later on, the Coronation Stakes at Royal Ascot could be a possibility."

Puissant is a Galileo brother to Adelaide. He won a Redcar maiden in October after finishing runner-up at Newcastle two weeks earlier.

"He was a breeze-up horse and took a while to settle with us – he was a little nervous. He's done very well through the winter though, chilled out, grown and trained on.

"We'll start him off at the Newmarket Craven meeting in a Listed race over a mile and one furlong. It's early days but he's in the French Derby and the English Derby is a possible. At this stage we have high hopes."

Astrelle ran nine times as a two-year-old, winning twice and finishing in the frame three times, including a close runner-up in the Group 3 Oh So Sharp Stakes at Newmarket to the Godolphin hotpot Local Time, who has won her last six races and is a strong Guineas fancy.

Not surprisingly, Botti describes Astrelle as tough and consistent and is full of hope: "I'm really pleased with her – she's done very well over the winter. She's in the Irish Guineas and will go for one of the trials. We'll also give her an entry in the German Guineas.

"I'm confident she'll make a Group 1 filly. We'll put her in all the major races and concentrate on improving her black type. Her best trip will be seven furlongs to a mile. I don't think she'll stay further."

Soluble is another of Botti's two-year-olds from last year that is exciting him, and not just because of his 400,000gns price tag.

Weak and backward as a juvenile, the Galileo colt out of an unraced sister to top-class Shirocco grew and strengthened over the winter and was given his first outing in a Wolverhampton maiden in mid-February.

He won in a three-way photo-finish to Botti's delight and shock. "We didn't expect him to win first time out. It was a surprise because we thought he'd need the race, although we knew he was stronger," Botti says. "He was very game and stuck his neck out. He'll get at least a mile and a quarter and there's a lot more improvement to come."

He is entered in the two Tattersalls sales races at the Craven meeting but Botti is considering the handicap route for Soluble, probably Class 3 over 1m2f.

Another entrant for those races is the unraced Cape Cross filly *Talawat*, who cost 260,000gns.

"She's working well and we have her quite forward, so it won't be long before we see her on the track. We'll start her off over a mile

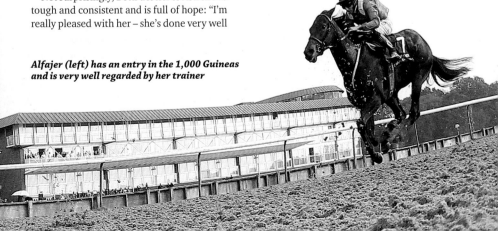

Alfajer (left) has an entry in the 1,000 Guineas and is very well regarded by her trainer

and a quarter," says Botti. "She could go for a Newbury fillies' maiden at the Greenham meeting. We've entered her for the French Oaks but whether she'll be a black-type filly time will tell."

Fanciful Angel won his maiden and was considered good enough to tackle the Group 3 Sirenia Stakes at Kempton in September, where he finished fourth of ten, before ending the season with third place in a York Listed race.

"He'll start in a Listed race to see if he's up to earning black type, then it will be decision time," says Botti.

The trainer is not renowned for having early two-year-olds, preferring not to rush them, but he has a couple who are already beginning to raise his hopes.

One is an unnamed colt by Champs Elysees out of Dahama, a half-brother to impressive Group 2 Rockfel winner Al Thakhira, setting a record for the opening day of the Tattersalls December Foal Sale when selling for 160,000gns.

"He's a nice type who is bigger than his half-sister," says Botti. "He's a good mover and has more scope than her. I don't think he'll be a sprinter from what I've seen, so he'll probably start out over seven furlongs some time in June."

Another juvenile getting Botti excited is an unnamed Lawman filly out of Rose De France, who cost €520,000 at Goffs. She is a three-quarters sister to last year's Dewhurst Stakes runner-up Cable Bay bought by Saleh Al Homaizi and Imad Al Sagar, owners of Derby winner Authorized.

"I can see why she was so expensive. She's a lovely filly with plenty of class and is very easy to deal with. She won't be a sprinter but she's showing plenty of class so far," he says.

"She's pleasing me. She's very straight-forward and enjoying things."

Another unnamed two-year-old for the notebook is a Zoffany colt out of Attalea, who could be interesting according to Botti.

"He's quite big for a two-year-old, so I see him starting out over six furlongs, but he'll definitely get a mile in time. He looks a really smart horse with a great temperament. He could be a Royal Ascot horse."

The Dandy Man juvenile *Onesie* is a nice type who looks a proper two-year-old, according to his trainer: "I'm very pleased with him and he could be one of our early two-year-olds. He's going well and has a great attitude. He's showing some speed, so we'll start him off over five or six furlongs."

MARCO BOTTI
NEWMARKET, SUFFOLK

	No. of Hrs	Races Run	1st	2nd	3rd	Unpl	Per cent	£1 Level Stake
2-y-o	41	129	19	18	27	65	14.7	-2.81
3-y-o	70	276	40	43	28	165	14.5	-90.40
4-y-o+	40	174	21	22	20	111	12.1	-30.57
Totals	151	579	80	83	75	341	13.8	-123.78
2013	149	541	89	92	84	275	16.5	-21.11
2012	105	372	52	48	45	227	14.0	-13.13

BY MONTH

2-y-o	W-R	Per cent	£1 Level Stake	3-y-o	W-R	Per cent	£1 Level Stake
January	0-0	0.0	0.00	January	1-8	12.5	-4.50
February	0-0	0.0	0.00	February	3-16	18.8	-4.79
March	0-0	0.0	0.00	March	4-18	22.2	-5.90
April	0-0	0.0	0.00	April	5-51	9.8	-13.60
May	0-4	0.0	-4.00	May	4-44	9.1	-27.23
June	0-10	0.0	-10.00	June	7-38	18.4	-1.25
July	1-12	8.3	-9.90	July	4-27	14.8	-14.17
August	6-20	30.0	+11.02	August	1-23	4.3	-12.00
September	3-24	12.5	-11.75	September	3-18	16.7	-2.50
October	7-29	24.1	2.82	October	4-18	22.2	-2.00
November	2-13	15.4	+36.00	November	2-12	16.7	-6.38
December	0-17	0.0	-17.00	December	2-3	66.7	+3.91

4-y-o	W-R	Per cent	£1 Level Stake	Totals	W-R	Per cent	£1 Level Stake
January	3-17	17.6	-8.58	January	4-25	16.0	-13.08
February	3-13	23.1	+10.25	February	6-29	20.7	+5.46
March	1-10	10.0	-8.50	March	5-28	17.9	-14.40
April	1-14	7.1	-9.50	April	6-65	9.2	-23.10
May	3-26	11.5	+15.50	May	7-74	9.5	-15.73
June	1-16	6.3	-12.00	June	8-64	12.5	-23.25
July	2-11	18.2	+2.75	July	7-50	14.0	-21.32
August	2-15	13.3	+14.00	August	9-58	15.5	+13.02
September	1-14	7.1	-9.67	September	7-56	12.5	-23.92

DISTANCE

2-y-o	W-R	Per cent	£1 Level Stake	3-y-o	W-R	Per cent	£1 Level Stake
5f-6f	3-34	8.8	-23.65	5f-6f	8-48	16.7	+5.33
7f-8f	15-91	16.5	+9.84	7f-8f	17-109	15.6	-51.00
9f-13f	1-4	25.0	+11.00	9f-13f	14-115	12.2	-48.24
14f+	0-0	0.0	0.00	14f+	1-4	25.0	+3.50

4-y-o	W-R	Per cent	£1 Level Stake	Totals	W-R	Per cent	£1 Level Stake
5f-6f	1-21	4.8	-16.50	5f-6f	12-103	11.7	-34.82
7f-8f	6-54	11.1	-36.75	7f-8f	38-254	15.0	-77.91
9f-13f	12-83	14.5	+23.18	9f-13f	27-202	13.4	-14.06
14f+	2-16	12.5	-0.50	14f+	3-20	15.0	+3.00

TYPE OF RACE

Non-Handicaps	W-R	Per cent	£1 Level Stake	Handicaps	W-R	Per cent	£1 Level Stake
2-y-o	13-113	11.5	-15.25	2-y-o	6-16	37.5	+12.44
3-y-o	17-127	13.4	-78.34	3-y-o	23-149	15.4	-12.07
4-y-o+	12-60	20.0	+36.00	4-y-o+	9-114	7.9	-17.75

RACE CLASS

	W-R	Per cent	£1 Level Stake
Class 1	11-77	14.3	-28.98
Class 2	11-122	9.0	-24.08
Class 3	10-47	21.3	-11.23
Class 4	20-102	19.6	+21.61
Class 5	25-204	12.3	-70.46
Class 6	3-27	11.1	-10.63
Class 7	0-0	0.0	0.00

FIRST TIME OUT

	W-R	Per cent	£1 Level Stake
2-y-o	1-41	2.4	-7.00
3-y-o	7-70	10.0	-33.01
4-y-o+	5-40	12.5	-22.75
Totals	13-151	8.6	-62.76

Astrelle (below right) has wintered well and is expected to improve at three

MARCO BOTTI: ASSESSING THE STATS

Marco Botti is one of the more progressive trainers on the Flat. The 80 winners he sent out in 2014 wasn't as high as the 89 the previous term but there was a significant increase in prize-money. In 2013, Botti broke the £1 million barrier for the first but he beat that comfortably last season, amassing over £1.5m, *writes Kevin Morley*.

That was largely to his impressive team of handicappers led by De Rigeur and Suegioo, with the latter's Chester Cup victory the highlight in that respect. Botti also knows how to get the job done in Pattern company with Guest Of Honour's win in Ascot's Group 2 Summer Mile his highest achievement on these shores.

However, the Newmarket handler is no stranger to Group 1 success abroad. Botti has had winners at the highest level in America, Canada and France, and Tac De Boistron securing his second successive Prix Royal-Oak at the Arc meeting was probably the stable's proudest moment last year. To take his career to the next stage Botti needs to break the century barrier and score a first British Group 1.

Most of Botti's winners last season came with three-year-olds, but the strike-rates are fairly even in all age groups. Handicappers provide most of the successes, with the juveniles standing out in this respect from a level-stake perspective, but the trainer also has solid strike-rates in Group races, maidens, even sellers and claimers. He also sends out plenty of winners over a variety of distances although he is best followed in races between a mile and 1m4f.

Most of the yard's winners are ridden by Martin Harley but better profits are secured by backing the mounts of Andrea Atzeni. It is worth watching out for the few occasions when Ryan Moore is in the saddle.

Unlike most leading Flat yards, Botti sends out plenty of winners on the all-weather. He keeps himself particularly busy on the artificial surfaces during the winter months and his string often has a fitness advantage at the beginning of the turf season. He has a high turnover of runners at Lingfield, Kempton and Wolverhampton with his figures at the latter venue significantly better than any of the other sand tracks.

On turf, Botti's record at Ascot catches the eye, especially when considering the competitive nature of racing at the Berkshire venue. At a lower level, watch out for his raids to Yorkshire as he boasts decent records at Beverley, Redcar and Thirsk.

Tac De Boistron landed the Prix Royal-Oak at Longchamp for the second time last season

Powerful yard might be missing a star but another early start is on the cards

I**T IS no secret Richard Fahey likes to get the turf season off to a flyer and this year will be no exception.**

The former journeyman jockey, who once said he gave up riding before it gave him up, is now in his 22nd season as a trainer and is held in high regard by his peers and punters alike, *writes Lawrie Kelsey.*

So the powerful raiding party he will launch on Town Moor from his Musley Bank stables in Malton, North Yorkshire, will be scrutinised forensically by punters well aware Fahey knows precisely what is needed to land Doncaster's two major handicap prizes – the Lincoln and Spring Mile.

This year he has nine entered in the Lincoln but take particular note of *Gabrial's Kaka*, owned by Marwan Koukash, another man who takes pleasure in targeting the Doncaster meeting.

The five-year-old was beaten a little over five lengths carrying 8st 10lb in last year's race, then won the Newbury Spring Cup on his next outing two weeks later. He has been allotted 9st 1lb this year.

In the same ownership and due to carry 1lb less is *Gabrial*, winner of the Doncaster Spring Mile in 2013 and rated 111 when third in that year's Group 3 Diomed Stakes.

He tumbled to a mark of 94 after a moderate season last year but is now on a rating of 100 after landing a Leicester handicap in October.

The third Lincoln entry to note is *Spirit Of The Law* (8st 5lb), who won a well-contested

York handicap in June and ended last season finishing runner-up in another good handicap on the Knavesmire.

After a memorable year in 2014 which brought a record 192 winners and a couple of pay packets under £3m in prize-money, this year is unlikely to reach such heights, as Fahey admits.

"I think we might be lacking in a bit of quality this year – no Group 1 horses," he says, but nevertheless he hopes *Akeed Champion* can live up to his promise.

He opened his career with an impressive second in a September Ascot maiden but was only fourth in a York maiden a month later when the team expected victory.

"He's ground dependent and it was very soft at York that day, which he didn't like. He'd have won with better ground," the trainer says.

"He's quite a nice horse. He's in the 2,000 Guineas and will definitely go for a trial. He's very well and we're very hopeful with him."

Lacing's victory in the Tattersalls Millions Fillies' Stakes at Newmarket and runner-up in a similar sales race over course and distance a fortnight later helped towards the Fahey annus mirabilis in 2014.

The aim this season is to earn some black type to boost her paddock value but there is no racing plan mapped out as yet, save for precautionary entries in the two Tattersalls sales races at the Newmarket Craven meeting.

The same entries have been made for the gelding *Ballymore Castle*, who stepped up on an encouraging third in a Newbury

Gabrial's Kaka is likely to be in action early this season

DID YOU KNOW

Richard Fahey has been a trainer for over 20 years, but he started out as a jockey and rode over 100 winners under both codes. Fahey won the conditional jockeys' title one year.

maiden to land a similar contest at Chester last May before finishing second in the Woodcote Stakes at Epsom.

"He's a nice, progressive type. He's wintered well and we're pleased with him, although we haven't done too much with him yet. He could get further, eventually, maybe a mile," says Fahey.

There are few secrets surrounding the seven-year-old gelding *Alben Star*, whose 33 races have brought seven victories, four seconds and three thirds, amassing more than £180,000 in prize-money and earning that well-worn epithet 'grand old servant'.

He has little to prove to connections, but Fahey is aiming to pick up a handicap this season and his first target is Lingfield's All-Weather Championship on Good Friday.

"He's been a little disappointing this winter but he's in good form now and we're hopeful for Lingfield. After that he'll be entered in all the big handicaps," says Fahey.

Eastern Impact had a good campaign last year, beginning on a mark of 93, dropping to 91 after two moderate runs, then rising to 105 by the season's end after winning a pair of Newmarket handicaps and being pipped in a third.

There is little wonder Fahey has plenty of time for the four-year-old gelding, whom he not surprisingly describes as progressive.

"He'll probably run at the Guineas meeting in a handicap, then we might think about Group races – he's knocking on the door," says Fahey.

Duke Of Clare Tachophobia nce ran only three times last season, opening with a seventh in the Chester Cup and finishing with very close seconds in big handicaps at York and Newmarket to earn a rating of 101. He

will be aimed at the Chester Cup again in the hope of going one better than the owner's Angel Gabrial in last year's race.

"He's had a little setback but he's been back in training for the last couple of months. He's a nice staying handicapper," says Fahey.

For a filly who was "always going to be a three-year-old" *Home Cummins* had an impressive juvenile season.

Costing €75,000 as a foal, the daughter of Rip Van Winkle out of a French Listed winner up to 1m1f was well backed on her debut and was just run out of it close home with the rest of the field eight lengths away.

She duly obliged next time at Redcar at odds of 1-2 before a creditable fourth in a hot Newmarket nursery in August after a two-month break. She then landed a Doncaster nursery before ending the season with a disappointing eighth of nine in the Group 2 Rockfel at Newmarket.

"She's a very nice filly and we're very pleased with the progress she's making," says her trainer. "She'll get seven furlongs."

Liberty Sky, another daughter by Rip Van Winkle, is a half-sister to four winners, including Missit, who won a Grade 2 in America. She is well regarded at Musley Bank and had only one outing last year when third in a Doncaster maiden in June. She ran unsurprisingly green but realised what was required of her late on and finished to good effect, albeit more than four lengths off the winner.

It was a run full of promise, however, and she has progressed over the winter to Fahey's satisfaction. "She's big but she's a nice filly

Lacing (right) did well last season and will be sent in pursuit of black type this year

who could be anything," he says. "She probably won't be out too early."

Abbey Angel ran green on her debut at Haydock towards the end of May, wanting to lug left under Tony Hamilton from over one out, yet she still finished within two lengths of the winner.

The run promised much, particularly as she is a half-sister to a couple of winners and, although she could finish only fourth at Doncaster next time out, the progression was showing.

She ended the season with victory in a Pontefract nursery, earning a rating of 90.

"She's a nice, progressive filly," says Fahey. "She's come through the winter well but there are no plans. We'll just see how she goes."

Arcano Gold began his career with two undistinguished runs at York, but then perked up with a couple of thirds at Newcastle and Leicester before hitting form with a close second in a Doncaster nursery to stablemate *Tachophobia*.

He finally broke his duck by winning at Nottingham in November over 1m½f and earning the description of "nice, progressive handicapper" from his trainer.

The colt has wintered well and is expected to improve further this season.

One Musley Bank inmate who could be anything is *Flashy Memories*, particularly after an impressive debut in a Redcar maiden in November, which he won in eyecatching style by three lengths.

"It was no surprise he won as he did because he'd been working well at home," reveals Fahey. "He's by Dubawi, so he'll get better with age. He's still learning and will get a mile-plus. He's done well over the winter."

Heaven's Guest is one of the toughest old handicappers in Fahey's yard and proved it by landing the Bunbury Cup on Newmarket's July Course last July, one of the most difficult handicaps of the season.

That followed four handicap wins the previous year, bringing his tally to six from 24 outings, as well as a couple of runner-up spots.

"He'll go the same route as last year, starting in a six-furlong race at Doncaster. We're always ready early and have plenty of ammo for Donny, and he'll be part of the team" says Fahey.

The agenda for Heaven's Guest after that could take in the Victoria Cup, Buckingham Palace Stakes and the Ayr Gold Cup.

RICHARD FAHEY

MUSLEY BANK, N YORKS

	No. of Hrs	Races Run	1st	2nd	3rd	Unpl	Per cent	£1 Level Stake
2-y-o	117	473	68	68	53	281	14.4	-19.07
3-y-o	84	482	65	61	57	298	13.5	-30.08
4-y-o+	78	547	59	77	66	343	10.8	-70.08
Totals	279	1502	192	206	176	922	12.8	-119.23
2013	240	1287	164	162	155	803	12.7	-84.97
2012	235	1294	142	158	135	856	11.0	-187.44

BY MONTH

2-y-o	W-R	Per cent	£1 Level Stake	Hurdles	W-R	Per cent	£1 Level Stake
January	0-0	0.0	0.00	January	2-14	14.3	-10.20
February	0-0	0.0	0.00	February	2-11	18.2	-5.88
March	0-0	0.0	0.00	March	1-14	7.1	-10.75
April	4-18	22.2	-4.27	April	6-53	11.3	-24.75
May	10-48	20.8	-7.28	May	11-80	13.8	+4.78
June	8-61	13.1	-3.27	June	14-84	16.7	+36.83
July	8-77	10.4	-32.59	July	8-62	12.9	-14.25
August	12-77	15.6	-13.63	August	11-60	18.3	+0.88
September	11-94	11.7	-13.50	September	2-44	4.5	-29.25
October	8-64	12.5	-3.13	October	6-38	15.8	+28.00
November	5-21	23.8	-2.40	November	2-14	14.3	+2.50
December	2-13	15.4	+61.00	December	0-8	0.0	-8.00

4-y-o+	W-R	Per cent	£1 Level Stake	Totals	W-R	Per cent	£1 Level Stake
January	6-32	18.8	+20.50	January	8-46	17.4	+10.30
February	1-12	8.3	-9.13	February	3-23	13.0	-15.01
March	3-20	15.0	+7.00	March	4-34	11.8	-3.75
April	6-49	12.2	+12.25	April	16-120	13.3	-16.77
May	6-77	7.8	-39.50	May	27-205	13.2	-42.00
June	10-73	13.7	+6.88	June	32-218	14.7	+40.44
July	4-48	8.3	-9.50	July	20-187	10.7	-56.34
August	11-69	15.9	-1.17	August	34-206	16.5	-13.92
September	3-70	4.3	-34.50	September	16-208	7.7	-77.25
October	5-58	8.6	-13.67	October	19-160	11.9	+11.20
November	4-22	18.2	+7.75	November	11-57	19.3	+10.25
December	0-17	0.0	-17.00	December	2-38	5.3	-25.00

DISTANCE

2-y-o	W-R	Per cent	£1 Level Stake	3-y-o	W-R	Per cent	£1 Level Stake
5f-6f	45-323	13.9	+26.14	5f-6f	16-147	10.9	-50.42
7f-8f	23-148	15.5	-43.22	7f-8f	29-219	13.2	-29.37
9f-13f	0-2	0.0	-2.00	9f-13f	19-108	17.6	+51.71
14f+	0-0	0.0	0.00	14f+	1-8	12.5	-2.00

4-y-o	W-R	Per cent	£1 Level Stake	Totals	W-R	Per cent	£1 Level Stake
5f-6f	17-156	10.9	+12.88	5f-6f	78-626	12.5	-11.40
7f-8f	22-200	11.0	-41.79	7f-8f	74-567	13.1	-114.38
9f-13f	17-155	11.0	-33.67	9f-13f	36-265	13.6	+16.04
14f+	3-36	8.3	-7.50	14f+	4-44	9.1	-9.50

TYPE OF RACE

Non-Handicaps	W-R	Per cent	£1 Level Stake	Handicaps	W-R	Per cent	£1 Level Stake
2-y-o	47-358	13.1	-52.95	2-y-o	21-115	18.3	+33.88
3-y-o	11-106	10.4	-47.59	3-y-o	54-376	14.4	+17.51
4-y-o+	4-47	8.5	+5.00	4-y-o+	55-500	11.0	-58.67

RACE CLASS / FIRST TIME OUT

	W-R	Per cent	£1 Level Stake		W-R	Per cent	£1 Level Stake
Class 1	2-60	3.3	-50.00	2-y-o	16-117	13.7	+53.10
Class 2	25-278	9.0	+11.50	3-y-o	7-84	8.3	-41.70
Class 3	26-210	12.4	-3.19	4-y-o+	6-78	7.7	24.00
Class 4	47-345	13.6	-97.50				
Class 5	67-470	14.3	+0.54	Totals	29-279	10.4	-12.60
Class 6	25-139	18.0	+19.41				
Class 7	0-0	0.0	0.00				

Tough Heaven's Guest will be plying his trade in the big sprints again this season

RICHARD FAHEY: ASSESSING THE STATS

Last year was record-breaking for Richard Fahey on the numbers front. With 192 winners on the board and over £2.8 million amassed in prize-money, the Musley Bank handler continues to gradually improve his yard's output. The only disappointing aspect from his stable's performance was the lack of success at pattern level with Sandiva's win in the Nell Gwyn the only one in Group company in 2014, *writes Kevin Morley*.

What Fahey does best though is to win handicaps and it was business as usual in some of the biggest races last term. Baccarat (Wokingham), Angel Gabrial (Northumberland Plate) and Heaven's Guest (Bunbury Cup) secured some of Britain's premier handicaps, while Eastern Impact also landed two decent prizes at Newmarket. Fahey also has a decent record in the valuable juvenile sales contest and picked up another at Doncaster's Leger meeting with Bond's Girl.

Fahey is multi-skilled when it comes to winning races with different age groups, although it is very hard to profit from his older horses. The best method to profit from his handicappers is to focus on the youngsters as he returned a level-stake profit in nurseries over the last five seasons and did better than ever in this category in 2014.

Fahey is able to keep the winners ticking all year round but does particularly well early in the turf season with the months of April and May often particularly successful.

Unsurprisingly, Fahey sends out most winners in races from 5f to a mile, but it is only his juveniles who punters can back blind and secure a profit. His runners aged three and above often catch out the layers in staying races.

Riding duties have been shared more evenly since Paul Hanagan took the retainer for Hamdan Al Maktoum, with Tony Hamilton now riding most of the yard's winners. Hanagan's services are still called upon regularly and he returned a level-stake profit for Fahey last term. The mounts of promising apprentice Jack Garritty are worth looking out for, as are the rare occasions when Graham Lee is booked.

Most of Fahey's winners tend to come in the north with his figures at Musselburgh standing out ahead of Pontefract and Newcastle. His runners in the south are best followed at Epsom.

On the way to and from exercise at Richard Fahey's Musley Bank stables in North Yorkshire

Plenty of Classic firepower as jockey decision shows Godolphin mean business

WITH the signing of William Buick and James Doyle as principal retained riders for the season, Godolphin have made a big statement of intent for 2015.

While a generous retainer might have played a part in the two jockey's decisions, both are accustomed to riding good horses in good races. For trainers Charlie Appleby and Saeed Bin Suroor, the task is to provide a consistent stream of quality for their ambitious duo, *writes Scott Burton*.

Even before the contracts were signed Buick had proved his worth to Godolphin in guiding **Charming Thought** to success in the Middle Park Stakes, a first European Group 1 win for Appleby.

"Charming Thought has wintered well and we're delighted," says Appleby. "I'm really happy with where he is and the plan is to step him up to seven furlongs in the Greenham."

Appleby has a good group of three-year-old colts to spread around the various Guineas trials and has already begun to tentatively assign targets.

Secret Brief has joined Godolphin from Mark Johnston's yard and will bid to put a disappointing run in the Dewhurst behind him having previously won two of the Tattersalls Millions sales races at Newmarket.

Appleby says of the Shamardal colt: "He arrived with us in the new year and he looks a good honest horse who will put his head down and try. We were impressed with his win in the sales race because we think a bit of our **Outlaw Country**, who was second. The Craven might be the place to start him off."

Another recruit from Johnston is **Jungle Cat**, who was beaten only a nose in the Group 2 Gimcrack at York before getting bogged down at Newbury on his final start at two.

Appleby reasons: "The experience we've had with horses by Iffraaj is they don't like soft ground, and William Buick said he hated

Festive Fare streaks home at Kempton in February to make it two out of two

it in the Mill Reef. He could start off in the Free Handicap as I'm not fully convinced he'll be a miler."

Festive Fare didn't reach the track until January but has won on the Polytrack over a mile at both Lingfield and Kempton.

Appleby might be looking at trips in excess of the Guineas for Festive Fare and clearly holds the son of Teofilo in high regard.

"It's done him the power of good having those two runs over the winter," he says. "He's a big horse and we gave him time last summer. He's done physically well since his second run on the all-weather and we'll look towards the Fielden Stakes as a likely starting point on turf."

Saeed Bin Suroor might lack a star name from last season among his Classic generation colts but has a goody body of horses from which one could emerge this spring.

Maftool scored in the Group 3 Somerville Tattersalls Stakes at Newmarket in September before proving his adaptability when landing the UAE 2,000 Guineas on the dirt at Meydan.

"He'll run in the UAE Derby and we'll keep our options open after that with regard to British Classics," says Bin Suroor.

Future Empire mixed it with some good sorts last season, just losing out to Aktabantay in the Group 3 Solario Stakes before chasing home Commemorative in the Autumn Stakes.

Best Of Times didn't fly quite so high but is two from three ahead of the new campaign, having missed his intended Group 1 assignment at Doncaster at the end of last season.

Bin Suroor says: "Future Empire is in very good form so we'll look at giving him a run at Group level. We'll see how he gets on but he could be one for the Classics.

"Physically Best Of Times has done very well and looks better than he did in the week of the Racing Post Trophy. He's started off nicely now he's back in work. We might look for a Listed race at Newmarket for him."

Bin Suroor looks extremely strong among the three-year-old fillies, with *Local Time* at the head of the yard's pretenders for the Qipco 1,000 Guineas after cutting a swathe through the opposition with three wins in Dubai over the winter.

The daughter of Invincible Spirit also scored in the Oh So Sharp Stakes last September, a race won by subsequent 1,000 Guineas Miss France in 2013.

"We want to run her in the English Guineas," says Bin Suroor. "She's unbeaten since her debut and, following her win in the UAE Oaks, she's stayed in full training and is in quarantine with Newmarket as the target."

A half-sister to the Group 1 winning duo of Mandean and Wavering, *Winters Moon* came agonizingly close to joining the family

DID YOU KNOW

The operation's founder Sheikh Mohammed rode in his first horse race at the age of 12, earning a reputation for being able to master the wild ones considered untrainable by others. The Sheikh went to watch his first race in Britain in 1967 and ten years later he had his first winner as an owner in the UK at Brighton.

club when losing out by half a length and a nose in the Dubai Fillies' Mile last October.

"She's doing really well and we hope she'll be up to running in a Classic," reports Bin Suroor. "I see her as a more of a mile-and-a-quarter or mile-and-a-half filly."

Aside from Local Time and Winters Moon, the yard houses a trio of much darker horses for the fillies' Classics.

Elite Gardens was two from three last term, with a disappointing run in the Albany Stakes the only blot on her record. *Very Special* ran a fine third to the well-regarded Osaila at Newmarket on her second start while *Beautiful Romance* ran out a nine-length winner of her sole start at Doncaster's Racing Post Trophy meeting.

Bin Suroor summarises the trio: "Elite Gardens has done well in Dubai. She's done only easy work at the moment to get her ready for the European season but there's no plan with her at the moment. Very Special is quite a small filly but she's shown class from day one in her work and I think she'll be running in some nice races this season. *Beautiful Romance* will obviously need to step up a lot but she won her first race really well. She'll face much better horses next time but so far I'm happy with her."

Appleby's two entries for the 1,000 Guineas include *Mistrusting*, a daughter of

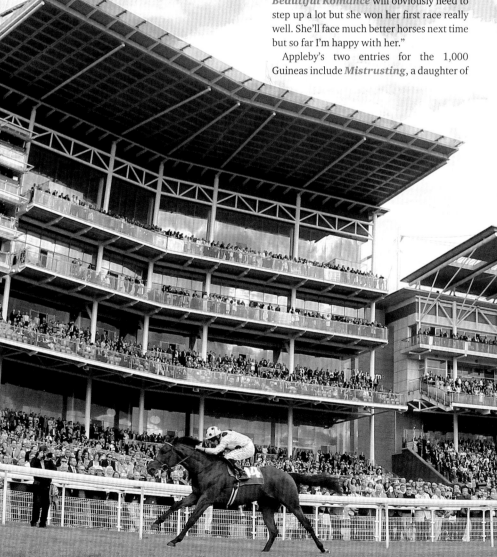

Cherry Hinton heroine Misheer by New Approach.

"We put her in the Guineas but I wouldn't be bold enough to say she'll definitely get a mile," he cautions. "There's a lot of speed on the dam's side and she's shown that herself. We'll aim at a trial."

Joining Mistrusting in the list for the fillies' Classic is *Risen Sun*, who finished her juvenile campaign when second to Best Of Times at Salisbury.

Appleby says: "She joined us from Mark Johnston's and is from a family that get's a trip. She's a big filly and we're not pushing too many buttons yet. I think she might want a mile and a quarter."

Size is a recurring theme among a trio of Appleby's Classic-entered colts yet to earn black type.

"*Latharnach* won his last two starts nicely He's a big horse, up around the 570 kilo mark. We'll look at one of the trials but I don't want to force him towards a certain date. I'll let him tell me if he's ready for a trial or the Guineas because he's exciting and is only going to get better at three and four.

"*Rare Rhythm* has wintered very well and, as a big son of Dubawi, is in the same case as Latharnach, I won't be rushing him. *Legend's Gate* put up two nice performances and I think we bumped into a decent horse of

Hugo Palmer's at Kempton. He needs to break his maiden but, on what he's done so far and on his home work, he looks potentially up to standard."

The spring tends to persuade the mind towards dreams of Classic glory but both Appleby and Bin Suroor have a few older horses who will be worth keeping an eye on.

Bin Suroor will once again be targeting the biggest night of the Dubai season.

"*African Story* won the last Al Maktoum Challenge and will run in the World Cup. *Prince Bishop* was second and will go the same way. They will need a break after that."

Safety Check has really come of age during the Dubai winter, reeling off a pair of Group 2 successes in the Al Fahidi Fort and the Zabeel Mile. Now Appleby is preparing the four-year-old son of Dubawi for a domestic campaign this summer: "He's in quarantine and will be coming back early April. He'll have a break and then we'll look at a race like the Lennox Stakes at Goodwood during the summer. He's a seven-furlong specialist and has won on the track which is always an advantage."

Two of Godolphin's Derby runners from last year will also be looking to make their mark.

"*Sudden Wonder* is a bit ground dependent as he wants cut," says Appleby. "Like *Pinzolo*, who won on his comeback at Lingfield, the Derby took a lot out of him and we'll be feeling our way with both of them."

*Secret Brief (red cap)
finishes second in a York
maiden before winning
three races on the bounce*

GODOLPHIN: ASSESSING THE STATS

Not much separated Godolphin's trainers last term. Charlie Appleby had 102 winners compared to Saeed Bin Suroor's 93 although the latter secured lightly more prize-money, amassing just over £1.5 million, *writes Kevin Morley*.

Appleby and Bin Suroor score at a similar rate with three-year-olds but there are clear discrepancies with their output regarding two-year-olds and those aged four and over. Appleby fares much better with the youngsters and Bin Suroor's statistics favour the older horses.

Appleby's most notable victory last term came courtesy of a juvenile when Charming Thought landed the Group 1 Middle Park at Newmarket, while Bin Suroor's leading moneyspinner was veteran stayer Cavalryman, who landed two Group 2s.

Aside from exploits at Meydan last year, which included victory for African Story in the Dubai World Cup, 2014 was moderate

CHARLIE APPLEBY
NEWMARKET, SUFFOLK

	No. of Hrs	Races Run	1st	2nd	3rd	Unpl	Per cent	£1 Level Stake
2-y-o	81	245	51	41	30	123	20.8	-31.47
3-y-o	57	216	42	33	37	104	19.4	-41.62
4-y-o+	33	88	9	10	15	54	10.2	-40.05
Totals	171	549	102	84	82	281	18.6	-113.14
2013	131	304	60	43	33	168	19.7	-10.50
2012	0							+

BY MONTH

2-y-o	W-R	Per cent	£1 Level Stake	3-y-o	W-R	Per cent	£1 Level Stake
January	0-0	0.0	0.00	January	0-0	0.0	0.00
February	0-0	0.0	0.00	February	0-0	0.0	0.00
March	0-0	0.0	0.00	March	0-0	0.0	0.00
April	0-3	0.0	-3.00	April	3-21	14.3	-8.58
May	4-19	21.1	-0.84	May	4-33	12.1	-21.38
June	5-28	17.9	-16.57	June	4-37	10.8	-14.88
July	4-29	13.8	-8.47	July	8-34	23.5	+6.03
August	9-44	20.5	-7.26	August	2-26	7.7	-15.00
September	15-50	30.0	+1.10	September	4-26	15.4	-5.00
October	5-35	14.3	+7.99	October	3-15	20.0	+0.83
November	6-23	26.1	+3.88	November	6-9	66.7	+4.93
December	3-14	21.4	-8.30	December	8-15	53.3	+11.42

4-y-o	W-R	Per cent	£1 Level Stake	Totals	W-R	Per cent	£1 Level Stake
January	0-0	0.0	0.00	January	0-0	0.0	0.00
February	0-0	0.0	0.00	February	0-0	0.0	0.00
March	0-0	0.0	0.00	March	0-0	0.0	0.00
April	1-4	25.0	-1.80	April	4-28	14.3	-13.38
May	2-21	9.5	-11.00	May	10-73	13.7	-33.22
June	2-17	11.8	+3.50	June	11-82	13.4	-27.95
July	1-15	6.7	-11.75	July	13-78	16.7	-14.19
August	0-10	0.0	-10.00	August	11-80	13.8	-32.26
September	1-9	11.1	-5.00	September	20-85	23.5	-8.90
October	1-9	11.1	-4.00	October	9-59	15.3	+4.82
November	1-3	33.3	0.00	November	13-35	37.1	+4.93
December	0-0	0.0	0.00	December	11-29	37.9	+11.42

DISTANCE

2-y-o	W-R	Per cent	£1 Level Stake	3-y-o	W-R	Per cent	£1 Level Stake
5f-6f	19-81	23.5	-9.25	5f-6f	3-12	25.0	-6.00
7f-8f	30-154	19.5	-18.22	7f-8f	16-89	18.0	+0.68
9f-13f	2-10	20.0	-4.00	9f-13f	23-113	20.4	-34.30
14f+	0-0	0.0	0.00	14f+	0-2	0.0	-2.00

4-y-o	W-R	Per cent	£1 Level Stake	Totals	W-R	Per cent	£1 Level Stake
5f-6f	0-10	0.0	-10.00	5f-6f	22-103	21.4	-25.25
7f-8f	4-39	10.3	-21.30	7f-8f	50-282	17.7	-38.84
9f-13f	5-37	13.5	-6.75	9f-13f	30-160	18.8	-45.05
14f+	0-2	0.0	-2.00	14f+	0-4	0.0	-4.00

TYPE OF RACE

Non-Handicaps	W-R	Per cent	£1 Level Stake	Handicaps	W-R	Per cent	£1 Level Stake
2-y-o	42-213	19.7	-25.95	2-y-o	9-32	28.1	-5.52
3-y-o	13-99	13.1	-60.33	3-y-o	29-117	24.8	+18.71
4-y-o+	6-45	13.3	0.00	4-y-o+	3-43	7.0	-28.75

RACE CLASS / FIRST TIME OUT

	W-R	Per cent	£1 Level Stake		W-R	Per cent	£1 Level Stake
Class 1	6-76	7.9	-32.25	2-y-o	8-81	9.9	-24.25
Class 2	11-67	16.4	-3.53	3-y-o	7-57	12.3	-24.25
Class 3	14-58	24.1	-13.60	4-y-o+	3-33	9.1	-10.80
Class 4	30-147	20.4	-16.43				
Class 5	37-192	19.3	-50.47	Totals	18-171	10.5	-59.30
Class 6	4-9	44.4	+3.13				
Class 7	0-0	0.0	0.00				

Charlie Appleby: has good record with juveniles

for Godolphin, especially in Britain.

In handicaps, Appleby seems better to follow from a level-stake view, especially with the three-year-olds, while Bin Suroor has the much higher strike-rate with the older brigade, particularly in Group races.

One similarity between the trainers is the distances over which their respective strings excel. Both have much better figures in races at 1m2f and beyond.

Both used a wide variety of jockeys last term and there were quite a few names who were profitable to follow. Silvestre de Sousa had a solid record for Bin Suroor in 2014 but so did Freddie Tylicki and Richard Hughes, while apprentice Kevin Stott also posted some eyecatching numbers.

Appleby preferred the services of William Buick, while Phillip Makin and Shane Gray had excellent strike-rates from a handful of opportunities – but by far the best jockey to follow was Adam Kirby.

SAEED BIN SUROOR

NEWMARKET, SUFFOLK

	No. of Hrs	Races Run	1st	2nd	3rd	Unpl	Per cent	£1 Level Stake
2-y-o	53	124	30	25	15	54	24.2	-19.93
3-y-o	41	160	41	25	19	75	25.6	+18.16
4-y-o+	41	121	22	19	11	69	18.2	-23.97
Totals	135	405	93	69	45	198	23.0	-25.74
2013	200	523	106	86	67	263	20.3	-18.28
2012	125	436	85	71	65	214	19.5	-57.49

BY MONTH

2-y-o	W-R	Per cent	£1 Level Stake	3-y-o	W-R	Per cent	£1 Level Stake
January	0-0	0.0	0.00	January	0-0	0.0	0.00
February	0-0	0.0	0.00	February	0-0	0.0	0.00
March	0-0	0.0	0.00	March	0-0	0.0	0.00
April	0-0	0.0	0.00	April	6-14	42.9	+3.75
May	1-3	33.3	+6.00	May	4-17	23.5	+4.45
June	0-4	0.0	-4.00	June	4-22	18.2	-7.63
July	3-16	18.8	-5.75	July	5-28	17.9	-3.75
August	5-22	22.7	-6.24	August	5-21	23.8	+4.50
September	7-26	26.9	-0.82	September	7-18	38.9	+18.63
October	11-33	33.3	+3.14	October	7-31	22.6	+1.08
November	1-12	8.3	-8.50	November	2-8	25.0	-3.38
December	2-8	25.0	-3.75	December	1-1	100.0	+0.50

4-y-o	W-R	Per cent	£1 Level Stake	Totals	W-R	Per cent	£1 Level Stake
January	0-0	0.0	0.00	January	0-0	0.0	0.00
February	0-0	0.0	0.00	February	0-0	0.0	0.00
March	0-1	0.0	-1.00	March	0-1	0.0	-1.00
April	0-2	0.0	-2.00	April	6-16	37.5	+1.75
May	3-17	17.6	+2.83	May	8-37	21.6	+13.28
June	1-19	5.3	-15.00	June	5-45	11.1	-26.63
July	6-26	23.1	-0.08	July	14-70	20.0	-9.58
August	2-24	8.3	-16.50	August	12-67	17.9	-18.24
September	4-18	22.2	-2.52	September	18-62	29.0	+15.29
October	5-12	41.7	+6.80	October	23-76	30.3	+11.02
November	1-2	50.0	+3.50	November	4-22	18.2	+0.12
December	0-0	0.0	0.00	December	3-9	33.3	+0.50

DISTANCE

2-y-o	W-R	Per cent	£1 Level Stake	3-y-o	W-R	Per cent	£1 Level Stake
5f-6f	8-39	20.5	-6.65	5f-6f	1-4	25.0	+2.00
7f-8f	22-82	26.8	-10.28	7f-8f	10-64	15.6	-24.05
9f-13f	0-3	0.0	-3.00	9f-13f	28-89	31.5	+39.71
14f+	0-0	0.0	0.00	14f+	2-3	66.7	+0.50

4-y-o	W-R	Per cent	£1 Level Stake	Totals	W-R	Per cent	£1 Level Stake
5f-6f	1-16	6.3	-12.25	5f-6f	10-59	16.9	-16.90
7f-8f	2-28	7.1	-21.33	7f-8f	34-174	19.5	-55.66
9f-13f	17-59	28.8	+19.82	9f-13f	45-151	29.8	+56.53
14f+	2-18	11.1	-10.20	14f+	4-21	19.0	-9.70

TYPE OF RACE

Non-Handicaps	W-R	Per cent	£1 Level Stake	Handicaps	W-R	Per cent	£1 Level Stake
2-y-o	24-108	22.2	-26.68	2-y-o	6-16	37.5	+6.75
3-y-o	20-67	29.9	+12.53	3-y-o	21-93	22.6	+5.63
4-y-o+	13-63	20.6	+39.00	4-y-o+	9-58	15.5	-13.38

RACE CLASS / FIRST TIME OUT

Race Class	W-R	Per cent	£1 Level Stake	First Time Out	W-R	Per cent	£1 Level Stake
Class 1	12-76	15.8	-21.42	2-y-o	6-53	11.3	-22.25
Class 2	12-69	17.4	-22.39	3-y-o	11-41	26.8	+3.46
Class 3	17-56	30.4	+18.46	4-y-o+	7-41	17.1	+1.74
Class 4	24-81	29.6	+12.34				
Class 5	28-115	24.3	-4.73	Totals	24-135	17.8	-17.05
Class 6	0-8	0.0	-8.00				
Class 7	0-0	0.0	0.00				

Saeed Bin Suroor has the knack with his runners aged four and over

Classic hope Faydhan has big boots to fill as Gosden seeks new flagbearers

WITH Kingman having been retired to stud, John Gosden begins the season not only with the task of having to replace the irreplaceable, but also the likes of Oaks and King George winner Taghrooda, four-time Group 1 winner and stable stalwart The Fugue, and Nassau heroine Sultanina.

The now-retired quartet landed eight Group 1s between them last season but Gosden has potential superstars queuing up to take on the mantle of their illustrious former stablemates, headed by one of the winter 2,000 Guineas favourites in *Faydhan*, *writes Ben Hutton*.

Like Taghrooda he is owned by Hamdan Al Maktoum and, although he ran just once as a two-year-old, winning a Haydock maiden, his price for the first Classic of the season contracted with each subsequent run from six-length runner-up Dutch Connection, who went on to win the Group 3 Acomb Stakes at York.

The son of War Front, sire of Declaration Of War, missed the rest of the campaign with a leg injury, although Gosden is reassuring in that regard: "His injury was pretty minor, he had something done to him when he was a baby in America and it was a slight recurrence of that.

"He's cantering away, he's in good order, and we might look at a race like the European Free Handicap."

Faydhan will get to run off a mark of 102 in that 7f contest at Newmarket on April 15 and could be just one of several Gosden contenders in Guineas trials, with Chesham Stakes winner *Richard Pankhurst* also set to embark on such a path.

Like a number of Gosden's inmates, the Raven's Pass colt will now be racing in the royal blue of Godolphin, many having formerly run in the green colours of Princess Haya of Jordan, and when Richard Pankhurst reappears he will be making just his third start, having been unraced since Royal Ascot.

Gosden explains: "He's very happy on top of the ground – like his father he doesn't like soft, so I couldn't really run in the big two-year-old races in the autumn like the Dewhurst. He's got a lot of speed and we might look at a race like the Craven."

Fannaan was two from two as a juvenile and the trainer reports: "He's a nice type, he won well at Newmarket and we'll be looking at one of the Guineas trials with him. His mother Titian Time was a miler and he looks like a mile will be his trip. He's strong and he's done well during the winter."

Another possible contender for a trial is *Golden Horn*, successful on his debut at Nottingham in October over 1m½f: "He's promising – he won his only start and he would have run earlier but for a small problem with mucus on his lungs.

"He's interesting tripwise – we might look at a Guineas trial but we'll see how his work goes and we could start him back at a mile and a quarter."

Gosden's fifth and final 2,000 Guineas

Faydhan wintered as one of the favourites for the 2,000 Guineas

Lap Of Luxury has reportedly done well during the winter and will head to a Classic trial

entry is Group 1 Criterium International runner-up *Johnny Barnes*, about whom the trainer says: "He loves cut in the ground. He ran well in France last time out and we'll send him where the ground is."

Clarehaven Stables also have an interesting hand in the Derby, headed by the unbeaten *Christophermarlowe*, with the trainer reporting him as being "in good form. His father Tapit is not perhaps known as a mile-and-a-half sire but his mother stayed well and he looks more like her, by Galileo, than his sire.

"He'll go straight to a mile and a quarter and you could possibly see him in a race like the Classic Trial at Sandown or even the Derby Trial at Epsom, where he's won before."

Another of Gosden's Derby entries is the strapping *Jack Hobbs*, winner of a Wolverhampton maiden in December: "I'd be confident he'd stay a mile and a quarter like his father Halling, I wouldn't know whether he'd stay beyond that. He's an interesting dark horse for the season."

Of the yard's three-year-old fillies *Star Of Seville* is the most prominent in the ante-post Classic betting and Gosden reports of the six-length Doncaster maiden winner: "She's in good order and we might take a look at a race like the Fred Darling. She's a strong galloper and I see her as a mile- to a mile-and-a-quarter filly."

Lap Of Luxury, also in the 1,000 Guineas, is owned by the Coolmore triumvirate of Tabor, Smith and Magnier, and she beat a good yardstick on her sole start at Haydock in September: "She's done well through the winter and we'll look to run her in a trial.

"Like her half-brother Dutch Art she's got a fair bit of speed. She might get a mile and a quarter but we'll start her out over a mile."

Jellicle Ball and *Lady Correspondent* are also in the first fillies' Classic and Gosden says: "Both have run once and won once, they've had good winters and if they're going nicely we could look at a trial for them."

Moving on to the older horses, one of Gosden's flagbearers for the season will be *Eagle Top*, who will begin his four-year-old campaign having raced just four times. Among those starts, though, was a Group 2 win in the King Edward VII Stakes at Royal Ascot and a fourth place behind Taghrooda in the King George when last seen in July.

IT'S LIKE THE RACING POST ON AN iPAD BUT EVEN BETTER

It's a newspaper you can bet through, search our comprehensive database, get the latest up-to-the-minute news and follow horses using Horse Tracker.

FREE 30-DAY TRIAL. ON THE APP STORE NOW

Gosden excels when it comes to finding improvement from his older horses, and an exciting season surely lies ahead for the Pivotal colt, who could make his reappearance at Sandown in May, with the trainer reporting: "He's in good form and we'll aim for a race like the Brigadier Gerard and then go back to Royal Ascot."

St Leger runner-up *Romsdal* is one of the horses who raced for Princess Haya last year but will appear in the Godolphin blue this season. After winning his maiden at Kempton in April the colt was a nose runner-up in the Chester Vase, and then third in the Derby, and Gosden says: "He's in good order and we could look at a race like the John Porter [Newbury, April 18] with him.

"He's had a good winter and he's got the option of conditions races too – he ran very well in some Group races last year without winning."

Forever Now was sixth in the Leger having previously won the Listed March Stakes at Goodwood, and Gosden issues a positive report about his subsequent development: "He ran a nice race when he won at Goodwood, he was still a bit weak last season but he's had a good winter and we'll be looking at some nice staying races from April onwards."

Western Hymn concluded his three-year-old campaign with a fourth place in the Champion Stakes at Ascot, having landed a Group 2 and a Group 3 earlier in the season, also on testing ground. A similar prize could be his initial target, with Gosden saying: "We'll look to start him off in a race like the Gordon Richards Stakes [Sandown, April 24]."

Muwaary showed some very good form during his three-year-old season, filling fourth in the French 2,000 Guineas and second in the Jersey Stakes at Royal Ascot, all despite pulling hard in his races. He was injured when fifth in the Prix Jean Prat but is expected to be back in training in April.

Another Gosden inmate who could develop into a Group 1 winner is *Wannabe Yours*, who Gosden nominated as a possible future contender for the Sussex Stakes after he won the Group 3 Thoroughbred Stakes, also at Glorious Goodwood, in August.

Now four, he ran below form when last seen at Newmarket in September but there was an excuse: "He scoped badly after the Joel Stakes, having been clean going in. We'll be starting a fresh year with a fresh horse."

Eagle Top (red colours) could start off in the Brigadier Gerard Stakes

JOHN GOSDEN

NEWMARKET, SUFFOLK

	No. of Hrs	Races Run	1st	2nd	3rd	Unpl	Per cent	£1 Level Stake
2-y-o	73	171	37	25	21	88	21.6 -	14.26
3-y-o	102	362	78	55	50	179	21.5	-33.08
4-y-o+	20	80	17	13	10	38	21.3	+22.70
Totals	195	613	132	93	81	305	21.5	-24.64
2013	157	525	108	98	64	253	20.6	-26.95
2012	166	629	119	101	100	307	18.9	+54.37

BY MONTH

2-y-o	W-R	Per cent	£1 Level Stake	3-y-o	W-R	Per cent	£1 Level Stake
January	0-0	0.0	0.00	January	2-10	20.0	-4.05
February	0-0	0.0	0.00	February	1-7	14.3	-3.50
March	0-0	0.0	0.00	March	2-8	25.0	+2.50
April	1-1	100.0	+10.00	April	17-56	30.4	-1.38
May	0-5	0.0	-5.00	May	7-59	11.9	+1.45
June	1-4	25.0	+7.00	June	12-63	19.0	-18.29
July	1-13	7.7	-11.09	July	10-49	20.4	-13.74
August	3-16	18.8	-5.25	August	12-40	30.0	+9.50
September	9-32	28.1	+19.67	September	6-30	20.0	+8.50
October	7-44	15.9	-22.52	October	4-25	16.0	-9.25
November	5-31	16.1	-10.19	November	3-8	37.5	-0.95
December	10-25	40.0	+3.13	December	2-7	28.6	-3.86

4-y-o	W-R	Per cent	£1 Level Stake	Totals	W-R	Per cent	£1 Level Stake
January	0-1	0.0	-1.00	January	2-11	18.2	-5.05
February	0-1	0.0	-1.00	February	1-8	12.5	-4.50
March	0-4	0.0	-4.00	March	2-12	16.7	-1.50
April	2-7	28.6	-1.42	April	20-64	31.3	+7.20
May	5-17	29.4	+12.07	May	12-81	14.8	+8.52
June	3-13	23.1	+1.75	June	16-80	20.0	-9.54
July	1-8	12.5	+1.00	July	12-70	17.1	-23.83
August	4-9	44.4	+18.80	August	19-65	29.2	+23.05
September	2-11	18.2	+5.50	September	17-73	23.3	+33.67
October	0-7	0.0	-7.00	October	11-76	14.5	-38.77
November	0-2	0.0	-2.00	November	8-41	19.5	-2.95
December	0-0	0.0	0.00	December	12-32	37.5	-3.86

DISTANCE

2-y-o	W-R	Per cent	£1 Level Stake	3-y-o	W-R	Per cent	£1 Level Stake
5f-6f	8-33	24.2	+6.16	5f-6f	2-13	15.4	-8.00
7f-8f	28-132	21.2	-16.67	7f-8f	34-169	20.1	-3.83
9f-13f	1-6	16.7	-3.75	9f-13f	41-168	24.4	-14.25
14f+	0-0	0.0	0.00	14f+	1-12	8.3	-7.00

4-y-o	W-R	Per cent	£1 Level Stake	Totals	W-R	Per cent	£1 Level Stake
5f-6f	1-4	25.0	+2.00	5f-6f	11-50	22.0	+0.16
7f-8f	2-15	13.3	-4.50	7f-8f	64-316	20.3	-25.00
9f-13f	12-50	24.0	+21.45	9f-13f	54-224	24.1	+3.45
14f+	2-11	18.2	+3.75	14f+	3-23	13.0	-3.25

TYPE OF RACE

Non-Handicaps	W-R	Per cent	£1 Level Stake	Handicaps	W-R	Per cent	£1 Level Stake
2-y-o	33-156	21.2	-13.76	2-y-o	4-15	26.7	-0.50
3-y-o	57-226	25.2	+17.21	3-y-o	21-136	15.4	-50.29
4-y-o+	12-58	20.7	+77.00	4-y-o+	5-22	22.7	+16.83

RACE CLASS

	W-R	Per cent	£1 Level Stake
Class 1	23-117	19.7	+6.82
Class 2	10-55	18.2	-3.00
Class 3	14-41	34.1	+12.11
Class 4	24-157	15.3	-65.46
Class 5	56-228	24.6	+25.31
Class 6	5-15	33.3	-0.42
Class 7	0-0	0.0	0.00

FIRST TIME OUT

	W-R	Per cent	£1 Level Stake
2-y-o	13-73	17.8	+6.01
3-y-o	24-102	23.5	+26.31
4-y-o+	6-20	30.0	+11.58
Totals	43-195	22.1	+43.90

DID YOU KNOW

John Gosden was a top sportsman in his university days. A man of many talents, he won blues for both discus and javelin while at Cambridge. Gosden is also a keen music fan, in particular of Neil Young, Bob Dillon and the Rolling Stones and is mates with Ronnie Wood.

JOHN GOSDEN: ASSESSING THE STATS

John Gosden achieved his first trainers' championship in 2012 sending out 119 winners and amassing over £3.7 million in prize-money and, although he couldn't add a second title last term, he recorded impressive figures. The Newmarket handler secured a tally of 132 winners in 2014, earning £4.2m, *writes Kevin Morley*.

As those numbers might suggest, Gosden enjoyed plenty of big-race success. Kingman proved himself to be the leading miler, landing the Irish Guineas and St James's Palace before beating his elders in the Sussex Stakes, Taghrooda was victorious in the Oaks and King George, while The Fugue won her fourth Group 1 in the Prince of Wales's at Royal Ascot.

That trio have now been retired but Gosden has a steady conveyer belt of talent flowing through his yard and it is unlikely to be long before those voids are filled, especially considering the 37 juvenile winners he saddled in 2014, striking at 22 per cent.

Although he never enjoyed many notable victories with his two-year-olds last season, Gosden has never been one to rush his youngsters. Kingman, for example, had never won anything more than a weakly contested Group 3 before his Classic campaign so it is likely Gosden has a few types who could make massive strides at three.

Leading hopes for the early Classics this year appear to be Richard Pankhurst (2,000 Guineas) and Star Of Seville (1,000 Guineas) although it wouldn't be a surprise to learn some of their inmates have surpassed them in their homework in the meantime.

Three-year-olds provide most of the stable's victories and although a level-stake loss would be incurred if backing them blind, there are certain angles that can be followed profitably. Those running in Group races have a good strike-rate, particularly those running over a mile and beyond. But the best category for backing Gosden's string is his older handicappers who provide a mammoth level-stake profit over the last five seasons.

A decent strike-rate is maintained by Paul Hanagan who rides those in the ownership of Hamdan Al Maktoum, while Dane O'Neill also posted some eyecatching figures for the stable last year. Frankie Dettori will be figuring in that list soon enough now he is set to ride plenty of runners for the stable following William Buick's move to Godolphin.

The size of Gosden's string means he can now have a solid strike-rate all year round although it is noticeable he is particularly strong at the backend of the turf campaign.

Gosden's best figures come at Ascot, Haydock and Newbury, while he has a high strike-rate on all the all-weather tracks.

Celebrating after The Fugue's success in the Prince of Wales's Stakes

Tiggy Wiggy one of many stars for yard brimming with talent in every area

CHAMPION in his first year as a trainer, Richard Hannon is looking for more of the same this season.

Hannon took over from the incumbent titleholder, father Richard, at the start of 2014, and the Herridge and Everleigh stables continued where they left off, with 17 Group winners in Britain and nearly £4.7 million in prize-money narrowly eclipsing the yard's tallies from the year before, *writes Ben Hutton.*

Such fantastic success helped to propel Richard Hughes to his third champion jockey title in a row, although this season will be the last in which the formidable Hannon-Hughes axis will combine as the rider is set to become a trainer in his own right in 2016.

One of the stars unearthed by Hannon last season was the Cartier Two-Year-Old Filly of the Year *Tiggy Wiggy*, and she is one of many big names who have the ability and potential to fill the void left by retired trio Olympic Glory, Toronado and Sky Lantern.

The highlight of her six successes was the Group 1 Cheveley Park at Newmarket in September and, although she is unraced beyond 6f, her initial path will be one that aims to lead to the 1,000 Guineas.

Hannon says: "We don't know whether she'll stay, and that's why we want to run her in a trial to see if she gets seven furlongs. She stays six well, so seven may not be a problem, and then we'd hopefully stretch her to a mile.

"She's already had experience of Newmarket and doesn't have to carry a penalty for her Group 1 win if she goes for the Fred Darling at Newbury, although she has got other options. It depends on the ground and what sort of form she's in at the time."

Confidence in the stamina of Hannon's chief hopes for the 2,000 Guineas is greater, with *Ivawood* heading the contenders. He was beaten on soft ground in the Middle Park but had previously picked up a pair of Group 2s in impressive fashion on good to firm ground in July.

Hannon reports: "He's in good form. It's not essential for him to have a run before the Guineas but the Craven and the Greenham are options, or he could go straight there. I think he'll stay a mile, I don't see a problem with that."

The trainer is also positive about fellow dual Group 2 winner *Estidhkaar*: "He's done very well over the winter. He's lengthened, and thickened out quite well, and he's moving very well at home.

"He'll probably have a trial on his way to the 2,000 Guineas – we're favouring the Greenham at Newbury but that could change."

As well as this trio, Hannon also has a potentially deep supporting cast for the 2,000 and 1,000 Guineas, including *Marsh Hawk*, fourth in the Fillies' Mile, and *Osaila*, third in the Breeders' Cup Juvenile Fillies Turf.

Of the former Hannon says: "She was never a very big filly, and she pulled a bit too hard in the Fillies' Mile, but she's very good and will probably have a trial on the way to the Guineas, and go from there. I'm not sure which one yet."

The trainer adds of Osaila: "She's definitely going to stay a mile. I'm not sure whether she's going to be quite ready for a trial but if she is she'll go there and, if not, she'll go straight to the 1,000. She was third at the Breeders' Cup and won a nice Group 3, and she's a good filly. She'd have a chance."

Three-year-old colt *Kool Kompany* had a busy first campaign featuring five wins, and Hannon reports: "We'll probably go to Newmarket or Newbury with him for a trial and then we'll be looking at the Guineas.

"He's a little bit more relaxed now than he was last year, he had a lot of racing so he's had a good break."

About *Smaih (pictured)*, who landed the Group 3 Horris Hill Stakes at Newbury when last seen in October, Hannon says: "He won his Group 3 last year, I'm not sure how strong that race was. He's done okay over the winter and he might struggle with his Group 3 penalty all year, but we'll run him in a Guineas trial and we'll see how it goes. If there

was soft ground at Newbury, for instance, he could have a chance."

Another Guineas entry, *Baitha Alga*, won the Group 2 Norfolk Stakes at Royal Ascot before suffering two heavy defeats, and Hannon is hopeful he can rediscover his earlier promise: "He lost his form last year but he's had a good break since. He got quite upset in his last couple of runs, so he's wearing a hood now and he can hopefully recapture some of his form."

Moheet caught the eye when easily winning his maiden at Salisbury in October and Hannon reports: "He's won his maiden so we'll be looking at conditions races early on for him, but we hope he can be a Guineas or Derby horse."

A Derby entry with more substantial form is *Basateen*, an easy Doncaster maiden winner who was third in the Group 3 Acomb Stakes at York in August, his third and final start as a two-year-old.

The way Hannon speaks of him suggests he is highly thought of: "We've deliberately given him a bit of time and a nice break, and hopefully he can repay us this year in some good races."

A darker horse among the Hannon Derby entries is *Ya Hade Ye Delil*, a slow-starting third on his sole start in a Goodwood maiden in September, and a half-brother to Group/Grade 2 winners Spacious and Dimension: "He's a very nice horse. We've taken our time with him and he'll get a trip, but we have to win a maiden with him first before we start thinking of Derbys and good races like that."

Along with this clutch of compelling three-year-olds, Hannon will be looking for flag-bearing four-year-old *Night Of Thunder* to significantly bolster his charge to a second trainers' title.

The only horse ever to beat Kingman, when landing the 2,000 Guineas, Night Of Thunder failed to win in four subsequent starts but still showed excellent form to be placed in three Group 1s over a mile, and will now race in the royal blue of Godolphin.

Hannon says of his stable star: "It's great he's staying in the yard. He's done very well over the winter and we're getting him ready for the Lockinge, he'll go straight there."

The yard has been responsible for the winner of the Newbury Group 1 in three of the last five seasons and could well go double-handed, with *Toormore* another possible contender.

After a predominantly disappointing 2014 he returned to form with a close third in the QEII at Ascot when last seen in October, one spot behind Night Of Thunder having not enjoyed the best of runs. Hannon says: "His third in the QEII was his best run for a long time. He'll have an entry in the Group 2 Bet365 Mile at Sandown but we're leaning to going straight to the Lockinge with him."

A direct trip to Newbury for Toormore will make the life of stablemate *Shifting Power* easier, given his intended initial target. He showed some solid form in defeat in Group 1s last season before running below par at Goodwood in August, a performance attributed to him not handling the track.

The trainer reports: "He ran three or four super races on the way into Glorious Goodwood, he was second or third in two Group 1s, and he's going to Sandown for the Group 2 Betfred Mile."

Over further *Pether's Moon* will be bidding to add to his three Group 2 or 3 victories gained last season over 1m4f before possibly being stepped back up in grade, with his ability to win on both soft and good to firm ground a commendable asset: "He'll be going over the same ground hopefully, in Group 2s and Group 3s, and go where the prize-money is. He travels very well and appears to be in good form. Once he's gone and won another Group 2 we'll try and find a Group 1 for him."

One of Pether's Moon's wins came in Turkey, and *Coulsty* was another to make a successful European raid, in his case to France for a Group 3 at Deauville in August, his final start of 2014. Hannon says of the win: "That was a massive performance. He'll be going for races like the Diamond Jubilee at Royal Ascot if he's good enough, and earlier races like the Group 2 Duke of York Stakes. He's effective over six and seven furlongs but I think five is a bit sharp for him."

Ninjago failed to threaten on his two starts at Meydan in February but last year's Stewards' Cup runner-up will be back for more of the same this season: "He's coming back from Dubai for some of the nice sprint handicaps like the Wokingham and the Stewards' Cup. He'll be fit and be able to start the year running hopefully."

The yard is not known for its stayers but one of his horses about whom the trainer is most excited is St Leger fourth *Windshear*, who could be in for a big season judged by Hannon's comments: "He could be a very good horse this year and could be the real deal as a stayer. He'd get any trip and appears to go on any ground, and he's very tough. The John Porter at Newbury might be a good race to start him off in."

Night Of Thunder and Kieren Fallon after winning the 2,000 Guineas

RICHARD HANNON: ASSESSING THE STATS

It would be hard to say last season was anything but a big success for Richard Hannon. Having seen his father send out over 200 winners in each of the previous four seasons, a period in which he secured three trainers' championships, Hannon managed an impressive total of 206 winners in 2014, which also saw him land the trainers' title at the first attempt, *writes Kevin Morley*.

Even more staggering was his prize-money tally of over £4.7 million. Highlights included Night Of Thunder's 2,000 Guineas success and Toronado's Royal Ascot victory in the Queen Anne, while Tiggy Wiggy rounded up a hugely successful campaign by landing the Cheveley Park.

Juveniles continue to provide the backbone of the yard's success with 119 two-year-olds accounting for over half of the total winners last term. A 19 per cent strike-rate with the youngsters in 2014 was decent although a heavy level-stake loss was accrued given the vast turnover. However, a profit could have been secured by focusing on Hannon's juveniles in Group races. It is not always easy to find ways to profit from and this was one of the few ways to gain an edge, along with the stable's rare forays into sellers. The yard is also known to target big juvenile sales races and enjoyed success again in Newbury's Weatherbys Super Sprint with Tiggy Wiggy.

It is also difficult to nail down a distance over which the stable's runners can best be followed although surprisingly, two-year-olds struck often when asked to race beyond a mile with five of 19 runners last term in this area obliging.

Richard Hughes continues to ride the lion's share of winners and has been champion jockey for the last three years thanks to the stable's backing. However, from a punting perspective, the mounts of Frankie Dettori were more profitable, and even more impressive figures were posted by James Doyle. The demand for Doyle appears to be ever increasing across a number of yards and it is clear Hannon likes to utilise his services when the opportunity arises.

Hannon's juveniles are always well drilled before they first set foot on a racecourse and his decent record with youngsters at tricky tracks such as Lingfield and Brighton is noticeable. Newmarket is the most common venue for success though with the two-year-olds excelling on the Rowley Mile, while three-year-olds do better on the July course.

A group of two-year-olds work their way up the gallops at Richard Hannon's Herridge Stables near Marlborough

RICHARD HANNON

EAST EVERLEIGH, WILTS

	No. of Hrs	Races Run	1st	2nd	3rd	Unpl	Per cent	£1 Level Stake
2-y-o	157	638	119	94	103	322	18.7	-159.60
3-y-o	117	595	70	81	75	369	11.8	-123.29
4-y-o+	29	171	17	23	17	113	9.9	-82.35
Totals	303	1404	206	198	195	804	14.7	-365.24
2013	0							+
2012	0							+

BY MONTH

2-y-o	W-R	Per cent	£1 Level Stake	3-y-o	W-R	Per cent	£1 Level Stake
January	0-0	0.0	0.00	January	2-15	13.3	-8.00
February	0-0	0.0	0.00	February	0-5	0.0	-5.00
March	1-2	50.0	-0.39	March	4-10	40.0	+3.75
April	5-16	31.3	+2.54	April	10-67	14.9	-13.05
May	16-48	33.3	+19.93	May	13-105	12.4	+43.75
June	21-83	25.3	-16.50	June	14-108	13.0	-23.44
July	18-105	17.1	-53.09	July	9-87	10.3	-47.51
August	24-125	19.2	-24.12	August	6-84	7.1	-38.25
September	18-115	15.7	-22.35	September	7-54	13.0	-19.04
October	11-100	11.0	-41.50	October	3-38	7.9	-13.00
November	0-27	0.0	-27.00	November	0-12	0.0	-12.00
December	5-17	29.4	+2.88	December	2-10	20.0	+8.50

4-y-o	W-R	Per cent	£1 Level Stake	Totals	W-R	Per cent	£1 Level Stake
January	0-4	0.0	-4.00	January	2-19	10.5	-12.00
February	0-1	0.0	-1.00	February	0-6	0.0	-6.00
March	0-6	0.0	-6.00	March	5-18	27.8	-2.64
April	3-15	20.0	+3.00	April	18-98	18.4	-7.51
May	2-27	7.4	-21.88	May	31-180	17.2	+41.80
June	4-27	14.8	+3.80	June	39-218	17.9	-36.14
July	1-21	4.8	-18.38	July	28-213	13.1	-118.98
August	2-25	8.0	-17.40	August	32-234	13.7	-79.77
September	2-14	14.3	-6.25	September	27-183	14.8	-47.64
October	1-13	7.7	-9.75	October	15-151	9.9	-64.25
November	2-9	22.2	+4.50	November	2-48	4.2	-7.50
December	0-9	0.0	-9.00	December	7-36	19.4	-0.50

DISTANCE

2-y-o	W-R	Per cent	£1 Level Stake	3-y-o	W-R	Per cent	£1 Level Stake
5f-6f	84-345	24.3	-26.04	5f-6f	16-132	12.1	-22.39
7f-8f	31-283	11.0	-142.05	7f-8f	34-304	11.2	-48.69
9f-13f	4-10	40.0	+8.50	9f-13f	19-154	12.3	-51.54
14f+	0-0	0.0	0.00	14f+	1-5	20.0	-0.67

4-y-o	W-R	Per cent	£1 Level Stake	Totals	W-R	Per cent	£1 Level Stake
5f-6f	2-40	5.0	-15.50	5f-6f	102-517	19.7	-63.93
7f-8f	12-94	12.8	-41.20	7f-8f	77-681	11.3	-231.94
9f-13f	3-37	8.1	-25.65	9f-13f	26-201	12.9	-68.69
14f+	0-0	0.0	0.00	14f+	1-5	20.0	-0.67

TYPE OF RACE

Non-Handicaps	W-R	Per cent	£1 Level Stake	Handicaps	W-R	Per cent	£1 Level Stake
2-y-o	100-519	19.3	-143.76	2-y-o	19-119	16.0	-15.84
3-y-o	32-201	15.9	+41.17	3-y-o	38-394	9.6	-164.46
4-y-o+	8-80	10.0	+12.00	4-y-o+	9-91	9.9	-45.25

RACE CLASS / FIRST TIME OUT

	W-R	Per cent	£1 Level Stake		W-R	Per cent	£1 Level Stake
Class 1	26-203	12.8	-4.17	2-y-o	17-157	10.8	-55.62
Class 2	22-175	12.6	-46.32	3-y-o	18-117	15.4	-7.53
Class 3	17-158	10.8	-71.86	4-y-o+	4-29	13.8	-12.82
Class 4	48-354	13.6	-100.39				
Class 5	80-432	18.5	-125.28	Totals	39-303	12.9	-75.97
Class 6	13-82	15.9	-16.23				
Class 7	0-0	0.0	0.00				

Last season's Richard Hannon-trained Queen Anne Stakes winner Toronado arrives for stallion duties at the National Stud in Newmarket

Massive squad should ensure plenty more big paydays this season

MARK JOHNSTON: THIS SEASON'S BRIGHTEST HOPES

IF YOU want to make money in racing, some would say the best way to do it would be to back a Mark Johnston horse at Goodwood. The trainer's superb record at the Sussex track continued last season with victory in the Celebration Mile, and this year Johnston is confident of more high-profile success, not just at Goodwood, but across Britain.

With a team of over two hundred horses and growing all the time, there are few stables in England that can boast such quality in depth, *writes Tom Bull.*

The horse who won the Celebration Mile for Johnston last season was Bow Creek but, like many of the trainer's better inmates last season, he has moved on to Godolphin. Other stars from last season who have also moved there or to foreign stables include the Tattersalls Millions 2yo Trophy winner Secret Brief, International Stakes winner Heavy Metal and Bahrain Trophy winner Hartnell. Muteela, Johnston's star filly last season, has been retired, while Alex My Boy has gone to Germany and Salutation has moved on.

To an average trainer these losses would be catastrophic, but this is simply the way Johnston goes about his business. The trainer has struck up a healthy partnership with some top Arab owners, and contained within this partnership is the understanding that, as well as parting with some of his stable stars, Johnston will be allowed to keep others.

One such star still housed in the Middleham stables, and one that has Johnston very excited, is black type-winner *Muraaqaba*. The Dubawi filly made the perfect start to her career when beating a good field in a Newmarket maiden, and she has since gone on to add a Group 3 to her tally. Although she was beaten either side of those performances, she had excuses, and there is little doubt that is more to come from this lightly raced three-year-old.

"Muraaqaba is very well in herself and I would say she is very much one of my brighter lights for the season," says Johnston.

"She's rated only 104 which is quite low for a Group 3 winner but my gut feeling is that we'll take her to the 1,000 Guineas. It's possible she will go for a Guineas trial but I think it's more likely we'll go straight to the Newmarket race without a prep run. I'd say out of the whole of our team we're most excited about her."

Another of the trainer's winners from last season who has realistic Group race aspirations is *Mister Universe*. The highly tried three-year-old has clearly shown enough ability at home to warrant an Investec Derby entry, and it is likely the Abdulla Al Mansoori-owned colt will again be pitched in against some of the classiest of his generation this season. Out of a Group 1 winner at four, there are reasons to expect the son of Cape Cross to improve with age.

"I was very excited about him last season and I actually thought he was among the nicest two-year-olds I had at the time," says the trainer.

"Unfortunately he was disappointing at Newmarket, and at Salisbury I don't think he stayed the trip. He's done well over the winter and I'll be starting him off over a mile although I don't have a target for him yet. I imagine we'll probably be aiming him at some black type this season."

It would be difficult to find any horse who epitomises Johnston's skill quite as much as the astonishing *Maid In Rio*. Her achievements might not be on a par with the best horses that Johnston has seen come through his yard, but the speed of her improvement last season – from selling race to valuable handicap – was remarkable. To put her achievements into perspective, in May last year she was rated 65, but just two months later she was competing off a mark of 96.

"She went up dramatically in the handicap for her win in the Brown Jack at Ascot and she couldn't quite compete in that sphere from then on - she was in a ball park that was beyond her I think. She didn't look like she stayed in the Goodwood Stakes when she went there at the Glorious meeting. She'll be looking for black type again as she's so high in the handicap, and I'd imagine her first target of the season will be the Further Flight Stakes at Nottingham [April 9]."

As is the norm with the winter lull, Johnston has had a number of runners on the all-weather both in England and overseas. One of those who has been recently campaigned in Meydan is the admirably hardy *Fire Fighting*. Although he wasn't quite as good in his final two races, there was much to be gained from his Meydan debut.

"He's been running in Dubai and put up a great performance against a horse of

Godolphin's, Al Saham, on his first start out there. He was disappointing on his next outing but last time was all wrong as he went off very fast and Silvestre de Sousa couldn't hold on to him."

There are some valuable prizes on the all-weather at this time of the year, culminating in the Good Friday Championship races at Lingfield, and it seems that is the likely route for the Alan Spence-owned four-year-old.

"He's back in England now and had his first start over two miles at Chelmsford City as a prep run for a tilt at the championship long-distance race on Good Friday."

Another who has had a stint in Dubai is *Sennockian Star*. Like many of the trainer's horses, he was campaigned as though having a rest were not an option, lining up 14 times last year and proving very consistent. His performances in Dubai have

not been as good, but vibes are positive that the Cheveley Park-bred gelding can rediscover the winning thread this season.

"He's been running in Dubai as well as Fire Fighting, but the handicapper has been rather strange with him. He was rated 101 but after being reassessed has been dropped only 2lb. He had a great year here last season and was on a high for most of it. He'll be aimed at handicaps again."

Another of Johnston's battalion that will be aimed at high-class handicaps is *Oriental Fox*. Among other tough assignments last year he competed in the Ascot Gold Cup finishing sixth but promoted to fifth – and it appears the drop to a more realistic level will be the aim this year.

"He's been for a break over the winter and hasn't started anything fast yet. I imagine we'll take him along slowly and aim for a race

Sennockian Star (second left) will be plying his trade in handicaps again after a busy campaign last year

this season like the Northumberland Plate. He's already shown he can win a race of that nature when he finished second, beaten a short head, two years ago in the same race."

One horse who has featured on the all-weather over the winter at a good level is *Lyn Valley*. Although the four-year-old by Shamardal could manage only one victory last season, that win was in a good handicap at Goodwood, and he showed what he is capable of on synthetics when finishing a gallant second to the high-class Maverick Wave in November. Although he's not run since, his final run will have satisfied connections, and there is definite cause to be hopeful this season.

"Lyn Valley is a very in-and-out horse who has been doing some fast work. He'll be campaigned over middle distances but at the moment he has no particular target. Unfortunately he's currently very high in the handicap as he went up from a mark of 90 to 96 after winning at Goodwood in the summer."

Blue Wave is another who has flirted with the Polytrack. A triple winner at Lingfield last winter, he coupled that with a victory at Southwell, and the Sheikh Hamdan-owned five-year-old is clearly no stranger to the winner's enclosure. However, he has not yet been seen this year and it looks as though the bigger handicaps in the summer will be the target.

"Blue Wave has had a slight setback but all seems well now. He's had some respite from the handicapper, who has taken him down from a mark of 102 to a mark of 97 and I imagine the targets this season will be the big handicaps and I hope he'll be competitive."

Among the vast army of Johnston two-year-olds there are usually one or two who are a cut above the others – last year Muraaqaba and Pallister shone out – and this season there is already one who has caught Johnston's eye.

"It's very difficult to say which of our two-year-olds has the best prospects as this year we have a huge number – 120 – it's really too early to tell. They've only just started galloping but one that has caught my eye and stood out a bit is a horse of Hamdan Al Maktoum's called *Muatadel*. He could be one for the future."

On the gallops at Mark Johnston's Middleham stables

MARK JOHNSTON
MIDDLEHAM MOOR, N YORKS

	No. of Hrs	Races Run	1st	2nd	3rd	Unpl	Per cent	£1 Level Stake
2-y-o	69	303	43	46	45	169	14.2	-104.02
3-y-o	92	698	116	97	108	377	16.6	-112.56
4-y-o+	51	343	48	34	36	225	14.0	-65.32
Totals	212	1344	207	177	189	771	15.4	-281.90
2013	253	1557	216	200	190	951	13.9	+37.17
2012	211	1344	215	158	151	815	16.0	-11.38

BY MONTH

2-y-o	W-R	Per cent	£1 Level Stake	3-y-o	W-R	Per cent	£1 Level Stake
January	0-0	0.0	0.00	January	9-19	47.4	+14.78
February	0-0	0.0	0.00	February	5-26	19.2	-8.38
March	0-0	0.0	0.00	March	12-36	33.3	-5.76
April	1-7	14.3	-0.50	April	9-63	14.3	-19.10
May	3-21	14.3	+5.10	May	11-91	12.1	-5.65
June	13-40	32.5	+32.13	June	14-99	14.1	-7.92
July	7-53	13.2	-27.89	July	26-116	22.4	+5.34
August	7-49	14.3	-16.33	August	14-101	13.9	-27.04
September	9-64	14.1	-42.77	September	14-85	16.5	-3.34
October	1-43	2.3	-37.50	October	2-44	4.5	-37.50
November	1-23	4.3	-17.00	November	0-14	0.0	-14.00
December	1-3	33.3	+0.75	December	0-4	0.0	-4.00

4-y-o	W-R	Per cent	£1 Level Stake	Totals	W-R	Per cent	£1 Level Stake
January	7-26	26.9	-8.17	January	16-45	35.6	+6.61
February	4-23	17.4	-7.90	February	9-49	18.4	-16.28
March	9-36	25.0	+7.60	March	21-72	29.2	+1.84
April	9-57	15.8	-21.69	April	19-127	15.0	-41.29
May	5-54	9.3	-26.00	May	19-166	11.4	-26.55
June	5-53	9.4	-18.50	June	32-192	16.7	+5.71
July	7-34	20.6	+48.00	July	40-203	19.7	+25.45
August	0-27	0.0	-27.00	August	21-177	11.9	-70.37
September	2-16	12.5	+5.33	September	25-165	15.2	-40.78
October	0-15	0.0	-15.00	October	3-102	2.9	-90.00
November	0-1	0.0	-1.00	November	1-38	2.6	-15.00
December	0-1	0.0	-1.00	December	1-8	12.5	-5.00

DISTANCE

2-y-o	W-R	Per cent	£1 Level Stake	3-y-o	W-R	Per cent	£1 Level Stake
5f-6f	25-154	16.2	-27.29	5f-6f	10-63	15.9	-19.98
7f-8f	16-139	11.5	-71.06	7f-8f	33-246	13.4	-40.34
9f-13f	2-10	20.0	-5.67	9f-13f	67-358	18.7	-43.16
14f+	0-0	0.0	0.00	14f+	6-31	19.4	-9.08

4-y-o	W-R	Per cent	£1 Level Stake	Totals	W-R	Per cent	£1 Level Stake
5f-6f	1-6	16.7	+1.00	5f-6f	36-223	16.1	-46.27
7f-8f	15-134	11.2	-29.25	7f-8f	64-519	12.3	-140.65
9f-13f	23-153	15.0	-16.35	9f-13f	92-521	17.7	-65.18
14f+	9-50	18.0	-20.72	14f+	15-81	18.5	-29.80

TYPE OF RACE

Non-Handicaps	W-R	Per cent	£1 Level Stake	Handicaps	W-R	Per cent	£1 Level Stake
2-y-o	34-235	14.5	-75.85	2-y-o	9-68	13.2	-28.17
3-y-o	20-149	13.4	-51.12	3-y-o	96-549	17.5	-61.45
4-y-o+	7-42	16.7	+6.00	4-y-o+	41-301	13.6	-48.66

RACE CLASS

	W-R	Per cent	£1 Level Stake
Class 1	9-78	11.5	-27.17
Class 2	26-252	10.3	-30.50
Class 3	16-168	9.5	-67.03
Class 4	60-336	17.9	-46.66
Class 5	75-423	17.7	-102.22
Class 6	21-87	24.1	-7.33
Class 7	0-0	0.0	0.00

FIRST TIME OUT

	W-R	Per cent	£1 Level Stake
2-y-o	7-69	10.1	-26.17
3-y-o	21-92	22.8	-25.85
4-y-o+	12-51	23.5	-11.82
Totals	40-212	18.9	-63.84

DID YOU KNOW

Mark Johnston worked for three years as a vet before he began training. Now his yard is a winning machine. Johnston became the first to send out 200 winners in a season in 2009 and he has passed that landmark on four occasions since then, including last year.

MARK JOHNSTON: ASSESSING THE STATS

A total of 207 winners in 2014, more than any other trainer last term, was par for the course for Mark Johnston although the £2.9 million earned in prize-money was a personal best. That was part in thanks to Secret Brief, a useful juvenile who landed a couple of valuable sales contests, *writes Kevin Morley*.

After winning those big pots at Newmarket in the autumn, Secret Brief came up short when upped in class in the Dewhurst and his exploits highlight what has been missing from the yard for quite some time.

While Johnston continues to have handicap winners galore, his runners consistently came up short at the top level and you have go to back as far as 2009 to find his last Group 1 winner in Britain when Awzaan landed the Middle Park.

In fairness to the Middleham handler, he often loses some of his promising types to Godolphin. As such, Classic or any kind of success at the highest level will be tough to achieve again this term unless a talented juvenile emerges within his ranks.

Johnston has his share of winners at Listed and Group level but the best way to profit from his string is to focus on the stayers. All three-year-olds running between 1m2f and 1m4f returned a profit, and it is a similar story with all older horses running in excess of 1m4f.

The majority of the yard's horses tend to excel on fast ground so it is no surprise to learn the stable is at its busiest during the summer. June and July were particularly profitable months for Johnston last term, much to the benefit of punters.

With such a big string, Johnston uses a wider range of jockeys than most. Joe Fanning, Silvestre de Sousa and Franny Norton are all given plenty of rides but none return a level-stake profit. Johnston's more selective use of Adam Kirby is worth looking out for, but the most impressive figures were posted by Dane O'Neill (11 from 27, 41 per cent) and Paul Mulrennan (four from six, 67 per cent).

Johnston enjoys plenty of success at run-of-the-mill meetings close to his North Yorkshire base and he boasts excellent figures at Beverley and Catterick. However, his favourite track is Goodwood. He continues to provide a solid strike-rate and profit at the Sussex track and his runners at the Glorious meeting in the summer are always respected.

Rapid progress of G Force and Custom Cut show O'Meara has magic touch

DAVID O'MEARA'S ability to transform horses who have lost enthusiasm for racing, coupled with his capacity for improving those who appeared to have reached their limit are both qualities that have marked him out as a trainer to follow in recent seasons.

On top of that, last term O'Meara demonstrated he could compete with the most powerful stables on the biggest stage of all, saddling his stable star *G Force* to win the Group 1 Betfred Sprint Cup at Haydock in September, *writes Tom Bull.*

G Force's ascension of the sprinting ranks last year was achieved at lightning pace, and there are few who would have predicted that when he narrowly won a Newcastle maiden in April he would be competing and winning at the highest level just a few months later. Understandably, O'Meara and his team are confident of more top-tier success now their best horse has broken his Group 1 duck, and a route for the season has already been marked out.

"G Force is in good order and has had a nice break," says O'Meara. "The aim will be to start him off in the Temple Stakes at Haydock and then we'll go on to look at races like the King's Stand at Royal Ascot. He'll go down the Group 1 route over the minimum distance and I think he will improve further this season."

Another of O'Meara's squad who acquitted himself admirably at Group level last season was the phenomenally consistent *Custom Cut.* Before the six-year-old by Notnowcato had arrived at O'Meara's stables, he had looked exposed as a good handicapper and occasional Listed winner. But, as is the case with so many, Custom Cut was transformed by the northern trainer's handling, and last season he racked up a series of victories that culminated in a Group 2 success at Newmarket.

"Custom Cut was a star for us last season. He showed admirable toughness on a number of occasions and it takes a good horse to win five races in a row at any level, but he managed to do it in Listed and Group races. At Ascot on Champions Day the ground was against him and I'm not sure if he'll go for a Group 1 this season or not but we'll try to find good races for him over a mile."

It wasn't just Group races that propelled O'Meara to his most successful season thus far. He also gained a number of top handicap victories, including bagging the Ayr Gold Cup with *Louis The Pious*.

O'Meara says: "Louis The Pious was great for us last year and showed he's best in big-field handicaps when winning the Ayr Gold Cup towards the end of the season. However, because of that he's now pretty high in the handicap and I think we'll look to start him off in a conditions race. He might go for some black type this year and maybe he'll have a go in some Group races. We might have to go down that route as his handicap mark is now so high".

The 2014 season started off perfectly for *That Is The Spirit*, with three straight victories that ended in a Listed race win at Epsom, and O'Meara is confident his gelding can rediscover the winning thread this year. Although only in his first season last year, the four-year-old was pitched into Group 1 company on his final start and is clearly held in some regard.

"That Is The Spirit progressed well last season and probably reached his peak at Epsom in the Listed Surrey Stakes. I imagine the target this season will be Group races over six or seven furlongs."

Another of O'Meara's top handicap successes came courtesy of the strong-travelling *Out Do* in the Great St Wilfrid at Ripon. There is little doubt the horse's consistency will be rewarded again this season at some point, and the trainer is looking forward to targeting similar races later in the campaign.

"Out Do had a good success at Ripon last season when he won the Great St Wilfrid.

The target this year will be another top six-furlong handicap, and we could aim him at the Ayr Gold Cup as he has plenty of speed and likes a bit of cover so the race could suit him down to the ground."

O'Meara trained the tough *Move In Time* to win the Prix de l'Abbaye last year, providing him with a second Group 1 success of the season.

"Move In Time is doing well and comes alive at the back end of the season which is where his main targets will be. The Prix de l'Abbaye could be on the agenda again," the trainer says.

O'Meara has also had horses in Dubai over the winter, and one who has plied his trade there is the Middleham Park-owned *Earth Drummer*. Despite not putting his best foot forward in the Gulf, there are reasons to be hopeful for a successful season ahead.

"He's had a long season and now is having a bit of a break. He's done well on the all-

Louis The Pious: Ayr Gold Cup winner will try his hand in Group races this season

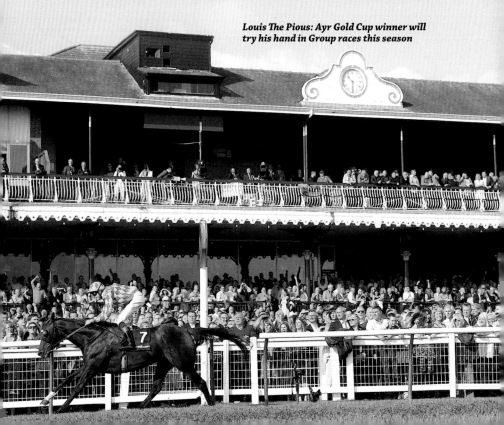

weather in England and Dubai and I think he'll go for targets on synthetics later in the year."

Joining Earth Drummer in Dubai was the seven-year-old *Robert The Painter*. Last season proved to be a fruitful one for the consistent gelding, with a third in the Lincoln accompanying a good victory in a Thirsk handicap.

"Robert The Painter has been running in Dubai and is back now. He had a good year last year and will have a prep run on the all-weather at some point. He takes his racing well as he showed in April and May last year, where he had four starts in two months."

Another of O'Meara's charges who could be aimed at some black type this season is *Balducci*. There is undoubtedly a lot of talent hiding in the son of Dansili but extracting it has proved to be a difficult task, but this year vibes are good that Balducci can get back on track.

"Balducci is one of our older horses who needs fast ground. We may aim him at the Melrose Stakes at York but it could be quite a challenge for him. We'll also be looking at good mile handicaps for him this season."

One of the stars in recent seasons for O'Meara's stable has been *Penitent*. A durable horse who has been campaigned at a similar level for the last few years, he again proved last season that he has ability left in the locker with a Group 3 victory, and it is likely he will be aimed at similar contests this year.

"The likelihood is Penitent will be aimed at the Lincoln. He's been working well and will want a bit of cut in the ground. He won a Group 3 last season but then his form tailed off. The Lincoln will be a good guide as to where we stand with him at the moment."

Among the brace of good handicappers housed in the Arthington Barn stables is the somewhat frustrating *Two For Two*. Although he has brought home good prizes on a number of occasions, the style of his running means he needs a lot of luck, and in a couple of races last year he was blocked off

when he was just about to make his challenge.

O'Meara says: "Two For Two is a 95-100 rated horse who needs a strongly run race and a good gallop. He has a very high cruising speed and just needs to switch off, and I think the contest that could suit him is the Heritage Handicap."

Another handicapper who needs a bit of luck is *Highland Acclaim*. The four-year-old by Acclamation ran some fantastic races last season, including a very close second in the Coral Sprint Trophy at York, and hopes are high at Helmsley he can get back in the winning groove this season.

"Highland Acclaim needs a good gallop in a big field because in a small field he can be too free. The faster they go the better and last season he kept improving and the aim will be good handicaps with a large number of runners."

One of the more hardened handicappers at the O'Meara stables is *Frontier Fighter*. The Fibresand specialist has put up some good performances this year and his trainer thinks there are some good contests to be won with him later in the season: "Frontier Fighter is back working now and is fit and well. He's being aimed at a 0-105 handicap at Goodwood over seven furlongs. He goes well fresh."

O'Meara's stable size is growing year on year, and with success upon success there is every chance his operation will keep expanding. With that in mind, there are naturally a number of two-year-olds and lightly raced horses who have either not yet seen the racecourse or have gone under the radar. The trainer nominates one from his battalion he is excited about this season:

"One who sticks out a bit is *Hail The Hero*, who came from Ballydoyle. He's been given a Guineas entry and looks a nice prospect."

Penitent: likely to be sent in search of further success at Group 3 level

DAVID O'MEARA: ASSESSING THE STATS

David O'Meara is probably the most progressive trainer in Britain. The Nawton handler has smashed the century barrier for the past two seasons and, although last term's tally of 112 winners wasn't as high as his previous 136, the prize-money column increased from £1.1 million to £1.7m, *writes Kevin Morley*.

As those figures suggest, O'Meara managed to secure some bigger prizes last term. Handicaps remain the staple diet of his yard's success, with the victories of Louis The Pious in the Buckingham Palace at Royal Ascot and the Ayr Gold Cup the highlights.

But O'Meara boosted his standing last term thanks largely to his performances in Group races. Custom Cut landed five Pattern contests on the bounce, ranging from Listed to Group 2, but what caught the eye more was the Betfred Sprint Cup success of G Force, a first Group 1 winner in Britain for O'Meara. Not settling for that, he also sent out Move In Time to land the Prix de l'Abbaye to give him a first Group 1 prize abroad.

As his highest-profile wins suggest, O'Meara is at his most effective in races over a mile and shorter, with the sprinters in particular standing out. All runners aged three and older and running at 5f or 6f have been profitable to follow over the past five seasons.

If there is one aspect in which the yard could improve it would be with juvenile output. Two-year-olds aren't the strongest category but an improvement in this area would certainly see O'Meara progress further as a trainer.

He isn't the fastest out of the gate for the turf season's early exchanges and he doesn't have an end-of-season flourish, but he is very strong between the months of May and September when the Flat season is at its busiest.

Danny Tudhope rides most of the yard's winners to a decent strike-rate although the mounts of Silvestre de Sousa have proved more profitable to follow over the past five seasons.

O'Meara has a high strike-rate when sending his string north of the border, boasting decent figures at Ayr, Musselburgh and Hamilton. However, he sends most of his winners to Ripon and has returned a level-stake profit at the track over the past five seasons.

David O'Meara's string enjoy a trip to the gallops at Malton

DAVID O'MEARA

NAWTON, N YORKS

	No. of Hrs	Races Run	1st	2nd	3rd	Unpl	Per cent	£1 Level Stake
2-y-o	19	92	9	14	16	53	9.8	-49.15
3-y-o	37	220	30	27	30	133	13.6	-63.47
4-y-o+	78	518	73	46	63	336	14.1	+10.47
Totals	134	830	112	87	109	522	13.5	-102.15
2013	152	905	136	85	109	575	15.0	-59.30
2012	95	542	69	64	64	345	12.7	-33.45

BY MONTH

2-y-o	W-R	Per cent	£1 Level Stake	3-y-o	W-R	Per cent	£1 Level Stake
January	0-0	0.0	0.00	January	0-3	0.0	-3.00
February	0-0	0.0	0.00	February	0-7	0.0	-7.00
March	0-0	0.0	0.00	March	1-8	12.5	-1.00
April	0-0	0.0	0.00	April	4-18	22.2	-4.00
May	0-5	0.0	-5.00	May	6-28	21.4	-11.23
June	0-8	0.0	-8.00	June	5-29	17.2	-2.80
July	1-16	6.3	-8.00	July	2-25	8.0	-16.67
August	4-21	19.0	-4.25	August	5-37	13.5	-7.50
September	3-17	17.6	-3.40	September	4-29	13.8	+1.23
October	0-12	0.0	-12.00	October	1-21	4.8	-12.00
November	1-6	16.7	-1.50	November	0-5	0.0	-5.00
December	0-7	0.0	-7.00	December	2-10	20.0	+5.50

4-y-o	W-R	Per cent	£1 Level Stake	Totals	W-R	Per cent	£1 Level Stake
January	3-17	17.6	-5.25	January	3-20	15.0	-8.25
February	3-13	23.1	+8.75	February	3-20	15.0	+1.75
March	2-19	10.5	-11.25	March	3-27	11.1	-12.25
April	7-38	18.4	+14.38	April	11-56	19.6	+10.38
May	9-75	12.0	-2.17	May	15-108	13.9	-18.40
June	14-82	17.1	+18.72	June	19-119	16.0	+7.92
July	8-69	11.6	-18.50	July	11-110	10.0	-43.17
August	12-59	20.3	+5.25	August	21-117	17.9	-6.50
September	9-56	16.1	+27.03	September	16-102	15.7	+24.86
October	2-51	3.9	-32.00	October	3-84	3.6	-56.00
November	3-25	12.0	+14.00	November	4-36	11.1	+9.00
December	1-14	7.1	-8.50	December	3-31	9.7	-3.00

DISTANCE

2-y-o	W-R	Per cent	£1 Level Stake	3-y-o	W-R	Per cent	£1 Level Stake
5f-6f	5-56	8.9	-29.00	5f-6f	18-101	17.8	+6.10
7f-8f	4-35	11.4	-19.15	7f-8f	8-77	10.4	-49.30
9f-13f	0-1	0.0	-1.00	9f-13f	3-39	7.7	-22.77
14f+	0-0	0.0	0.00	14f+	1-3	33.3	+2.50

4-y-o	W-R	Per cent	£1 Level Stake	Totals	W-R	Per cent	£1 Level Stake
5f-6f	17-106	16.0	+37.05	5f-6f	40-263	15.2	+14.15
7f-8f	29-265	10.9	-39.63	7f-8f	41-377	10.9	-108.08
9f-13f	26-120	21.7	+36.04	9f-13f	29-160	18.1	+12.27
14f+	1-27	3.7	-23.00	14f+	2-30	6.7	-20.50

TYPE OF RACE

Non-Handicaps	W-R	Per cent	£1 Level Stake	Handicaps	W-R	Per cent	£1 Level Stake
2-y-o	6-68	8.8	-40.15	2-y-o	3-24	12.5	-9.00
3-y-o	10-64	15.6	-20.93	3-y-o	20-156	12.8	-42.54
4-y-o+	13-75	17.3	+76.00	4-y-o+	60-443	13.5	-15.44

RACE CLASS / FIRST TIME OUT

RACE CLASS	W-R	Per cent	£1 Level Stake	FIRST TIME OUT	W-R	Per cent	£1 Level Stake
Class 1	7-47	14.9	+30.60	2-y-o	1-19	5.3	-11.00
Class 2	15-187	8.0	-43.25	3-y-o	3-37	8.1	-24.00
Class 3	23-115	20.0	+16.13	4-y-o+	11-78	14.1	-8.13
Class 4	27-161	16.8	+1.04				
Class 5	25-204	12.3	-88.83	Totals	15-134	11.2	-43.13
Class 6	15-115	13.0	-16.84				
Class 7	0-1	0.0	-1.00				

Custom Cut strikes in the Joel Stakes at Newmarket for David O'Meara

Gatsby out to sprinkle more stardust for yard with fine mix of talent

WITH an exciting crop of young talent, a smattering of established performers and a bona fide European power, Kevin Ryan looks to have struck on the perfect blend for the season.

For all the quality housed at Hambleton Lodge, there is no mistaking the stable's leading light after *The Grey Gatsby* sprinkled the stardust on another sparkling campaign, *writes Andrew Dietz*.

Although the total number of winners was the lowest for a decade, quality superseded quantity as Ryan maintained his steady stream of big-race winners.

In the past he has relied on juveniles and sprinters to carve out his niche as a trainer to fear at the top level, but The Grey Gatsby changed all that during a sensational 2014.

Having dented some lofty reputations in the Dante, the distinctive grey delivered his trainer's first Classic victory in the Prix du Jockey Club before turning round the form of the Juddmonte International to beat Australia in his own backyard in the Irish Champion Stakes.

That performance under an inspired Ryan Moore earned The Grey Gatsby the title of joint European champion in last year's World Rankings alongside Australia and Kingman, and out of that trio he is the only one still in training.

"He's a top-class horse and hopefully he'll have a very good year again," says Ryan.

"He's done marvellous over the winter and hasn't lost any of his speed but I've no doubt he'll stay a mile and a half. He likes fast ground and although he'll go on ground with a bit of cut, he hates it soft."

Ryan has signalled his intention to start The Grey Gatsby's four-year-old campaign on Dubai World Cup night before heading to Royal Ascot.

"After Dubai he's likely to go to Royal Ascot and his season is pretty much mapped out after that. He'll head back to York for the Juddmonte and on to the Irish Champion Stakes again."

Crack sprinter *Hot Streak* gave Ryan another high point last season when winning the Group 2 Temple Stakes at Haydock.

He followed that with a solid third in the King's Stand Stakes at Royal Ascot and although his season fizzled out on four more Group 1 starts, Ryan expects further improvement from a horse he has described on occasions as the best he has trained.

"There's going to be loads more to come from him," the trainer says. "He's grown and strengthened and is a very genuine and classy horse with a lot of speed.

"He'll be going for the Group 1 sprints this season and will probably take the same route to Royal Ascot as last year with Newmarket [Palace House Stakes] and Haydock coming first.

"Both sprint distances come the same to him and he copes with most conditions, although he doesn't want rattling quick ground."

Astaire came close to gaining a Group 2 sprint of his own last season only to go down by half a length in the Duke of York Stakes, which will be the early-season target again.

He has however already gained victory at the highest level when edging out Hot Streak in the Middle Park Stakes as a juvenile and the four-year-old adds more depth to the sprinting team.

"He's really developed over the winter and has grown into himself and filled his frame," Ryan says.

"He ran some cracking races last year including in the Duke of York and that would be one of his main aims with a prep run.

"I wouldn't rule out seven furlongs now he's a year older but for the first half of the year he'll go sprinting."

Like Astaire, *Blaine* is a former Gimcrack Stakes winner and he could be another sprinter to keep tabs on as he bids to make the step up to Pattern level.

The five-year-old came back to his best last year with victories at Hamilton and York, the highlights in a string of solid displays in some of the season's biggest sprint handicaps.

"He ran incredibly well all year and was an unlucky third in the Ayr Gold Cup as he got locked up on the rail before coming home really well," Ryan says.

"He's improved over the winter and will start off sprint handicapping for the first half of the season and then we might end up going travelling for a Listed or Group 3 race."

One horse to have already made a splash overseas is *Glory Awaits*, who brought home the International Topkapi Trophy as a souvenir from his trip to Turkey in September.

Earlier in the season, the 2013 2,000 Guineas runner-up had won a Listed race at Chester but more globetrotting appears to be on his itinerary.

"The race he won in Turkey will be his main aim this year and I wouldn't rule out taking him to America to try and win a Grade 1," says Ryan.

"He's a solid horse who turns up and runs his race. He always wanted top of the ground but he won in Turkey on ground on the easy side so it seems as he gets older he copes with it better."

Following an influx of breeze-up purchases, Ryan had his biggest team of two-year-olds last season and although he raced only once, £260,000 purchase *Flaming Spear* could prove the pick of them.

His sole outing in a York maiden in which Ryan has a history of unleashing his top juvenile talent was successful as he followed The Grey Gatsby and Blaine on to the roll of honour.

The strapping son of Lope De Vega can be backed at 20-1 for the Qipco 2,000 Guineas. He was not sighted in action again after his debut win, but connections are hoping their patient approach pays dividends.

"He was big and backward last year and we think the decision to give him time will benefit him in the long run," says Ryan. "He did what we expected at York and Ryan Moore was impressed with him.

"He's really filled out and looks absolutely fantastic and we're quite excited by him. All things being equal he'll go to Newbury for the Greenham. For such a big horse he's very fast and we wouldn't be going further than a mile with him."

A Classic run is also in the pipeline for filly *Calypso Beat*, who struck at Listed level before finishing second in two Group 3s over 7f.

She ended last season finishing last of nine in the Rockfel Stakes but she had previously shown enough to suggest she could develop into a smart performer.

"She did very well last year and was possibly a bit unlucky not to win a Group race in France as the ground came up very heavy," says Ryan.

"She's grown, which is something you like to see in a filly, and seems more relaxed. Although she needs to step up to be a Guineas filly, she's in both the English and French versions.

"There's no reason why there shouldn't be a lot more improvement in her and we'll possibly go back to France to start her off in April."

Having shown blistering speed in handicap successes at Glorious Goodwood and York's Ebor meeting, *Online Alexander* looks capable of taking her form to another level this season.

Ryan says: "She ran two solid races on her last starts at Listed level on ground she hated. She has to have fast ground and it's a case of the faster the better for her. She was always a little weak and backward and she's definitely a better filly this year.

"It's all about getting black-type and we'll try to win a Listed race before stepping up to Group level."

Speed is also a key component for the appropriately named *Fast Act*, who won a Carlisle maiden before making the frame in the Weatherbys Super Sprint and Molecomb Stakes.

He proved too headstrong when stepped up to 6f at York but returned to form with a fourth-place finish in the Group 2 Flying Childers on his last start.

"He has a lot of speed and has done particularly well over the winter," says Ryan.

"He's grown and has definitely got stronger. He'll have plenty of opportunities and I'm very hopeful he will progress."

Salateen was killing time as a two-year-old last year but he still showed ample ability, rounding off a promising campaign finishing a five-length third behind subsequent Racing Post Trophy winner Elm Park in the Group 2 Royal Lodge Stakes.

Before Newmarket he had won two of his five starts and he maintained his upward trajectory throughout the season.

"He ran really well in the Royal Lodge," says Ryan. "He led into the Dip and quickened up really nicely – the ground was just a bit quick for him and he didn't let himself down on it.

"He was quite weak last year and we're looking forward to him. He's in the English and French Guineas and, while a good surface is not a problem, he wouldn't want any firm in the ground."

Another colt who continued to improve throughout his two-year-old campaign was *Teruntum Star*, who struggled in two starts in Pattern company but advertised his potential with a comprehensive victory in a Haydock nursery.

"He put up some very good performances

Salateen (noseband) should come into his own at three

last year and he's done really well from two to three," says Ryan.

"He was a bit over the top on his last start of the season at York but there's a lot more to come from him and he looks a stronger horse now and will probably start off in a conditions race somewhere."

Time got the better of *Weld Al Emarat* last season but Ryan still managed to squeeze in a juvenile start and, although he won only a Southwell maiden in December, his trainer is looking forward to getting him on grass.

"He's a huge horse and was a slow-burner last season," Ryan says. "He did some nice bits of work at the end of August but unfortunately wasn't ready to go but he did it quite well at Southwell."

Captain Colby, a half-brother to the stable's Group 3-winning sprinting stalwart Benbaun, landed two of his four starts, rounding off his campaign with victory in a Chester nursery.

Ryan says: "He was a big backward two-year-old who showed lots of speed and you'd like to think he'll keep progressing."

The form of *Charlie Croker* received a sizeable boost when Charming Thought

DID YOU KNOW

Frankie Dettori and Graham Lee were two of the earliest jockeys to record Pattern victories for Kevin Ryan. Dettori won the Group 3 Greenlands Stakes in Ireland for the Hambleton trainer in 1999, while Lee landed the Grade 2 John Smith's Hurdle for the yard in his days as a jump jockey. Nowadays most of Ryan's horses are ridden by Phillip Makin and daughter Amy.

pierced the bubble of Ivawood in the Middle Park. The Carlisle maiden winner finished three and a quarter lengths behind the Godolphin colt in a novice stakes at Leicester before finding the step up in class at York too stern a test.

"He had only a few runs last year and won his maiden before finishing third in a conditions race not beaten far," Ryan says. "He's done really well over the winter."

The trainer has proved to be a dab hand in the top sprint handicaps over the years and *Lexington Abbey* fits the mould as the type of horse he excels with.

"He's a big horse and it was only in the second half of the season he learned how to race. We dropped him in and the more he learned to settle, the better he came home.

"We're looking forward to him and hopefully he'll be one for the better sprint handicaps."

The pick of *Bogart's* eight winless starts last year was chasing home the exciting Muthmir in the Portland Handicap at Doncaster, and he looks well capable of exploiting a current mark of 94.

"He ran some solid races," Ryan says. "He'll go for all the big sprint handicaps and he's certainly not badly handicapped."

The trainer enjoyed some great days with Amadeus Wolf and although *Lesha*, one of the talented sprinter's offspring, might not reach the level of his sire, he could make an impact in handicaps.

"He started very early last season and held his form all the way through," Ryan says. "A mile and quarter might be his trip this year and Epsom and Chester might suit him."

KEVIN RYAN
HAMBLETON, N YORKS

	No. of Hrs	Races Run	1st	2nd	3rd	Unpl	Per cent	£1 Level Stake
2-y-o	63	231	29	25	28	149	12.6	-41.60
3-y-o	33	216	31	28	18	139	14.4	-39.37
4-y-o+	29	187	18	16	22	131	9.6	-89.79
Totals	125	634	78	69	68	419	12.3	-170.76
2013	140	781	94	86	73	528	12.0	-28.12
2012	154	789	95	74	78	539	12.0	-69.01

BY MONTH

2-y-o	W-R	Per cent	£1 Level Stake	3-y-o	W-R	Per cent	£1 Level Stake
January	0-0	0.0	0.00	January	1-10	10.0	-7.75
February	0-0	0.0	0.00	February	1-9	11.1	+12.00
March	0-0	0.0	0.00	March	5-13	38.5	+1.71
April	1-7	14.3	+3.00	April	3-25	12.0	-8.50
May	1-22	4.5	-18.50	May	4-25	16.0	-4.00
June	4-19	21.1	+40.25	June	2-30	6.7	-21.25
July	6-36	16.7	-5.65	July	4-29	13.8	+4.21
August	5-53	9.4	-18.25	August	5-33	15.2	-6.38
September	7-49	14.3	-12.57	September	3-21	14.3	-1.50
October	3-28	10.7	-20.50	October	1-10	10.0	-2.00
November	1-6	16.7	-3.38	November	2-7	28.6	-1.92
December	1-11	9.1	-6.00	December	0-4	0.0	-4.00

4-y-o	W-R	Per cent	£1 Level Stake	Totals	W-R	Per cent	£1 Level Stake
January	3-17	17.6	-5.00	January	4-27	14.8	-12.75
February	2-8	25.0	-1.90	February	3-17	17.6	+10.10
March	1-11	9.1	-7.00	March	6-24	25.0	-5.29
April	4-32	12.5	-12.89	April	8-64	12.5	-18.39
May	0-29	0.0	-29.00	May	5-76	6.6	-51.50
June	0-21	0.0	-21.00	June	6-70	8.6	-2.00
July	4-18	22.2	+5.00	July	14-83	16.9	+3.56
August	4-24	16.7	+9.00	August	14-110	12.7	-15.63

DISTANCE

2-y-o	W-R	Per cent	£1 Level Stake	3-y-o	W-R	Per cent	£1 Level Stake
5f-6f	21-144	14.6	+6.40	5f-6f	14-107	13.1	-35.47
7f-8f	8-87	9.2	-48.00	7f-8f	16-84	19.0	+11.10
9f-13f	0-0	0.0	0.00	9f-13f	1-23	4.3	-13.00
14f+	0-0	0.0	0.00	14f+	0-2	0.0	-2.00

4-y-o	W-R	Per cent	£1 Level Stake	Totals	W-R	Per cent	£1 Level Stake
5f-6f	9-83	10.8	-39.54	5f-6f	44-334	13.2	-68.61
7f-8f	4-78	5.1	-53.00	7f-8f	28-249	11.2	-89.90
9f-13f	5-26	19.2	+2.75	9f-13f	6-49	12.2	-10.25
14f+	0-0	0.0	0.00	14f+	0-2	0.0	-2.00

TYPE OF RACE

Non-Handicaps	W-R	Per cent	£1 Level Stake	Handicaps	W-R	Per cent	£1 Level Stake
2-y-o	21-180	11.7	-39.47	2-y-o	8-51	15.7	-2.13
3-y-o	9-45	20.0	+3.30	3-y-o	22-171	12.9	-42.67
4-y-o+	3-27	11.1	-2.00	4-y-o+	15-160	9.4	-76.04

RACE CLASS / FIRST TIME OUT

	W-R	Per cent	£1 Level Stake		W-R	Per cent	£1 Level Stake
Class 1	5-40	12.5	+8.00	2-y-o	5-63	7.9	-36.90
Class 2	7-85	8.2	-35.25	3-y-o	3-33	9.1	-7.42
Class 3	6-64	9.4	-23.90	4-y-o+	4-29	13.8	-6.75
Class 4	16-125	12.8	-25.38				
Class 5	29-226	12.8	-85.21	Totals	12-125	9.6	-51.07
Class 6	14-93	15.1	-11.78				
Class 7	1-1	100.0	+2.75				

The Grey Gatsby will head to Royal Ascot before taking in other top races over middle distances this season

KEVIN RYAN: ASSESSING THE STATS

A total of 78 winners in 2014 was something of a disappointment for Kevin Ryan. Having sent out at least 94 winners in each of the seven previous years, a period during which he smashed the century barrier on four occasions, the numbers were down at Hambleton although Ryan still managed a respectable prize-money tally, securing nearly £1.2 million, *writes Kevin Morley*.

For Ryan, last year was mainly about one horse – The Grey Gatsby, who caused a few upsets in some major contests. Only one of those came in Britain when he won the Dante relatively unfancied. He showed that was no fluke when also upsetting the odds in the French Derby and later in the Irish Champion Stakes where he claimed the scalp of Epsom Derby winner Australia.

He was a rare top-class performer in middle-distance races for Ryan last term as the vast majority of his success usually comes in sprints. The Grey Gatsby aside, the likes of Hot Streak, Blaine, Hamza and Online Alexander were some of his leading earners who all picked up a variety of valuable handicaps and Group races between them over the shorter trips.

Ryan is a fine judge of precocious talent and has been no stranger to plenty of success with his juveniles over the years. It is somewhat surprising to see this fact often goes unnoticed by the layers as backing all of his two-year-olds over the past five seasons would have returned a hefty level-stake profit.

He turns over winners at a similar rate with his three-year-olds and older horses, especially in sprints although the benefit of backing these age groups blind isn't there for punters.

Ryan was a little slower than usual to get his string going last term and the winners didn't start to flow until July, something which might have contributed to his lower than usual seasonal tally. He usually hits form earlier with May and June proving particularly profitable months in previous years.

Ryan often relies on Jamie Spencer or Graham Lee for the big prizes, but Paul Mulrennan was a good jockey to follow for the yard last term. Not only did he ride the most winners for Ryan in 2014, he also managed to return a level-stake profit with a healthy strike-rate to boot.

Ryan doesn't boast outstanding figures at many tracks but his record at Hamilton catches the eye and his runners there often reward support. Also keep an eye out for any rare raids to Bath. He sent just two runners to the Somerset venue in 2014 and both obliged.

Hot Streak leads Kevin Ryan's string during exercise at the trainer's Hambleton stables

With Kingston Hill and co on board this could be Varian's best season yet

WITH his Kremlin House stables housing the St Leger winner and two of the most talented three-year-olds around, Roger Varian is entitled to feel excited as the days grow longer.

Last season was special enough with *Kingston Hill* delivering Varian a first Classic winner at the start of a golden seven-week spell in which he annexed four Group 1s. But with champion two-year-old Belardo and Moyglare winner Cursory Glance among the others to look forward to there is logic behind the belief that the 36-year-old has the potential to eclipse last year's record British prize-money haul of more than £2.2 million, *writes Mark Storey*.

"We're excited about Kingston Hill staying in training but also about the three three-year-olds in the camp who were Group 1 winners at two and who we hope can justify their ratings and do it again at three," says Varian, whose string for 2015 numbers 178.

"I think we have a strong team, with strength in depth to our three-year-olds and a good spread of two-year-olds, with older horses we know about already. I think we have the foundations for a good year."

Last year's Derby runner-up Kingston Hill again has the Prix de l'Arc de Triomphe, in which he finished four lengths fourth behind Treve in October, on his radar. Varian says: "He's been grand and has done very well through the winter. He's a stronger horse.

"We very much see him as a Leger winner with an optimum trip of a mile and a half rather than a two-mile stayer, and we'll be campaigning him like that, with middle-distance races possibly leading up to the King George and an autumn campaign with the Arc on the agenda.

"I could see him starting in something like the Tattersalls Gold Cup at the Curragh. The Coronation Cup at Epsom would also be on the radar, while if he came to hand quickly enough a ten-and-half furlong race at Longchamp on Guineas weekend could be the starting point. It will be one of those three. I won't have a problem running him on good to firm. When I pulled him out twice last year it was on firm."

Belardo was named champion European two-year-old following his impressive win in the Group 1 Dewhurst Stakes, although his rating of 119 is the joint-lowest for a juvenile champion since the classification began.

Godolphin were impressed enough by the two-length victory over Kodi Bear to buy a majority share for the Qipco 2,000 Guineas hopeful, and Varian says: "There are three Guineas in Europe and he'll be campaigned with those races in mind. We'll possibly be looking at a prep run in the Greenham.

"He carries high energy levels and a run might do him good mentally. He won in a hood in the Dewhurst and we might not reach for that straight away. I don't think he necessarily needs one. He looked good in that race last year and we would be very hopeful for him."

Belardo was not the only two-year-old colt

winning a Group 1 for the Newmarket trainer last season, with *Vert De Grece* landing the Criterium International at Saint-Cloud in October shortly after arriving at the yard from Joseph Murphy.

Varian says: "He's run once for me and although it has to be seen how strong the form is, to win by four and half a lengths he has to be a pretty good horse.

"He'll be looked upon as a Guineas horse, and afterwards possibly stretching him to ten furlongs.

"He could go French Guineas and French Derby or English Guineas and Irish Guineas. A bit of cut in the ground and a stiff mile might be ideal for him. He could run in the Craven first – options are open."

While Newmarket in May remains a possibility for Vert De Grece, that door closed for *Cursory Glance* when she suffered a fetlock injury this year. But Varian hopes to have his Moyglare Stud Stakes winner back for Royal Ascot where she claimed the Albany as a juvenile last June.

He said: "I think getting her back for Royal Ascot and the Coronation Stakes is achievable. While it's a blow to miss the 1,000 Guineas, it's not a disaster, as there is a lot of good racing after Royal Ascot. I think her form is as good as there is in the two-year-old fillies division.

"The Moyglare was as good a race there was run for fillies last year. You would have to argue she was among the top two or three fillies in Europe last year.

"Looking at her pedigree she will train on and I think a mile will be her trip. She's

Belardo: last year's Dewhurst winner will have lots of options this season

bred to get further but I'm not sure she will as she has a lot of speed."

Fellow three-year-old filly *Tigrilla*, fourth in the Group 2 Rockfel Stakes, landed a Listed contest at Deauville in August. Varian says: "She's a tough genuine filly who is pretty decent. She could have finished third in the Rockfel if she hadn't chased the pace. She could run in a trial. She's not in the English Guineas, her form wasn't good enough, but I've got a tentative plan to take her to the German Guineas."

Ambivalent retired after contesting the Melbourne Cup, while John Smith's Cup winner Farraaj has left to continue his career in the UAE, but Varian still has a powerful supporting cast with high hopes for six-year-old *Aljamaaheer*, who finished third in last year's Diamond Jubilee at Royal Ascot.

"We had a bit of a miss with him last year," says Varian. "He ran two or three fine races but didn't win. It's likely he'll step back up to seven furlongs and a mile. It will give Paul Hanagan a better chance to nail a Group 1 on him.

"We had a try at sprinting but at the highest level he just gets found out mid-race. We have the Lockinge in mind, with one run before. He was third in it two years ago. And there's no reason why he can't go back to Ascot for the Queen Anne afterwards in which he was second two years ago."

Steps, a Listed winner at Haydock last year, is back for another season aged seven along with six-year-old *Justineo*, who will also remain pointed at sprinting prizes.

"Steps is back with us. He's getting on in years but you wouldn't know it," Varian says. "He has the mind and body of a young horse. He needs his conditions to excel but when he does he's a pretty decent sprinter.

"Justineo is a decent sprinter too, a Listed to Group 3 horse, and we'll be trying to pick up those kind of prizes with him again."

Seven-furlong specialist *Eton Forever*, now eight, has won first time out in three of the last four seasons and Varian says: "His first run tends to be very good and we'll try to find a decent prize with him.

"He's very delicate and you'll only get two or three good runs out of him a year, but he's very capable on his day."

Not disgraced in the Jersey Stakes at Royal Ascot last year, Varian believes there is improvement to come from four-year-old *Toofi*, and says: "He's pretty decent on his day. He's got to rediscover his form but I'm sure he will. He's a six-furlong horse I think and I reckon he's more a stakes/conditions horse than a big-field handicapper. We'll possibly try to find a Listed race in May over six furlongs."

Varian thinks there is a big prize in *Battersea*, winner of two decent handicaps at Ascot last season, and says: "He did well last year and will improve from three to four. He's stronger this year. I think he's on a mark to win a big handicap, and I'd be hopeful he could progress to stakes races."

China Horse Club, which was founded by Derby winner Australia's part-owner Teo Ah Khing, have sent six two-year-olds to Varian, who had his first runner for the operation when *Bajan* was sixth in the Singapore Cup in February.

Varian says: "It's too early to name horses but they were bought at European sales – four colts and two fillies. None of them are screaming that they are particularly early. We're very lucky to have the support of the China Horse Club and they look a nice bunch at the moment.

"Of my other two-year-olds I've seen enough to like what I've got. I think I've got a good balance with some precocious early types, ones to push through midsummer and some late maturing types."

Varian, now in his fifth season, does not plan to appoint a retained rider following Andrea Atzeni's departure to join Qatar Racing, but there is a new face behind the scenes with Mike Marshall taking over from David Eustace as assistant trainer.

He adds: "It's very dangerous to set numerical targets because it can lead you to doing things you wouldn't normally do, but if we can better last season then we'll be in a good place."

ROGER VARIAN

NEWMARKET, SUFFOLK

	No. of Hrs	Races Run	1st	2nd	3rd	Unpl	Per cent	£1 Level Stake
2-y-o	51	131	19	22	21	68	14.5	-44.65
3-y-o	58	225	45	43	31	106	20.0	+1.72
4-y-o+	30	115	14	16	18	67	12.2	-37.77
Totals	139	471	78	81	70	241	16.6	-80.70
2013	123	402	89	62	52	199	22.1	-2.48
2012	112	398	72	55	59	210	18.1	-9.00

BY MONTH

2-y-o	W-R	Per cent	£1 Level Stake	3-y-o	W-R	Per cent	£1 Level Stake
January	0-0	0.0	0.00	January	0-1	0.0	-1.00
February	0-0	0.0	0.00	February	3-5	60.0	+7.30
March	0-0	0.0	0.00	March	4-9	44.4	-1.35
April	0-1	0.0	-1.00	April	6-34	17.6	+0.91
May	2-8	25.0	-2.59	May	6-35	17.1	+9.02
June	3-15	20.0	+3.34	June	10-51	19.6	-9.16
July	1-13	7.7	-11.27	July	7-29	24.1	+11.75
August	2-12	16.7	-1.75	August	2-22	9.1	-15.63
September	5-41	12.2	-21.63	September	5-21	23.8	+1.38
October	6-24	25.0	+7.25	October	1-13	7.7	-5.00
November	0-13	0.0	-13.00	November	1-3	33.3	+5.50
December	0-4	0.0	-4.00	December	0-2	0.0	-2.00

4-y-o	W-R	Per cent	£1 Level Stake	Totals	W-R	Per cent	£1 Level Stake
January	0-3	0.0	-3.00	January	0-4	0.0	-4.00
February	0-2	0.0	-2.00	February	3-7	42.9	+5.30
March	0-3	0.0	-3.00	March	4-12	33.3	-4.35
April	4-17	23.5	-3.88	April	10-52	19.2	-3.97
May	2-19	10.5	-6.50	May	10-62	16.1	-0.07
June	4-27	14.8	+7.75	June	17-93	18.3	+1.93
July	2-14	14.3	-4.75	July	10-56	17.9	-4.27
August	2-14	14.3	-6.40	August	6-48	12.5	-23.78
September	0-7	0.0	-7.00	September	10-69	14.5	-27.25
October	0-4	0.0	-4.00	October	7-41	17.1	-1.75
November	0-4	0.0	-4.00	November	1-20	5.0	+1.50
December	0-1	0.0	-1.00	December	0-7	0.0	-3.00

DISTANCE

2-y-o	W-R	Per cent	£1 Level Stake	3-y-o	W-R	Per cent	£1 Level Stake
5f-6f	9-60	15.0	-19.02	5f-6f	3-26	11.5	-13.87
7f-8f	10-69	14.5	-23.63	7f-8f	25-107	23.4	-10.95
9f-13f	0-2	0.0	-2.00	9f-13f	16-89	18.0	+26.29
14f+	0-0	0.0	0.00	14f+	1-3	33.3	+0.25

4-y-o	W-R	Per cent	£1 Level Stake	Totals	W-R	Per cent	£1 Level Stake
5f-6f	3-36	8.3	-9.90	5f-6f	15-122	12.3	-42.79
7f-8f	4-25	16.0	-12.50	7f-8f	39-201	19.4	-47.08
9f-13f	5-50	10.0	-17.50	9f-13f	21-141	14.9	+6.79
14f+	2-4	50.0	+2.13	14f+	3-7	42.9	+2.38

TYPE OF RACE

Non-Handicaps	W-R	Per cent	£1 Level Stake	Handicaps	W-R	Per cent	£1 Level Stake
2-y-o	16-121	13.2	-47.15	2-y-o	3-10	30.0	+2.50
3-y-o	26-117	22.2	-6.52	3-y-o	19-108	17.6	+8.24
4-y-o+	6-47	12.8	+13.00	4-y-o+	8-68	11.8	-29.13

RACE CLASS / FIRST TIME OUT

	W-R	Per cent	£1 Level Stake		W-R	Per cent	£1 Level Stake
Class 1	10-75	13.3	+11.83	2-y-o	2-51	3.9	-45.88
Class 2	6-38	15.8	+6.91	3-y-o	12-58	20.7	-7.94
Class 3	6-38	15.8	-19.80	4-y-o+	6-30	20.0	-5.88
Class 4	13-115	11.3	-48.08				
Class 5	42-185	22.7	-16.57	Totals	20-139	14.4	-59.70
Class 6	1-20	5.0	-15.00				
Class 7	0-0	0.0	0.00				

Justineo will be campaigned with a view to winning in Listed and Group 3 company

DID YOU KNOW

Roger Varian first started out as a point-to-point rider for Alan and Lawney Hill before moving to Josh Gifford's yard and becoming a conditional. He also went to Maryland to work for jumps trainer Jack Fisher before his training career took hold at Kremlin House.

ROGER VARIAN: ASSESSING THE STATS

Last year was a slight regression in terms of numbers with 78 winners in 2014 falling below Roger Varian's 2013 tally of 89, but that will not bother him too much as the £2.2 million prize-money accrued last season was a significant improvement on the £1.3m earned in the previous campaign, *writes Kevin Morley*.

Success at the highest level accounted for the surge in prize-money with Varian securing his first Classic with Kingston Hill in the St Leger while the surprise Dewhurst victory of Belardo was more than an added bonus. Previous Group 1 success for Varian had previously been confined to abroad, and he was on the mark again on the continent with Vert De Grece landing France's Criterium International. Cursory Glance landed the Curragh's Moyglare Stud Stakes, completing an excellent year for the Varian two-year-olds.

Although his juveniles excelled, Varian is generally better known for his exploits with three-year-olds. Kingston Hill's St Leger victory was the first Group-race success Varian has had with a three-year-old in Britain, though. This age group is usually best followed in handicaps where they strike frequently and often at rewarding odds while those running in maidens also return a profit. Varian rarely pitches his youngsters into Group company but the hint should be taken when he does.

One of the best ways to profit from backing his string regardless of age is to focus on those running over 7f up to 1m2f. His runners tends to have a good combination of speed and stamina and this is borne out by his record over these distances.

Unlike many yards, Varian is quieter than usual during the summer months, the height of the Flat season. Instead he focuses on a strong start to the turf season and a strong finish.

The Kremlin House handler has struck up an excellent association with Andrea Atzeni over the past few seasons and his mounts have secured handsome profit. Also take note on the few occasions he books Ryan Moore and Graham Lee, who both have an excellent record for the trainer.

Haydock remains a favourite track for Varian, while his figures for Newbury and Doncaster, both big, galloping left-handed tracks, are also impressive.

Vert De Grece scores at Leopardstown

O'Brien holds the key again with more Classic success a formality

THE build-up to the Cheltenham Festival was dominated by chat about Irish-trained horses – and our Flat cast commands a similarly lofty level of respect ahead of the 2015 Classics.

If Willie Mullins has a stranglehold on Irish jump racing, the dominance of Aidan O'Brien on the Flat is greater still. He had to endure a relatively poor run in the Epsom Derby after High Chaparral backed up Galileo's success in the great race in 2002 and had no winner until Camelot struck in 2012. This year, though, he is bidding for his fourth successive win in the race after Ruler Of The World and Australia kept the ball rolling. And, with that in mind, he has some fascinating contenders who gave the impression as juveniles that they had a great deal more to offer.

POTENTIAL STAR COLTS

There will be endless debate about who will emerge as the stable star in 2015. Bookmakers have decided *John F Kennedy* is the place to start. The son of Galileo was sure to capture the public's imagination with a name

JOHNNY WARD: VIEW FROM IRELAND

that honoured the former US president and it was not too big a deal when he was beaten on his debut as Ballydoyle's runners tend to come on markedly for their first start. After scoring in a Curragh maiden, he bolted up in a Leopardstown Group 3, achieving a Racing Post Rating of 113.

Moreover, he looks pretty certain to get a mile and a half. He is a brother to Tapestry, who shocked Taghrooda in the Yorkshire Oaks, and tends to finish his races strongly.

The question about stablemate *Ol' Man River* is whether he will get the Derby trip but I'm very much in the camp that he will.

For a start, Montjeu's progeny's median winning distance is just shy of 1m4f. Although Ol' Man River is out of a miler in the brilliant Finsceal Beo, she has already had a 1m2f winner in Too The Stars and he got a mile so easily at two. He looks liable to stay.

Interestingly, Joseph O'Brien says he is more worried about his stamina for the Derby trip than his speed for the Guineas, but

Montjeu horses aged three or more have a really poor record at a mile or less.

Two other potential Derby horses for the champion trainer are two sons of Galileo.

Giovanni Canaletto has only a maiden win to his name but his pace was quite extraordinary that day when he still appeared rather raw. He is a half-brother to Duke Of Marmalade and a brother to Ruler Of The World, further cementing his appeal.

Highland Reel won a Gowran maiden by 12 lengths in July and oozed class when dropping back to 7f in Goodwood's Vintage Stakes. He has a gorgeous pedigree, out of a Danehill mare who stayed 1m4f.

If there is a Guineas winner in Ballydoyle it is likely to be *Gleneagles*. Another son of Galileo, and a brother to Irish Guineas heroine Marvellous, Gleneagles is effectively unbeaten since his debut defeat.

He landed a Group 3, a Group 2 and the Group 1 National Stakes, while his performance reached a new level when he

Highland Reel:
Derby candidate is
very well bred

ran in the Prix Jean-Luc Lagardere. Although thrown out in a stewards' inquiry, Gleneagles was clearly the best horse on the day and is all the more intriguing because he tends not to do a great deal when hitting the front.

POTENTIAL STAR FILLIES

There is a great deal to like about *Found*. She had the distinction of winning on her debut, unfancied but brushing her Curragh foes aside under Seamie Heffernan, and she was beaten only three-quarters of a length in the Moyglare – a smashing performance as it came only about three weeks after her maiden success. She ran a little freely in the Prix Marcel Boussac on her only other start but looked all class, bolting up by two and a half lengths.

Found is out of Red Evie, a Lockinge winner. She could win the 1,000 Guineas but

there are other Irish challengers with a chance, notably *Lucida*. A daughter of Shamardal, she did end the season with a fairly disappointing run in the Fillies' Mile, but her previous win in a Newmarket Group 2 introduced her to the Classic picture.

Eddie Lynam has become familiar to British racegoers with his brilliant sprinters in recent years and he has a nice prospect in *Agnes Stewart*, who was second in the Fillies' Mile. She is bred to get a trip, being out of a 1m4f winner, but travels powerfully in her races and she definitely looks worth a shot at the 1,000 Guineas.

Found is also favourite for the Oaks but her stamina might be stretched at that distance. And there is further O'Brien dominance of the market. His *Words*, a daughter of Dansili, overcame inexperience to beat subsequent Group 2 winner Raydara on her debut and is towards the head of the betting

Catch me if you can: Free Eagle coasts clear of the Group 3 opposition at Leopardstown

for the Epsom Classic. Also right up there is **Together Forever**, who had Agnes Stewart and Lucida behind her when winning the Fillies' Mile and very much looks a type for middle distances.

THE OLDER STARS

Unfortunately, there is something of a paucity of older horses for racing aficionados can enjoy in 2015. The retirement of Australia reflects the ruthless nature of the Flat game: he ran only eight times and ended his career with that controversial Irish Champions Stakes defeat to The Grey Gatsby.

On that same day racegoers witnessed a breathtaking performance from **Free Eagle**, and the four-year-old looks set to make up for lost time this year. Given he had not run in around a year, that was an awesome display, and his subsequent third in the Champion

Stakes at Ascot showed he should be more than capable of striking at the highest level.

He might yet become the best of High Chaparral's progeny and Dermot Weld could have the smartest son of Nayef in **Forgotten Rules**. It seems incredible he started off in a bumper: a year later he heads the betting for the Gold Cup and that will be his target for 2015.

Weld won the Ascot race with Rite Of Passage in 2010, and Forgotten Rules has the potential to be even better than that fragile sort. He is likely to prep for Ascot in Leopardstown's Saval Beg Stakes and he seems pretty straightforward.

Admirable speedster **Sole Power** stays in training as an eight-year-old and appeals as one of those sprinters who loses none of his speed with age. The Tom Hogan-handled **Gordon Lord Byron** is also back for more.

Faydhan could be the one to give Gosden a full book of British Classics

EPSOM DERBY

The race every trainer wants to win on the Flat is the Derby. Unfortunately though if your name isn't Aidan O'Brien you haven't had a prayer in the last three years and the same is likely again this season.

O'Brien representatives occupy five of the first six berths in the betting market for the race so it's likely he will win it again, but with what?

The one I like is *Giovanni Canaletto*, who raced only twice last season and won a maiden, but could be capable of progressing a long way past that as a three-year-old.

An eyecatcher when third on his debut, he was under consideration for the Racing Post Trophy for a long time, but his trainer settled for a late-season maiden at Leopardstown which he won easily.

He was still fairly clueless in the early part of the race, but when Seamie Heffernan organised him he put the race to bed instantly, going away to win by six and a half lengths.

That success was over a mile, and his breeding suggests there should be a lot more to come over middle-distances this year as he is a brother to 2013 Derby winner Ruler Of The World, who didn't even make his debut until he was three, so Giovanni Canaletto is a step ahead already. He could be one to look out for in a trial at Chester, a course used to prepare Ruler Of The World for Epsom.

EPSOM OAKS

The situation is similar in the Oaks, with O'Brien horses Found, Words and Together

Forever at the head of the market. This time preference goes to *Found*, winner of two of her three starts last season and particularly impressive in the Marcel Boussac on her final run, quickening clear of Ervedya by two and a half lengths.

1,000 GUINEAS

Found might be quick enough for a 1,000 Guineas bid, but if she isn't then Mick Channon's *Malabar* certainly is.

Her form figures of 241144 would indicate she has her limitations but that is not necessarily the case. Fourth in the Albany Stakes at Royal Ascot on just her second start, she improved to win a Group 3 at Goodwood later in the season, and then didn't get the rub of the green in two Group 1s that ended her campaign.

In the Moyglare at the Curragh she repeatedly struggled to get a clear run in the home straight, eventually finishing fourth beaten just over a length.

Then in the Marcel Boussac against Found, she was in an awful position as the pace quickened and although she stayed on well, she finished fourth again but with the promise of so much more. A 25-1 shot for the Guineas, she could outrun those odds with a bit of luck.

2,000 GUINEAS

The only Classic John Gosden has yet to win is the 2,000 Guineas, and he probably should have done with Kingman last season. However, he could get another bite of the cherry this season with the once-raced *Faydhan*.

The War Front colt won his sole start in the manner of a very smart horse. In a Haydock maiden he quickened six lengths clear of Dutch Connection, who was rated 111 at the end of the season and was placed in a Group 1.

To do that on your debut is seriously smart and although it's a shame he was not seen again, if he can hit the ground running this spring then he could go right to the top.

Forgotten Rules (noseband) makes it three wins from three runs and will be a major player in the Ascot Gold Cup this summer

ROYAL ASCOT

Forgotten Rules is a smart stayer who will take all the beating in the Ascot Gold Cup if there is sufficient cut in the ground to enable him to run.

He has raced only three times, and one of those runs was in a bumper at Punchestown. However, he has quickly developed from there, winning at the Galway Festival before landing the Group 2 Long Distance Cup at Ascot in October.

He beat Biographer comfortably that day, should have little trouble with the 2m4f Gold Cup trip and still has endless scope to improve.

The sprint situation is a little more confusing with the retirement of Slade Power, but *Tiggy Wiggy* could be the one to follow.

She is all set for a Guineas campaign and if she is successful in that arena then sprinting probably wouldn't come into the equation. However, there has to be a chance that due to her extreme speed she won't last a mile, in which case she is very likely to do what she does best – run very fast.

She was electric in the Lowther Stakes at York last season and was also a comfortable winner of the Cheveley Park on her final start. She is very good and very quick.

Another sprinter to follow would be *G Force* after he made his breakthrough into Group 1 company when scooting home in the Sprint Cup at Haydock on his penultimate start.

He beat Gordon Lord Byron on that occasion so the form is strong, and although he disappointed at Ascot on his final outing last season, he wasn't drawn well and the ground was soft.

There is every chance he will resume his progress this spring, perhaps kicking off in the Duke of York in May.

G Force (right) became a force to be reckoned with when landing the Sprint Cup and can continue his progress this season

ONE TO FOLLOW

Christophermarlowe Convincing winner of starts at Sandown and Epsom and bred to appreciate middle distances. Overcame a tardy start at Esher and looked much more accomplished on the Downs. [Dave Edwards, Topspeed]

The formbook can take you so far – here's how to help make it really pay

JAMES PYMAN: HOW TO MAKE A PROFIT THIS SEASON

1. EARLY-SEASON STRATEGIES

With Doncaster's Lincoln meeting sandwiched between the Cheltenham Festival and Grand National, the start to the Flat season is a complete culture shock for many of us.

These initial weeks are tough for form students with match-fit horses who have been running on the all-weather competing against runners returning from the winter whose fitness will vary in accordance with the level of training they have received on the gallops, often in conditions a soft-ground staying chaser would relish.

Consequently, this is a period where it can pay dividends to adopt winner-finding strategies largely unrelated to the formbook.

Follow sires who get plenty of early two-year-old race winners

Two-year-old races are not everyone's favourite betting medium owing to the lack of form on offer, but they offer the pedigree-savvy punter an opportunity to get an edge as certain sires are considerably more likely to produce juveniles with the requisite speed and precocity to win these contests.

The table on page 82 shows the ten leading sires in terms of strike-rate (minimum 40 runs) this century with progeny in British and Irish two-year-old races run before June. Interestingly, we have four stallions from the Danzig sireline including Kodiac and Invincible Spirit who are closely related.

Kodiac produced Tiggy Wiggy, who last season shared the mantle as champion two-year-old filly in Europe with Found, and can lay claim to be one of the speediest juveniles we have seen in recent times.

Tiggy Wiggy was extraordinarily precocious, making her debut on the opening day of the season in a 5f maiden at Kempton which she won by seven lengths, and her sire's ability to produce fast-starters is underlined by the fact his progeny are showing a £1 level-stake profit of £38.45 in two-year-old races earlier than June with 23 per cent hitting the target.

The Royal Applause sireline is responsible for two of the stallions in our table. The first is Acclamation, a son of Royal Applause, and he is the sire with the best strike-rate (from a minimum of 50 runs) and most wins in these races. Acclamation's 2007 Middle Park winner Dark Angel has evidently inherited his sire's capacity to produce fast juveniles as Dark Angel's two-year-old offspring are showing a healthy 21 per cent strike-rate in March to May races.

Two of the more interesting first-season sires this season with regards to having immediate success are Zoffany and Lilbourne Lad. Zoffany is from the Danzig line and bloodstock experts are raving about his initial crop, while Lilbourne Lad is by Acclamation, so on paper at least looks a first-rate candidate to get early winners.

Aidan O'Brien is a slow starter

You should think twice about lumping on O'Brien's runners at short prices until later in the season when generally stakes are higher. This stable is typically slowly away from the

Table 1: LEADING SIRES BY STRIKE-RATE WITH THEIR EARLY 2YO RUNNERS (SINCE 2000, RACES STAGED EARLIER THAN JUNE IN GB-IRE)

Sire	Wins	Runs	%	Profit/loss
Acclamation (by Royal Applause)	39	165	24	+12.07
Dutch Art (by Machiavellian)	13	55	24	+30.04
Kodiac (by Danehill by Danzig)	34	151	23	+38.45
Oasis Dream (by Green Desert by Danzig)	13	59	22	-7.18
Invincible Spirit (by Green Desert by Danzig)	32	150	21	-11.64
Dark Angel (by Acclamation by Royal Applause)	17	81	21	-21.46
One Cool Cat (by Storm Cat)	15	72	21	+88.08
Footstepsinthesand (by Giant's Causeway by Storm Cat)	12	59	20	-2.65
Exceed And Excel (by Danehill by Danzig)	27	138	20	-23.23
Elusive City (by Elusive Quality)	11	60	18	+4.83

starting blocks and in recent years a lot of his well-fancied runners in the earlier weeks of the year were found out by a lack of fitness.

Table 2 gives a month-by-month account of how his Flat runners in Britain and Ireland sent off at 9-2 or shorter are performing since 2008. These runners are showing much lower strike-rates in March (18 per cent) and April (28 per cent) when compared against months comprising the core of the season. Their strike-rate is highest in July (38 per cent) which reflects how O'Brien trains many of his string to peak in midsummer.

His runners who started at 9-2 or shorter in March and April are returning a huge £1 level-stake loss of £66.12 in this period. During last season, for example, just two of his 15 runners who were not two-year-olds sent off no bigger than 9-4 to win a race run earlier than May rewarded backers (£1 level-stake loss of £11.76). You can back his hotpots with more confidence from May onwards.

On the gallops at Ballydoyle, from where runners should be treated with caution in the early part of the season

Table 2: RECORD OF AIDAN O'BRIEN'S GB-IRE RUNNERS AT 9-2 SP OR SHORTER BY MONTH (2008+)

Month	Wins	Runs	Strike-rate	Profit/loss
March	6	34	18	-14.32
April	49	178	28	-51.81
May	102	287	36	-27.97
June	110	311	35	-9.71
July	124	324	38	-8.68
August	96	277	35	-30.60
September	80	234	34	+0.98
October	80	223	36	+21.78
November	9	30	30	-0.57

2. O'BRIEN'S BID FOR BRITISH CLASSIC SLAM

The Ballydoyle maestro will almost certainly have a profound influence on this season's Classics both at home and in Britain given the embarrassment of riches he seemingly has in the three-year-old department.

In some bookmakers' winter ante-post markets, O'Brien trained the favourites for the two Newmarket Guineas, the Derby and the Oaks, and he appears to have a genuine shot at achieving a British Classics Slam, by winning all five races in the same season, for the first time.

O'Brien came mightily close to this milestone in 2012 when, with four Classics in the bag, his 2,000 Guineas and Derby winner Camelot missed out on becoming the first horse to complete the English Triple Crown since Nijinsky (1970) when finishing a close second to Encke in the St Leger.

Last season's two-year-old crop lacked standout performers – 2014 champion two-year-old Belardo is the joint lowest-rated since rankings began – which is fuelling

speculation this season's big three-year-old races will be at the mercy of Ballydoyle's later-maturing horses.

The problem is knowing which ones to back. A system proving a major money-spinner is to blindly follow O'Brien's horses who make winning debuts in British and Irish three-year-old Group races.

Since 2008 this strategy is showing a £1 level-stake profit of £37.08, courtesy of 28 wins from 115 bets. Interestingly, the horses who were running in Group 1s have made a significant contribution, with 15 wins from 66 bets netting a return of £29.07.

So we might get an edge following the O'Brien three-year-olds who won first time up at two in this season's Classics – and three runners with the right profile are *Ol' Man River*, *Found* and *Words*.

3. FOLLOW TOP FREELANCE JOCKEYS AT THE BIG MEETINGS

The majority of the Flat jockeys who finished in the higher strata of last season's British championship are retained this season by either a big-spending owner or powerful trainer and this could lead to an increase in demand from smaller shrewd stables for the services of top freelance jockeys, particularly at the bigger meetings on busier days.

Godolphin hired James Doyle and William Buick at the end of last season, Andrea Atzeni has replaced Jamie Spencer as Qatar Racing's number-one rider, Paul Hanagan has a retainer with Hamdan Al Maktoum, Frankie Dettori, who is retained by Al Shaqab Racing, will ride plenty of John Gosden's runners this season, while champion jockey Richard Hughes and Joe Fanning will continue to be backed by big trainers Richard Hannon and Mark Johnston respectively.

Ryan Moore will be kept busy riding for Sir Michael Stoute and O'Brien, and when you look at the jockeys who finished in the top ten in last season's title, probably only Graham

Ol' Man River (right) was a winner of boths starts at two and could be a major contender for Classic honours

ONE TO FOLLOW

Best Of Times Finished a promising sixth in a hot Newmarket maiden and then romped home at Goodwood in the best time of the day. Made hard work of landing the odds at Salisbury on his final start but might come into his own over 1m2f.
[Dave Edwards, Topspeed]

Lee, Adam Kirby and George Baker can be considered as proper freelancers.

Baker has seemingly become Roger Charlton's go-to jockey when Doyle is unavailable.

Last season Baker picked up two Group 1 rides for the trainer. He first guided Thistle Bird to a 4-1 success in the Pretty Polly Stakes at the Curragh before finishing runner-up on 16-1 Al Kazeem in a thrilling Champion Stakes at Ascot, losing a protracted battle with Noble Mission who was ridden by Al Kazeem's regular rider Doyle. Baker got the ride on Al Kazeem owing to Doyle's previous retainer with Noble Mission's owner Khalid Abdullah.

Baker has generally done well when picking up fancied rides in Group races. Since the start of 2010, his record when partnering horses sent off at 13-2 or shorter at this level is an impressive 13 wins from 37 mounts for a £1 level-stake profit of £18.68.

Lee finished third in the title last season, achieving the best placing of any northern-based jockey, and his rides this season in more valuable races at the northern courses merit close inspection. A trainer who clearly recognises his abilities is the super-shrewd William Haggas. Last season, Lee picked up five rides in handicaps with win prize-money of at least £10,000 for Haggas and four won for a £1 level-stake profit of £12.83.

The booking of Kirby for rides in valuable handicaps is also often proving significant. In the last three seasons, the jockey has an admirable 14 per cent strike-rate in such races worth £10,000-plus to the winner, on the back of 23 wins from 163 rides, netting a profit of £11.60 for every pound staked.

Interestingly, many of these successes came in straight-course handicaps featuring big fields. In this period he has won the Lincoln, Royal Hunt Cup, Bunbury Cup and Dash, run over Epsom's sharp five furlongs on Derby day, and he has enjoyed 14 wins from 87 rides (+£37.00) in handicaps worth at least £10,000 staged over a mile or shorter. Kirby is evidently adept at judging pace in a race run at a frantic pace.

Another freelancer likely to pick up plenty of quality rides this season is Jamie Spencer, who in December reversed the decision to retire he made in August last year. This former two-time British champion will be a popular choice with owners and trainers who adopt a 'best available' policy to booking jockeys.

Based on the handful of occasions Spencer has ridden in Britain since choosing to continue riding, three trainers who could supply him with plenty of winners this season are the upwardly mobile Hugo Palmer, Michael Bell and Jamie Osborne.

Spencer rides the straight course at Ascot particularly well. His record in races run over a mile or shorter at Royal Ascot since the track was relaid (2006 onwards) is a healthy 15 wins from 153 rides, for a £1 level-stake profit of £46.88.

4. TIMING IT RIGHT WHEN BACKING OVERSEAS RAIDERS

Royal Ascot is already a favoured destination for horses trained outside of Britain and Ireland, and Glorious Goodwood, which this season will be called the Qatar Goodwood Festival, is likely to attract more overseas runners given the prize-money on offer for the meeting's key eight races is now enormous having been boosted significantly by the new sponsors.

Home-based sprinters will conceivably face greater competition from overseas runners in this season's top races. This decade, four of the five King's Stand winners at Royal Ascot were British/Irish-trained, but this partly reflects an apparent loss of appetite from trainers of top-class sprinters from outside of Europe to target the race. Before 2010, six of the previous seven winners were from overseas with four of these non-European horses.

In the last five King's Stand renewals just five non-European-based sprinters have returned single-figure prices, compared to nine horses from outside of Europe starting at shorter than 10-1 in the five runnings between 2005 and 2009.

This season, prize-money in the 5f Group 2

George Baker celebrates Group 1 victory aboard Thistle Bird in the Pretty Polly Stakes at the Curragh

ONE TO FOLLOW

Terror Not many juvenile Warwick winners earn a Topspeed figure of 90 on their debut but this filly accomplished that feat when a wide-margin winner. Subsequently confirmed she was a cut above average and could develop into a top-class sprinter this summer. *[Dave Edwards, Topspeed]*

King George Stakes at Goodwood has been upped to £300,000, so trainers from Asia and the southern hemisphere might now be more tempted to map out a more prolonged campaign of races in Britain for their top sprinters starting with the King's Stand finishing with the Nunthorpe and in between taking in the King George Stakes and possibly even the July Cup.

Indeed, Australian sprinter Ortensia took this path three seasons ago. She was only ninth on her British debut in the King's Stand at Ascot, then finished fourth on unsuitably soft ground in the July Cup before achieving back-to-back wins in the King George Stakes and Nunthorpe.

Should the cream of sprinting talent from overseas descend on Britain this summer I will be in no hurry to oppose these runners.

The European Pattern Committee are this season beefing up the programme for three-year-old sprinters – this includes the inception of the 6f Group 1 Commonwealth Cup restricted to runners of the Classic generation at Royal Ascot. It is hoped these steps, by encouraging more sprinting two-year-olds to stay in training and not take up stud duties, will eventually improve the quality of European sprinting, but this is likely to be a slow process.

Newmarket is proving a favourite British destination for French trainers, who have enjoyed a lot of recent success in Group 1 mile races at both the Rowley Mile and July courses. This century, the record of French raiders in these contests is ten wins from just 41 runs, for a whopping £1 level-stake profit of £62.12. Nine of these wins came in fillies-only races, or contests for fillies and mares.

Additionally, the record of fancied French runners in Group 1 races of all distances at Newmarket courses since 2000 is really strong. Runners sent off at 9-2 or shorter have posted 11 wins from 28 runs (+£15.50).

French stables have also frequently targeted top-tier races at Ascot, although they are generally finding it much harder to capture Group 1s at the Berkshire course, this century posting ten wins from 116 runs (£1

ONE TO FOLLOW

Night Generation Shaped quite well on his Newcastle debut before completing a rapid-fire handicap education with two starts at Wolverhampton, beating home a total of only two horses. One to follow in handicaps.
[Simon Turner, Racing Post Ratings]

Australia's Ortensia is paraded at York in 2012 after landing the Nunthorpe

French raider Stacelita (right) finishes runner-up to Midday in the 2010 Sussex Stakes at Glorious Goodwood

level-stakes loss of £66.08).

The select bunch of horses from French stables who have competed at the highest level at Glorious Goodwood this century have fared pretty well.

From 1990 onwards, such runners have achieved finishing positions of 3671862 in the Sussex Stakes – Bigstone (Elie Lellouche) was their last winner in 1993 – while since the Nassau Stakes was promoted to a Group 1 in 1999, the French have suffered a string of near-misses in this 1m2f race. Ana Marie finished second in 2003, Mandesha found one too good in 2007, while Stacelita was runner-up to Midday five seasons ago. Two other runners were unplaced.

It seems a safe bet to expect a greater presence from France in future runnings of these landmark races given this season the Sussex and Nassau are offering substantially bigger total prize-money – £1,000,000 and £600,000 respectively.

TOMORROW'S TIPS
TOMORROW'S STATS
TOMORROW'S NEWS
TOMORROW'S FORM
TOMORROW'S BETTING
TONIGHT

The Racing Post iPad Edition, available on the iPad app from 8pm the night before it hits the newsagents.

FREE 30-DAY TRIAL. ON THE APP STORE NOW

Elm Park heads squad who can return a profit throughout the season

BARTEL Ed Vaughan

Ed Vaughan's three-year-old ran three fine races in 7f maidens last season and really should have been given the second of them in the stewards' room as he was beaten only a nose after taking a heavy bump. He made no mistake at Yarmouth next time, winning a 13-runner contest in ready fashion, and was put away afterwards. He is not going to be a superstar and his rating of 81 is pretty much in keeping with what he has achieved, but he ought to make a better three-year-old, will improve for the step up to a mile and might get 1m2f. He is one for handicaps.

DANZENO Michael Appleby

Michael Appleby made his name by improving recruits from other yards at a low level and winning stacks of all-weather races, particularly at Southwell, but there is more to the trainer than that, and Danzeno could be the one to put him on the big stage in 2015. He started last season by turning a competitive-looking 6f Newmarket handicap into a procession off a mark of 90 and continued to progress throughout the campaign, taking the small-field Group 3 Chipchase Stakes at Newcastle before running a head second off a mark of 105 in a Doncaster handicap and then being beaten the same margin by Lightning Moon in a Group 3 at Ascot. His last three runs saw him turn in consecutive career-bests on good to firm, good and soft ground, and that versatility marks him down as a horse to keep on side.

ELM PARK Andrew Balding

The stranglehold Aidan O'Brien and Coolmore have on the Derby market is scary, and Elm Park is only one of just a couple of British-trained horses in the top ten in the betting. He has the right profile having won the Racing Post Trophy at the end of last season in fine style and in doing so he became the first horse in 32 years to complete the Royal Lodge-Racing Post Trophy double. While he is also in the betting for the 2,000 Guineas, he is bred to be much better at middle distances. Very fast ground was considered to be against him but he handled it in the Royal Lodge at Newmarket, and if he could get away with it there he can get away with it anywhere. And in any case the ground is never allowed to get too fast at Epsom.

FANNAAN John Gosden

Was reportedly bought to be a Royal Ascot two-year-old, but picked up an early injury and did not finally make the racecourse until September, taking a 6f maiden in clearcut style (second, sixth and seventh have won since, while third and fifth have yet to run). He duly stepped up on that form with a comfortable 7f Newmarket win in a three-runner conditions race from the 104-rated Hawkesbury, who has since won easily in a similar contest at Kempton. The handicapper clearly didn't believe that form was up to much as Fannaan is rated 98 and it is fair to say Hawksbury did not really behave himself, but it was still a promising run. John Gosden was talking in terms of a Classic trial in the spring and, while his American sire Speightstown was a sprinter, he has been getting stacks of good winners at well over a mile.

GREATEST HITS John Gosden

Another late starter for John Gosden, he made his debut at Newmarket at the end of October, running a length second in what was not a particularly good 7f maiden for the course. However, he showed the benefit of the outing when defying a market drift on the all-weather at Kempton, making all to beat the well-punted odds-on favourite Pathway To Honour (easy winner since). He showed a good attitude there and that will stand him in good stead. Bred to be suited by middle distances, he surely has a workable mark of 83.

HERE COMES WHEN Andrew Balding

Andrew Balding's five-year-old has not had much racing, but is improving rapidly judging by his performances last season, and he might just be able to nick a Group 1 when he gets his favoured conditions, perhaps in Europe. The son of Danehill Dancer began last season with a handicap mark of 95 and duly bolted up on his return at Chester, before not showing much at all in the Royal Hunt Cup at Ascot. That was on fast ground, though, and he is a proper soft-ground performer as he proved when winning his last two starts, first in a Group 2 at Baden Baden and then at the same level in the Challenge Stakes at Newmarket. He was particularly impressive that day, winning going away, and if he maintains his rate of improvement a big race should come his way.

HIGHLAND REEL Aidan O'Brien

Unless you have a hotline to the ultra secretive Coolmore operation it is pure guesswork which of their vast array of talented three-year-olds will prove the cream of the crop, but this is my guess. He is a bit of a forgotten horse, having been displaced in the Derby market by John F Kennedy and Ol' Man River, but he is a genuine Classic contender in his own right and bred to get the Derby trip. After winning his maiden by 12 lengths on his second start at Gowran in July, he was sent to Britain for the Group 2 Vintage Stakes at Glorious Goodwood and, despite the drop to 7f, he duly bolted up. That might not have been a strong Group 2, but Highland Reel was always in control despite racing keenly early on and he clearly has plenty of pace despite being by Galileo out of a mare who stayed middle distances. It would be no surprise if he started off in the Qipco 2,000 Guineas, possibly first time out, and he's one to watch out for.

MUTHMIR William Haggas

Another sprinter who hasn't stood much racing, but is clearly very talented and very fast. William Haggas's five-year-old has always had a big reputation and in eight starts he has never been sent off at odds longer than 4-1, which is surprising when you consider his last three runs came in huge-field handicaps. Heavily backed on his seasonal reappearance at Newcastle in June, he dwelt at the start and then pulled extremely hard but still went down by only a neck. Made 4-1 favourite from a 6lb higher mark in a better race at York next time, he again broke a little slowly but this time it made no difference as he hacked up. He was then sent off one of the shortest-priced Stewards' Cup favourites in years (just 5-2 in a field of 24), but didn't pick up in the final furlong and finished fifth, the race probably having come too soon as it was only a week after York. He was back on track next time, though, winning the Portland Handicap by an easy two lengths despite a slow start and running into trouble. He is Group-class, perhaps Group 1-class, but must have fast ground.

STOKED Ed Walker

This could be another good handicapper this season and one who definitely looks well treated off a mark of 79. Fourth and second on hit first two starts at Newmarket and Newbury, he was upped to an extended mile at Nottingham on his final outing in October and made all for an easy win. The five-and-a-half-length third went close to winning off a mark of 75 over the winter and Stoked is bred to get better with age. He is the fourth foal of Es Que, who has produced one dud and two very good performers in sprinter/miler Es Que Love (best RPR 116) and Hong Kong Vase winner Dominant (119). Judging by the Nottingham success, Stoked won't be following Es Que Love's path and the chances are he's going to want more than a mile this season. Expect to see him taking in some good handicaps.

SYMPATHY Sir Michael Stoute

Owned by one of the many Highclere syndicates, this filly looks one to watch out for and it will be interesting to see how she is campaigned. She was set a really tough task on her debut as she ran in a conditions race against three previous winners and she wasn't knocked about by Shane Kelly to finish third, beaten just under five lengths by the 102-rated Elite Gardens. Partnered by Ryan Moore next time at Leicester, Sympathy was always in control and broke her maiden by an easy five lengths. She has an entry in the Irish Oaks but not the British equivalent, but either way you would think 1m4f would be too far. She has also been given an entry in the Qipco 1,000 Guineas, with a mile looking a more suitable trip, but if things don't work out she has a very fair handicap mark of 88. Gaining black type will probably be the plan, though, and she should have no problem achieving that.

TERROR David Simcock

David Simcock has this filly entered in the 1,000 Guineas, but it could be as a sprinter

ONE TO FOLLOW

Wrangler Soft ground brings out the best in this four-year-old, who caught the eye of clock-watchers when an emphatic Salisbury scorer in May. He followed up at Haydock later that month but was a disappointing Ascot favourite on his final start. A strapping individual, he has plenty more to offer and looks a smart stayer in the making. *[Dave Edwards, Topspeed]*

that she makes her name this season. A ten-length winner of a maiden at Warwick in August, she was supplemented into the Group 1 Cheveley Park the following month and ran a cracking race to finish fourth to Tiggy Wiggy, Anthem Alexander and High Celebrity. She bolted up in Listed company next, albeit at odds of 1-5 in a weakish race that she didn't need to improve to win. Her trainer plans to give her a run in one of the Guineas trials and there is no reason not to give her a chance of staying, but there are options for three-year-olds back at sprint trips this season, the obvious one being the new race at Royal Ascot and it wouldn't be a great surprise if that is where she ends up. She's promising wherever she goes, though.

TOUJOURS L'AMOUR William Haggas

Maidens trained by William Haggas are usually well supported if they are ready, so it is interesting this one managed to win at odds of 25-1 for the yard at Newmarket in September. That might not have been the best maiden, but the Authorized filly stayed on well to get up on the line and she improved when fifth in better company at the same track in November. That was in a Listed contest in which they went no pace early and Toujours L'Amour was again doing her best work in the closing stages. She has no fancy entries, but a mark of 87 looks fair and she ought to be a certainty to improve when she goes up in trip as she is out of a mare who won at Listed level over 1m5f on the all-weather.

Danzeno (left) could fly the flag in the top sprints for Michael Appleby this season

It's all in the pedigree – remember these names bred to make a splash

ABLAN Richard Hannon
3 b c Montjeu-Madeira Mist (Grand Lodge)

This year is marked by the penultimate crop of three-year-olds by the late, great Montjeu, and this Derby entrant boasts a fine pedigree as a brother to the sire's Grade 1-winning globetrotter Joshua Tree, who achieved the incredible feat of landing three consecutive runnings of the Canadian International. Bred by Lady O'Reilly's Castlemartin operation, he set the tone for the record-breaking 2013 Tattersalls Book 1 Yearling Sale when fetching 600,000gns as the first lot in the ring.

ALMELA Dermot Weld
3 b f Sea The Stars-Aliya (Darshaan)

Sea The Stars made the summer of 2009 his own, and last year his first three-year-olds made their mark. It was little surprise not to see his second-crop daughter Almela, bred and raced by the Aga Khan, out at two. A half-sister to the Prix du Cadran and Irish St Leger winner Alandi, she is out the Darshaan mare Aliya, winner of the 1m4f Listed Oyster Stakes – a race also won by her daughter Aliyfa. Almela has an entry in the Irish 1,000 Guineas, but another engagement in the Irish Oaks is more suited to her on pedigree.

FLAMING SPEAR Kevin Ryan
3 ch c Lope De Vega - Elshamms (Zafonic)

Showed an impressive attitude and turn of foot when winning his debut by two and three-quarter lengths at York in July, after which he was quoted between 20-1 and 33-1

for the 2,000 Guineas, although injury curtailed his season. He hails from the first crop of champion freshman sire Lope De Vega. The dual Classic-winning son of Shamardal improved vastly from two to three, so there are high hopes for his first three-year-olds.

LAP OF LUXURY John Gosden
3 ch f Galileo-Halland Park Lass (Spectrum)

Scored at 10-1 on her sole outing at Haydock last year, winning by half a length from odds-on Excilly. Although that 6f contest wasn't the strongest, there was a lot to like about the winner and a step up to a mile looks easily within her reach. By Galileo, she is a sister to Poule d'Essai des Pouliches second Up and a half-sister to Group 1 winner and sire Dutch Art – who finished third in the 2,000 Guineas – so a strong showing in top-class three-year-old company won't be unexpected.

LIKELY David Barron
3 ch f Exceed And Excel-La Pilaya (Pivotal)

Won easily on her debut from a subsequent Group 2 winner in Mattmu and, although not seen since, holds entries in the 1,000 Guineas on either side of the Irish Sea. Her sire Exceed And Excel is a reliable source of smart two-year-olds who progress well, most notably Excelebration and Helmet on opposite sides of the globe.

MCGUIGAN Jim Bolger
3 ch c Teofilo-Scribonia (Danehill)

Although his first outing left plenty to be desired, finishing 17th of 18 at Navan, two of

Mcguigan's four black type-performing siblings – Scintillula and Gile Na Greine – improved plenty at three, while another, Claiomh Solais skipped her juvenile season altogether. All four – completed by 1,000 Guineas runner-up Cuis Ghaire – are by Galileo, whose son Teofilo is the sire of Mcguigan. The Darley stallion has no shortage of top-flight performers including Irish Derby hero Trading Leather and Prix Jean Prat winner Havana Gold.

MOHEET Richard Hannon
3 b c High Chaparral-Abunai (Pivotal)

Another who made his mark from just one run, winning by seven lengths and earning an initial RPR of 87. A record-breaking 800,000gns breeze-up buy – a figure smashed the following day – Moheet holds entries in both the Newmarket and Irish 2,000 Guineas, but as a son of the late Derby hero High Chaparral out of a Pivotal half-sister to the top-class 1m2f peformer Miss Keller, a further step up in trip may prove more his forte. Also holds an entry in the Irish Derby.

OUTSTANDING Aidan O'Brien
3 b f Galileo-Absolutelyfabulous (Mozart)

This filly should have benefitted from another winter under her belt, as did her brother Magician – who was well beaten on three of his four starts at two but went on to land the Irish 2,000 Guineas and down The Fugue in the Breeders' Cup Turf at three. Another by Galileo, she is out of the 6f Listed winner Absolutelyfabulous from the wonderful family of Brigid, the dam of Group 1 winners Listen, Sequoyah, who produced Henrythenavigator, and record-breaking yearling Liffey Dancer.

STARS AND CLOUDS Freddy Head
3 b f Makfi-Ventura (Spectrum)

Something of a late starter when winning first time out in October at Chantilly, she is an interesting contender on this year's British and French scenes. With an entry in the 1,000 Guineas, it looks as though connections are confident she will improve on her initial RPR of 79. A half-sister to multiple Group 1 winner Moonlight Cloud and a descendant of the great Doff The Derby, she hails from the first crop of 2,000 Guineas hero Makfi who, like his daughter, debuted late in his juvenile season, and it is expected his progeny will step up this season.

SIR ISAAC NEWTON Aidan O'Brien
3 b c Galileo-Shastye (Danehill)

Despite failing to peg back the exciting Zawraq on his first and only time out last year, Sir Isaac Newton still looks one to watch as the season warms up – the pair pulled well clear of the field and both hold multiple Classic entries. A son of Galileo, he broke the record for a yearling sold in Europe when fetching 3.6 million guineas from MV Magnier at the Tattersalls October Book 1 Yearling Sale – albeit a record that stood for only 24 hours. He is a brother to dual Oaks runner-up Secret Gesture out of a Danehill half-sister to Arc winner Sagamix.

MY FAIRY John Oxx
3 b f Sea The Stars-Fairy Of The Night (Danehill)

Another daughter of Sea The Stars, My Fairy is a sister to the sire's first Group winner My Titania. Bred and raced by the Tsui family, whose colours were carried by the champion racehorse, My Fairy may be out of a 7½f Listed winner, but a longer trip might suit given relatives include Doncaster Cup winner Far Cry, globetrotter Grandeur and Champion Bumper and Supreme Novices' Hurdle runner-up Shaneshill.

NEW AGENDA Dermot Weld
3 b c New Approach-Prove (Danehill)

A homebred for Khalid Abdullah's Juddmonte Farms, New Agenda is among the unraced entrants for this year's Irish 2,000 Guineas. Although not hailing from the most illustrious of the operation's many families, his dam Prove, a Group 3 winner over 1m1f, is the dam of four winners from six runners, while sister Danefair is the dam of Group 3 winner and Dewhurst third Trade Fair, while half-sister Estala produced the multiple Grade 1 heroine Ventura.

A dozen names to have caught the eye away from the big meetings

ACOLYTE Roger Charlton

Having confirmed the promise of his Newbury debut over 7f behind smart Elm Park at Newbury when readily taking an all-weather maiden back down a furlong in September, Acolyte was very well backed to make a winning start in nurseries at York the following month. He never played a part that day and the tacky ground and more patient tactics were not for him. Connections fully expect him to exploit a mark in the mid-70s as a three-year-old. Indeed, he could run up a sequence and, in keeping with his pedigree, enjoy a stiffer test as he matures.

AGENT MURPHY Brian Meehan

Agent Murphy showed his Bath debut success at 33-1 absolutely no fluke when gamely following up on his handicap debut at Sandown in fair company last summer. He met defeat at Ascot on his two subsequent outings, but they both came in strong handicaps and it was his last run over 1m4f that really left the impression he could blossom in 2015 when growing into his imposing frame. Brian Meehan can place him to take another middle-distance handicap on a sound surface, before thinking about pattern races later on.

BOCCA BACIATA Jessica Harrington

This imposing filly caught the eye in two decent juvenile maidens last summer before making it third time lucky at Navan in October in another good-quality affair. She got a mile well at two and a Guineas campaign is not out of the question if she has matured physically as hoped over the winter. However, her dam was Group-placed over 1m4f she could well appreciate stepping up in trip as a three-year-old, so the Oaks might be the route to take. Her return is eagerly anticipated.

CONVEY Sir Michael Stoute

Considering Sir Michael Stoute's juveniles very often need an initial outing these days, it was telling to see such confidence behind Convey for his belated debut over 7f at Kempton last October. Sent off at odds of 4-6, the son of Dansili bolted up in a decent time and it was immediately clear Stoute had another potential star on his hands. His dam won a Listed race over a mile and stepping up in trip should be what he wants at three. Indeed, a 2,000 Guineas campaign is in the offing and, while he will have to win an early-season trial to become a strong candidate for that, there should be pattern races to be won with him providing he matures as expected.

FARHAM Richard Fahey

Considering he shaped so promisingly when runner-up in a fair Sandown maiden on his debut in July, it was somewhat disappointing this 200,000gns purchase failed to go one better on his next outing at Ayr in September. That came over an extra furlong in novice company, though, and the absence between outings was perhaps telling. Farham has plenty of size about him and is highly regarded, so trainer Richard Fahey has been minding him until he grows into his frame. Expect him to go on to better things, with a mile expected to be well within his compass at three.

NEW STORY Ismail Mohammed

New Story very much caught the eye in two strong three-year-old maidens when kicking off his career last season and registered an RPR of 93 when making it third time lucky at Salisbury in June. The manner in which he backed that up on his handicap debut at Haydock the following month, scoring by five lengths without being fully extended, was impressive. He was roughed off afterwards. It is as a four-year-old that this son of New Approach is expected to peak, and his pedigree gives hope for him relishing stepping up beyond 1m2f, the distance he was kept to in his initial season. Quick ground is ideal and he can make up into a pattern performer.

PUISSANT Marco Botti

A son of Galileo who might have gone under the radar thanks to him winning a maiden at the third attempt at Redcar in October. He has always been highly regarded by handler Marco Botti, who is no stranger to pattern success, and is certainly bred to be contesting Group races, being a brother to Cox Plate hero Adelaide. It wouldn't surprise to see him take in a Guineas trial on his seasonal return, yet middle-distances will ultimately be his optimum as a three-year-old. He handles deep ground well.

RAINBOW PRIDE Sir Mark Prescott

This grey colt showed little in three outings over 7f as a juvenile. However, each season his master trainer excels with such late-maturing types and, bred to come into his own over middle-distances, it would surprise were he not to sting bookmakers kicking off in handicaps over a suitably longer trip off an opening mark of 63.

SIRDAAB Barry Hills

Although restricted to just one outing as a juvenile and failing to make the frame, Sirdaab was an eyecatcher at Glorious Goodwood in July. He missed the kick before finishing with plenty left in the tank, over an inadequate 6f. His US pedigree suggests an all-weather maiden would be ideal for his seasonal return, and he looks a useful handicapper in the making.

TIGER JIM Jim Goldie

This late-maturing Jim Goldie-trained five-year-old had a decent time of it when switched to handicaps last year, winning twice over a straight 7f and improving 10lb to a mark of 75. His canny handler should be able to extract further progression out of him after another winter on his back, and there is most probably a decent big-field handicap to be won with him at some stage. Seems best suited by good ground.

TOE THE LINE John Kiely

Although a bumper winner on her debut at Listowel in 2013, two subsequent defeats in that division saw her connections aim towards a Flat campaign and it paid off in style. The six-year-old developed into a most consistent and progressive stayer, signing off with a game success upped to Listed company at the Curragh in September. She doesn't have too many miles on the clock, is adaptable regards going conditions and ought to be up to bagging a Group prize this season.

ZALTY David Marnane

Zalty was unlucky not to have landed the big-field handicap he promised last season. He often had the draw against him or faced a pace bias. As was the case when narrowly failing at the Curragh when last seen in 2014, he again found prominent racers just beyond recall when tackling the minimum trip, and a stiff 6f is his optimum. His running-on fourth to Group-class sprinter Muthmir at York, a very quick track, is well worth reviewing again. With that in mind and, given his rating in the high 90s, targeting the Wokingham at Royal Ascot in June, with the stiff finish to aim at, makes plenty of appeal.

Top honours could await these potential raiders from overseas

ABLE FRIEND John Moore (Hong Kong)
5g Shamardal - Ponte Piccolo

Blessed with a spectacular turn of foot, the world's top-rated miler sits right at the top of the Royal Ascot hitlist after a series of stunning displays in Hong Kong under superstar jockey Joao 'Magic Man' Moreira. He overwhelmed an international field to score by more than four lengths in the Hong Kong Mile, despite being allowed to coast home, then followed up with another pair of comfortable Group 1 wins in Stewards' Cup and Queen's Silver Jubilee Cup over 7f (had to get out of trouble pocketed on rail in latter 7f event before strolling home by a couple of lengths). Set for more local targets before going on his travels, with either the Yasuda Kinen in Japan or Queen Anne Stakes the overseas target. "The Queen Anne is the most likely path," says trainer John Moore. "The Yasuda Kinen in Tokyo was put to [owner] Dr Li as another option but his preference is for Royal Ascot, if the horse does travel."

AEROVELOCITY Paul O'Sullivan (Hong Kong)
6g Pins - Exodus

Presumably no-one needs reminding about the talent within the Hong Kong sprint division, which have provided a pair of Royal Ascot winners in Cape Of Good Hope and Little Bridge.

Having progressed through the Hong Kong handicap ranks, this New Zealand-bred broke like a shot from a gun when making all to beat an international field in the Hong Kong Sprint – an impressive display given

he was hassled by Australia's Buffering before having to stave off the favourite Peniaphobia.

"His next few months will be in Hong Kong, but he could venture elsewhere if things go well," said trainer Paul O'Sullivan.

BRAZEN BEAU Chris Waller (Australia)
3c I Am Invincible - Sansadee

Posted quick times in beating the best of his age group in the Roman Consul and Coolmore Stud Stakes over 6f in the spring, after which he was purchased by Darley. He had already been nominated as a Royal Ascot probable before shooting to the head of the formidable Australian sprint division with a breathtaking victory over established stars Chautauqua, Terravista and Lankan Rupee in the Newmarket Handicap at Flemington on March 14.

"He's beaten a world-class field and he's beaten them with a bit of contempt," said trainer Chris Waller.

Although Brazen Beau was getting weight from the older horses in that 6f event, his Racing Post Rating of 124 would be more than enough to make him a major factor in the King's Stand, his preferred target.

"If he brings this form anywhere, he will be competitive," said jockey Joao Moreira. "I would love to ride him at Royal Ascot."

CALIFORNIA CHROME Art Sherman (USA)
4c Lucky Pulpit - Love The Chase

Got be to regarded as a massive longshot to show up in Europe but Nick Smith, Royal

Ascot's head of international racing, has been wooing the US Horse of the Year's connections. On the plus side, last year's Kentucky Derby winner is already proven on turf, having won the Grade 1 Hollywood Derby on the Del Mar lawn in November. Less positively, he is a dual dirt Classic winner whose primary early-season target was the Dubai World Cup on dirt at Meydan.

There are many rivers to cross before he turns up in Berkshire but there would be no bigger marquee name at the royal meeting.

DEEP FIELD
Michael, Wayne & John Hawkes (Australia)
4c Northern Meteor - Listen Here

Long since regarded as a possible Royal Ascot hope, Deep Field was unbeaten before finishing a decent third on his first start for four months behind world champion sprinter Lankan Rupee in the Lightning Stakes. That Group 1 event is the first leg of the Global

California Chrome must be unlikely to run at Royal Ascot, but would be a huge attraction if making the trip

ROYAL ASCOT WINNERS TRAINED OUTSIDE EUROPE

2003 **Choisir**
(King's Stand, Paul Perry AUS)
Choisir (Golden Jubilee)

2005 **Cape Of Good Hope**
(Golden Jubilee, David Oughton HK)

2006 **Takeover Target**
(King's Stand, Joe Janiak AUS)

2007 **Miss Andretti**
(King's Stand, Lee Freedman AUS)

2009 **Scenic Blast**
(King's Stand, Danny Morton AUS)
Strike The Tiger
(Windsor Castle, Wesley Ward USA)
Jealous Again
(Queen Mary, Wesley Ward USA)

2012 **Little Bridge**
(King's Stand, Danny Shum HK)
Black Caviar
(Diamond Jubilee, Peter Moody AUS)

2013 **No Nay Never**
(Norfolk, Wesley Ward USA)

2014 **Hootenanny**
(Windsor Castle, Wesley Ward USA)

Sprint Challenge, a race that often produces a significant Ascot sprint contender (won by Choisir, Takeover Target, Miss Andretti, Scenic Blast and Black Caviar).

Young and inexperienced, Deep Field might well improve on his Racing Post Rating of 114, but he'll need to do so to get competitive.

Gold-Fun (below): would be suited by Royal Ascot's Golden Jubilee Stakes

DISSIDENT Peter Moody (Australia)
4c Sebring - Diana's Secret

Black Caviar's trainer could be back at Royal Ascot with Dissident, who is rated 121 in World Rankings and now a four-time Group 1 winner after three more top-level victories in 2014-15 to add to last season's triumph in the Randwick Guineas. Although he has plenty of form at a mile, the four-year-old is equally effective at 7f, the distance at which he comfortably landed the CF Orr Stakes at Caulfield in February, which leaves him slightly betwixt and between as far as the royal meeting is concerned. Perhaps the stiff 6f of the Diamond Jubilee might be more attractive than the Queen Anne.

DUBDAY Jassim Al Ghazali (Qatar)
5h Dubawi - Dayrose

Dubbed the Star from Qatar, former German-trained Dubday took his unbeaten record in Doha to six with an electrifying turn of foot from a near-impossible position under Frankie Dettori to win the nation's most prestigious thoroughbred race, the Emir's Trophy, in February. Drawn 16 of 16, he was forced wide all the way before beating last year's Irish Derby fourth Ponfeigh a neck. After a luckless trip to Meydan in 2014 where he was hampered by the ill-fated Mars and lost all chance in the Sheema Classic, the five-year-old is set to run in the two-mile Dubai Gold Cup before a staying campaign in Europe taking in both Ascot and Goodwood.

GOLD-FUN Richard Gibson (Hong Kong)
6g Le Vie Dei Colori - Goodwood March

Runner-up in the last two runnings of the Hong Kong Mile, this ex-Irish gelding shot towards the top end of the sprint division when dropped to 6f for the first time in his 22-race career for the Chairman's Sprint Prize at Sha Tin in February. Although Gold-

Fun struggled for pace in the early stages, the decision proved spot-on as he came through in a nail-biting finish to beat Hong Kong Sprint winner Aerovelocity by a short head to win his third Group 1 – and the form looks red-hot, with the rest of the territory's big-name speedsters further behind. Christophe Soumillon suggested 7f was his best trip, and he finished really well on his subsequent outing when marooned out wide behind top miler Able Friend. The stiff 6f of the Diamond Jubilee ought to suit and at this stage he is regarded as by far the most likely Hong Kong runner at Royal Ascot.

HOOTENANNY Wesley Ward (USA)
3c Quality Road - More Hennessy

It wouldn't be Royal Ascot without Wesley Ward these days, and the meeting's new Group 1 event, the Commonwealth Cup for three-year-old sprinters, could almost have been framed for Hootenanny, who routed a big field in last year's Windsor Castle Stakes. Carrying the colours of the Coolmore team, Hootenanny produced another fine effort to finish second to The Wow Signal in the Prix Morny, where he hated the ground, before Frankie Dettori harnessed his speed for an emphatic victory in the Breeders' Cup Juvenile Turf. That was over a mile but 6f is his game, as Dettori suggested at Santa Anita, saying: "I was afraid about the distance but I got him to switch off the first bit of the race." An extended European campaign would be no surprise.

LUCK OF THE KITTEN Wesley Ward (USA)
3c Kitten's Joy - Anura

Never worse than second in four career starts, Luck Of The Kitten was beaten for speed by Wesley Ward-trained stablemate Hootenanny at the Breeders' Cup, where he nevertheless ran a sound race in trying to make all in the Juvenile Turf before going down by just three-quarters of a length. He had already won twice over a mile – at Arlington and Cup venue Santa Anita – and is set to target Royal Ascot for his Anglophile owner Ken Ramsey, who remains desperate

for a winner at the royal meeting. The colt is in the right yard for that ambition to be fulfilled, even if he would need to improve markedly to figure in the St James's Palace Stakes, which offers the most likely option.

ONE AND ONLY Kojiro Hashiguchi (Japan)
4c Heart's Cry - Virtue

A leading player in the top flight of Japanese three-year-olds last term, One And Only enjoyed his finest hour when capturing the Tokyo Yushun (Japanese Derby) in June. Although his form dropped off a bit when he took on older horses in the Japan Cup and Arima Kinen, he has been earmarked for a crack at the King George after running in the Dubai Sheema Classic for his veteran trainer, set to retire at the end of the season. The colt is following the same path as his sire Heart's Cry, who scored in Dubai before being beaten a length into third behind Hurricane Run in the Ascot showpiece in 2006.

SPIELBERG Kazuo Fujisawa (Japan)
6h Deep Impact - Princess Olivia

A fast-finisher whose career has been interrupted by leg problems, Spielberg was sidelined for 14 months following the Japanese Derby of 2012 before a string of minor victories at his favourite track Tokyo, following his comeback in the second half of 2013. He hit the mark in Grade 1 company in November last year when he flew home to beat a top-class field in the Tenno Sho (Autumn), numbering Japan Cup winners Gentildonna and Epiphaneia among his victims. He was also a good third (behind Epiphaneia) in the Japan Cup on his most recent appearance in November. Assuming he comes through his seasonal debut okay in the Grade 2 Osaka Hai on April 5, Spielberg is in line for a summer campaign in Britain taking in both the Prince of Wales's Stakes at Royal Ascot and the Coral-Eclipse at Sandown. Rated 120 in last year's World Rankings, he is not a million miles away from what is likely to be required in those top British contests.

Head-Maarek has fine season in store with Treve and host of smart colts

TRAINER Criquette **Head-Maarek has proven herself one of Europe's finest trainers of fillies** down the years but, with the return of Group 1-winning juveniles Full Mast and Epicuris, she finds herself in the unusual position of having a much stronger hand to play in the colts' Classics this season.

Epicuris heads the hopefuls for Head-Maarek, whose career has enjoyed a thrilling renaissance thanks to the efforts of dual-Arc heroine Treve, herself set to pursue more history in 2015.

Unbeaten in three starts, the son of Rail Link rounded off his first season with a decisive success in the Criterium de Saint-Cloud, a race which could use all the ratings help it can get after being placed on the European Pattern Committee's watchlist for a possible downgrade.

The Prix du Jockey Club is the primary target for Epicuris, but it would be no surprise to see connections taking the precaution of adding him to the Investec Derby field at the second entry stage in April.

While Chantilly is the priority, Epsom could come under consideration if *Full Mast* – who like his stablemate is owned by Khalid Abdullah – were to set up the chance of a French Classic double with a win in the Poule d'Essai des Poulains.

Full Mast might not have received full credit for his success in the Prix Jean-Luc Lagardere owing to the disqualification of Gleneagles. But the Mizzen Mast colt is also unbeaten in three and counts the useful War Dispatch and Nucifera as his closest pursuers in a debut win at Deauville and the Group 3 Prix la Rochette.

A couple of names in the yard to receive less publicity are another Abdullah homebred, the as-yet-unraced *Clariden*, as well as Katsumi Yoshida's *Fontanelice*, the best filly in Italy when trained by Stefano Botti and a possible for the Qipco 1,000 Guineas.

As for *Treve*, last season's rollercoaster of injury and redemption showed both Head-Maarek's mastery of the trainer's art, as well as the sheer unpredictability of the sport.

Early plans are for a campaign which comprises just the Grand Prix de Saint-Cloud in June, followed by the Prix Vermeille and the Arc.

Flintshire's fine effort when chasing home Treve in the Arc pulled a 26th championship out of the fire for Andre Fabre, and the son of Dansili went on to claim international success with a second to Main Sequence in the Breeders' Cup Turf before returning to the Group 1 winner's circle in Hong Kong. Flintshire will go where the ground is fast in 2015 and that almost inevitably means he will race outside of France for much of the year.

The virus that struck last spring means Fabre has a number of unexposed older horses returning, two of which to note will be the Godolphin pair of *Fintry* and *Manatee*.

Three who Fabre tried at Group 1 level as juveniles can all be given another look.

High Celebrity was twice sent to Newmarket and will have learnt plenty ahead of her attempt on the 1,000 Guineas when chasing home Tiggy Wiggy and Anthem Alexander.

Alea Iacta might have been over the top when taking on the colts in the Criterium International but had previously impressed when scooting six lengths clear of Alpha Bravo in the Group 3 Prix Thomas Bryon. And *Territories* suffered arguably the worst interference of all in the Lagardere when delivering his challenge up the rail, yet still finished only half a length and a neck behind Gleneagles.

Among a raft of those tried in slightly shallower waters last autumn, the once-raced *Mexican Gold* and Group 3 runner-up *Baltic Comtesse* add extra punch to a battalion of promising fillies. That list must also include Al Shaqab's record-breaking purchase *Al Naamah*, who as a sister to Oaks heroine Was, will surely benefit from the move up to middle distances this season.

Make Believe has yet to meet serious opposition in two starts but the son of Makfi will surely be seen in a Classic trial in the spring.

Jean-Claude Rouget is once again likely to mount a stiff challenge to Fabre and can also welcome back his biggest earner from last season, *Avenir Certain*.

It would appear likely that the Pouliches and Prix de Diane heroine will be dropped in trip following her first career defeat in the Arc, when the daughter of Le Havre was almost the last horse to come off the bridle before subsiding tamely in the final furlong.

The case for Avenir Certain's stamina limitations is not quite so open and shut as would first appear since she didn't settle as well as usual from an unhelpful inside draw.

The yard will have an enormous wealth of three-year-old talent in terms of both quality and numbers. Drawing on and the example of Avenir Certain's progress from relative obscurity at two, attention should be paid to those who may have stayed away from Paris.

One such name to retain is *Rafaadah*, who showed toughness and class to win the Listed Grand Criterium de Bordeaux on her third and final start last season.

A first runner from Hamdan Al Maktoum's Prix Imprudence winner Joanna, Rafaadah looked to have a shade more stamina than her mother, who produced arguably her best display when dropped back to 6½f for the Prix Maurice de Gheest.

Rouget has shown a marked predilection for fillies in recent seasons, describing them as "more generous and sympathetic" in a Racing Post interview last October, so special attention should be paid on that front.

One colt who will be worth watching wherever he is sent from Rouget's Pau base is *War Dispatch*, who recovered from losing his opening skirmish with Full Mast to record three impressive victories in the colours of Joseph Allen.

Nominated for the Belmont Stakes and the UAE Derby, War Dispatch is likely to try and emulate Saonois, who went on from winning the Prix Policeman at the conclusion of Cagnes-sur-Mer's winter meeting in 2012 to claim Prix du Jockey Club glory. As a stepping stone Rouget has earmarked Chantilly's Prix de Guiche, which has been extended to the Jockey Club's full course and distance trip this season.

Ervedya was both Rouget and France's top-rated juvenile filly last season, despite being beaten in each of her two starts at Group 1 level.

Having closed rapidly behind The Wow Signal and Hootenanny to finish a good third in the Darley Prix Morny over 6f, Ervedya rounded off 2014 with an honourable second to Found in the Prix Marcel Boussac.

Her owner-breeder the Aga Khan can also look forward to an exciting season with *Vedouma*, a sister to Vadamar.

Alain de Royer-Dupre gambled on running her in the Listed Prix Isonomy at a soggy Chantilly late last November, and was rewarded with a six-length success.

While soft ground isn't a prerequisite for the daughter of Dalakhani, Royer-Dupre probably doesn't want an arid spring for Vedouma.

Dolniya overtook a pair of better-regarded fillies to emerge as the best of the Aga Khan's three-year-olds last season, finishing fifth in the Arc at the end of the year. She will be this year's project among the older horses for connections.

His Highness's emerald and red silks will also be carried by *Eesha*, who chased home Vedouma at Longchamp when the pair made their debut, and could help put a virus-hit 2014 firmly in the rear-view mirror for Mikel Delzangles.

One inmate who missed most of the middle part of the season through sickness was *Bookrunner*, who then had Group 2 targets at Deauville and Longchamp derailed by soft ground. A trip of 1m2f and a sound surface look to be the optimum conditions for the Tiznow colt, who failed to handle the undulations of the Rowley Mile in the 2,000 Guineas.

While Freddy Head couldn't match the Group 1 fireworks of his sister Criquette over the closing stages of last season, he did show off a pair of juveniles who could have a say when this year's top prizes are contested.

Migwar is clearly well forward for a potential Classic campaign, having opened his account for the season in early March at Saint-Cloud.

Stablemate *Stars And Clouds* made a huge impression on her Chantilly debut in October. A Makfi half-sister to the stable's mighty Moonlight Cloud, Stars And Clouds made light of a mile on her debut and looks to have inherited more stamina than her explosive sibling.

The last two seasons have been extremely positive for the Niarchos Family, thanks to the likes of Maxios and *Karakontie*, who races on for Jonathan Pease at four following his Breeders' Cup Mile heroics at Santa Anita.

Nucifera came up against the best at two and looks likely to be campaigned in a similar vein by Pease this term.

Pascal Bary also houses two major hopes that will carry the famous two-tone blue silks. A product of the dream union between Galileo and Six Perfections, *Faufiler* was making only her fourth career start when annihilating her rivals in a Listed race at the final meeting of Longchamp's 2014 season.

Tale Of Life ran away from his rivals in what has historically been a very good backend maiden at Saint-Cloud and his list of Classic engagements in France and Britain mark the son of Deep Impact down as very much one to watch.

Avenir Certain: big earner last season

Aces (Ire)

3 b c Dark Angel - Cute Ass (Fath)

Charlie Hills — Qatar Racing & Essafinaat

PLACINGS: 13- — RPR **109**

Starts	1st	2nd	3rd	4th	Win & Pl
2	1	-			£10,981
	8/14	Wind	6f Cls5 Mdn 2yo good		£2,911

Showed huge promise in just two starts last season, winning a good Windsor maiden before finishing within a length and a half when stepped up to 7f in Champagne Stakes; outstayed that day and looks more of a sprinter on pedigree (dam Group-placed twice over 5f).

Adelaide (Ire)

4 b c Galileo - Elletelle (Elnadim)

Aidan O'Brien (Ir) — Mrs J Magnier, W H Webb Et Al

PLACINGS: 1/2122131- — RPR **114**

Starts	1st	2nd	3rd	4th	Win & Pl
8	4	3	1	-	£1,432,325
	10/14	Moon	1m2f Gp1 good		£992,043
	8/14	Arlt	1m2f Gd1 3yo firm		£178,916
	5/14	Curr	1m2f Gp3 3yo soft		£35,208
	10/13	Leop	1m Mdn 2yo sft-hvy		£9,256

Due to return to Aidan O'Brien following his latest stint in Australia, where he won the Cox Plate last season having also landed the Secretariat Stakes in the USA; just beaten in his biggest tests in Europe (King Edward VII Stakes and Prix Niel) but looks good enough to challenge again in top middle-distance races.

Adventure Seeker (Ire)

4 gr c Dalakhani - Adventure (Unbridled's Song)

Ed Vaughan — Hamed Rashed Bin Ghadayer

PLACINGS: 6414/516262- — RPR **105**

Starts	1st	2nd	3rd	4th	Win & Pl
10	2	2		2	£47,521
78	5/14	York	1m4f Cls4 66-80 3yo Hcap good		£9,704
	9/13	Kemp	1m Cls5 Mdn 2yo stand		£2,911

Ran well in several top three-year-old handicaps last season, including when second in a heritage handicap on his final start at Newmarket after another second in the Melrose at York; still seems to be progressing and could well be a force in top staying handicaps.

Aetna

5 b m Indesatchel - On The Brink (Mind Games)

Mick Easterby — B Padgett

PLACINGS: 1081233/101301- — RPR **111**

Starts	1st	2nd	3rd	4th	Win & Pl
13	5	1	3	-	£65,479
	11/14	Donc	6f Cls1 List heavy		£26,116
92	5/14	York	6f Cls2 90-104 Hcap soft		£16,173
86	4/14	Newc	5f Cls3 81-95 Hcap soft		£9,057
74	6/13	Newc	5f Cls5 60-74 3yo Hcap good		£2,588
	3/13	Donc	7f Cls5 Mdn 3yo soft		£2,588

Progressive sprinter last season, winning a red-hot handicap at York in May and finishing with victory in a Listed event at Doncaster; won all three starts on soft or heavy ground but can cope with good, as she showed when an unlucky third in a handicap at Newmarket.

Agnes Stewart (Ire)

3 gr f Lawman - Anice Stellato (Dalakhani)

Eddie Lynam (Ir) — Clipper Logistics Group Ltd

PLACINGS: 1212- — RPR **109**

Starts	1st	2nd	3rd	4th	Win & Pl
4	2	2		-	£107,772
	9/14	Donc	1m Cls1 Gp2 2yo good		£39,697
	7/14	Fair	7f Mdn Auct 2yo gd-fm		£8,050

Showed a terrific turn of foot to win last season's

May Hill Stakes but didn't quite quicken as well on soft ground when second in Fillies' Mile next time; may well return to Newmarket for 1,000 Guineas but likely to improve when stepped up in trip (dam won over 1m4f).

Ainippe (Ire) *pictured below*
3 b f Captain Rio - Imitation (Darshaan)

Ger Lyons (Ir)					Qatar Racing Limited
PLACINGS: 1153-					RPR 102+

Starts	1st	2nd	3rd	4th	Win & Pl
4	2	-	1	-	£39,426
8/14	Curr	5f List 2yo good			£22,750
7/14	Naas	5f Mdn 2yo gd-fm			£8,338

Entered many notebooks when winning first two starts last season, even going off favourite for the Flying Childers, where she could manage only fifth; did better upped to 6f when an unlucky third at Ayr (denied a clear run) and remains a bright prospect.

Air Pilot
6 b g Zamindar - Countess Sybil (Dr Devious)

Ralph Beckett					Lady Cobham
PLACINGS: 2/212131-					RPR 115

Starts	1st	2nd	3rd	4th	Win & Pl
7	3	3	1	-	£91,341
11/14	NmkR	1m2f Cls1 List good			£20,983
87 9/14	Newb	1m2f Cls2 87-105 Hcap soft			£46,688
5/14	Thsk	1m4f Cls5 Mdn good			£2,588

Had run only once prior to last season but soon made up for lost time, running away with a good handicap at Newbury to earn a step up in grade and adding a Listed win at Newmarket; should continue to progress even as a six-year-old; yet to race on ground quicker than good.

Aktabantay
3 b c Oasis Dream - Splashdown (Falbrav)

Hugo Palmer					V I Araci
PLACINGS: 221216-					RPR 108

Starts	1st	2nd	3rd	4th	Win & Pl
6	2	3	-	-	£52,076
8/14	Sand	7f Cls1 Gp3 2yo gd-sft			£25,520
6/14	Newc	6f Cls4 2yo gd-fm			£6,469

No match for Estidhkaar in Superlative Stakes last season but managed to win a Group race in slightly weaker company when scrambling home in the Solario; didn't have any luck in running when sixth at Longchamp last time; trainer is sure he will be a lot better on quick ground.

Al Kazeem
7 b h Dubawi - Kazeem (Darshaan)

Roger Charlton					D J Deer
PLACINGS: 222/1/1111326/41502-					RPR 122

Starts	1st	2nd	3rd	4th	Win & Pl
20	8	6	1	1	£1,342,836
8/14	Wind	1m2f Cls1 Gp3 good			£34,026
7/13	Sand	1m2f Cls1 Gp1 gd-fm			£241,018
6/13	Asct	1m2f Cls1 Gp1 gd-fm			£283,550
5/13	Curr	1m2½f Gp1 gd-fm			£105,854
4/13	Sand	1m2f Cls1 Gp3 good			£34,026
5/12	NmkR	1m2f Cls1 Gp2 gd-sft			£56,710
95 5/11	Newb	1m2f Cls2 77-95 3yo Hcap gd-fm			£18,693
10/10	Newb	1m Cls4 Mdn 2yo gd-sft			£4,209

Came out of retirement last season having proved

subfertile at stud; failed to add to three Group 1 wins from 2013 but gradually recovered best form and went desperately close when second in Champion Stakes at Ascot; likely to be aimed at top 1m2f races once again.

Alea Iacta

3 b f Invincible Spirit - Almiranta (Galileo)

		Andre Fabre (Fr)			Miss K Rausing
PLACINGS: 115-					**RPR 104+**

Starts	1st	2nd	3rd	4th	Win & Pl
3	1	-	-	-	£49,291
	10/14	StCl	1m Gp3 2yo soft		£33,333
	9/14	Lonc	1m 2yo good		£10,000

Stunning six-length winner of a Group 3 at Saint-Cloud; over the top when fifth next time but fact she was sent off 5-4 for a Group 1 colt underlines the esteem in which she is held; by a great sire of milers but out of a Galileo mare so could get a bit further.

Aljamaaheer (Ire)

6 ch h Dubawi - Kelly Nicole (Rainbow Quest)

		Roger Varian			Hamdan Al Maktoum
PLACINGS: 1/41333/23218/33920-					**RPR 117**

Starts	1st	2nd	3rd	4th	Win & Pl
16	3	3	6	1	£294,084
	7/13	Asct	1m Cls1 Gp2 gd-fm		£56,710
	5/12	NmkR	7f Cls1 List 3yo gd-fm		£18,714
	10/11	Yarm	6f Cls5 Mdn 2yo good		£3,151

Has a desperate strike-rate for a horse of such ability, winning just one of his last 13, but is certainly capable of winning big races; won the Summer Mile at Ascot in 2013 and proved equally good back at 6f last season, finishing third in the Diamond Jubilee Stakes.

Aloft (Ire)

3 b c Galileo - Dietrich (Storm Cat)

		Aidan O'Brien (Ir)			
		Derrick Smith & Mrs John Magnier & Michael Tabor			
PLACINGS: 212-					**RPR 112**

Starts	1st	2nd	3rd	4th	Win & Pl
3	1	2	-	-	£53,548
	10/14	NmkR	1m Cls4 Mdn 2yo good		£5,175

Scrambled home in a maiden at Newmarket (looked green) but took a big step forward when second to Elm Park in the Racing Post Trophy on ground much softer than ideal; unlikely to figure among yard's best on that evidence but a smart prospect.

ONE TO FOLLOW

Flight Officer Slammed his rivals on his only start last term. Plenty to admire including that winning time and he can hold his own in much better company. *[Dave Edwards, Topspeed]*

Alonsoa (Ire)

3 ch f Raven's Pass - Alasha (Barathea)

		Henry Candy			Mrs Patricia J Burns
PLACINGS: 1148-					**RPR 97**

Starts	1st	2nd	3rd	4th	Win & Pl
4	2	-		1	£23,574
	7/14	Sand	7f Cls1 List 2yo gd-fm		£17,013
	6/14	Newb	7f Cls4 Mdn 2yo good		£3,881

Looked a smart prospect when winning a 7f Listed race at Sandown last season but failed to build on that subsequently; clearly amiss when last in the May Hill and had excuses (ground too soft) when fourth in Sweet Solera; capable of better.

Ansgar (Ire)

7 b g Celtic Swing - Jemmy's Girl (Pennekamp)

		Sabrina J Harty (Ir)			Ms Chynel Phelan & Shane Fox
PLACINGS: 1/808102427/3017116-					**RPR 117**

Starts	1st	2nd	3rd	4th	Win & Pl
26	6	4	3	1	£191,254
	9/14	Donc	7f Cls1 Gp2 good		£56,710
	8/14	Gdwd	7f Cls1 Gp3 good		£34,026
	7/14	Curr	7f Gp3 gd-fm		£32,500
93	6/13	Curr	7f m 76-101 Hcap gd-fm		£24,390
89	12/12	Dund	1m2¹/₂f 75-99 Hcap stand		£7,475
80	10/12	Dund	1m2¹/₂f 78-88 Hcap stand		£7,475

Has improved for being steadily dropped in trip with age and found niche over 7f last season having even been tried over hurdles in the past; enjoyed biggest win when pipping Aljamaaheer in a Group 2 at Doncaster (third Group win of the season); wants good ground or quicker.

Anthem Alexander (Ire)

3 ch f Starspangledbanner - Lady Alexander (Night Shift)

		Eddie Lynam (Ir)			Noel O'Callaghan
PLACINGS: 61132-					**RPR 115**

Starts	1st	2nd	3rd	4th	Win & Pl
5	2	1	1	-	£124,650
	6/14	Asct	5f Cls1 Gp2 2yo gd-fm		£56,710
	6/14	Tipp	5f Mdn 2yo gd-fm		£7,188

Beat Tiggy Wiggy to land last season's Queen Mary Stakes but no match for that rival when placed in Cheveley Park and Lowther Stakes; has plenty of size so should progress; will stick to sprinting and has new Group 1 sprint for three-year-olds at Royal Ascot as her aim.

Arab Spring (Ire) *pictured winning*

5 b h Monsun - Spring Symphony (Darshaan)

		Sir Michael Stoute			Ballymacoll Stud
PLACINGS: 2/11114-					**RPR 115+**

Starts	1st	2nd	3rd	4th	Win & Pl
6	4	1	-	1	£95,324
104	6/14	Asct	1m4f Cls2 93-104 Hcap gd-fm		£46,688
96	5/14	York	1m4f Cls2 81-97 Hcap good		£31,125
85	4/14	Donc	1m2¹/₂f Cls3 82-92 Hcap soft		£8,410
	3/14	Kemp	1m2f Cls5 Mdn stand		£2,588

Very progressive in first half of last season and

completed a hat-trick when easily defying a mark of 104 at Royal Ascot; disappointed next time in the Princess of Wales's Stakes but had looked every inch a Group horse as connections even mentioned the Arc as a target.

Arabian Queen (Ire)

3 b f Dubawi - Barshiba (Barathea)

David Elsworth   **J C Smith**

PLACINGS: **016156-**   RPR **101**

Starts	1st	2nd	3rd	4th	Win & Pl
6	2	-	-	-	£53,775
	7/14	NmkJ	6f Cls1 Gp2 2yo soft		£45,368
	5/14	Wind	5f Cls5 Mdn 2yo gd-fm		£2,911

Claimed notable scalp of High Celebrity in the Duchess of Cambridge Stakes last season, although there's a suspicion she made the most of a soft lead; disappointed twice subsequently but was suffering from sinus problems and trainer still feels she's a 1,000 Guineas filly.

Arod (Ire)

4 b c Teofilo - My Personal Space (Rahy)

Peter Chapple-Hyam   **Qatar Racing Limited**

PLACINGS: **3/12415-**   RPR **113+**

Starts	1st	2nd	3rd	4th	Win & Pl
6	2	1	1	1	£138,319
	7/14	Leic	1m2f Cls3 3yo gd-fm		£7,561
	4/14	Wind	1m2f Cls5 Mdn good		£2,588

Ran well in several good races last season, always leaving impression he was capable of better; fine second in the Dante despite finding ground too soft

(trainer reports he cannot have it fast enough) before not quite staying in the Derby and failing to settle in the Juddmonte.

Astaire (Ire) *below, white face*

4 b c Intense Focus - Runway Dancer (Dansili)

Kevin Ryan   **Mrs Angie Bailey**

PLACINGS: **16111/526000-**   RPR **113**

Starts	1st	2nd	3rd	4th	Win & Pl
11	4	1	-	-	£279,584
	10/13	NmkR	6f Cls1 Gp1 2yo gd-sft		£119,034
	8/13	York	6f Cls1 Gp2 2yo soft		£113,420
	7/13	NmkJ	6f Cls3 2yo gd-fm		£8,410
	5/13	York	6f Cls3 Auct Mdn 2yo good		£7,439

Top-class juvenile sprinter when winning four times including Middle Park Stakes; terrific second in Duke of York Stakes last season having failed to stay 7f first time out; lost way thereafter but talented enough to bounce back; has won on good to firm but seems better on soft.

Avenir Certain (Fr)

4 b f Le Havre - Puggy (Mark Of Esteem)

Jean-Claude Rouget (Fr)   **A Caro & G Augustin-Normand**

PLACINGS: **11/11110-**   RPR **118+**

Starts	1st	2nd	3rd	4th	Win & Pl
7	6	-	-	-	£784,813
	8/14	Deau	1m2f Gp2 3yo v soft		£61,750
	6/14	Chan	1m2½f Gp1 3yo good		£476,167
	5/14	Lonc	1m Gp1 3yo gd-sft		£214,275
	4/14	Chan	1m 3yo stand		£14,167
	10/13	Chan	1m 2yo stand		£11,789
	10/13	Bord	7f 2yo soft		£6,667

Brilliant French filly blessed with a devastating

turn of foot; won a Classic double last season and had won six in a row before suffering only defeat when 11th in the Arc (second entering final furlong before stamina gave way); should win more top races back at 1m2f.

Battersea

4 b c Galileo - Gino's Spirits (Perugino)

Roger Varian				H R H Sultan Ahmad Shah	
PLACINGS: 93/52110-				RPR **103**+	

Starts	1st	2nd	3rd	4th	Win & Pl
7	2	1	1	-	£130,084
90	9/14	Asct	1m4f Cls2 84-97 3yo Hcap gd-fm		£97,035
84	7/14	Asct	1m4f Cls2 84-105 3yo Hcap gd-fm		£31,125

Came of age last summer when winning a pair of competitive 1m4f handicaps at Ascot on good to firm ground; has the scope to carry on improving and seems likely to step up to Group races before long; should also stay further but may not be as effective on softer ground.

Beautiful Romance

3 b f New Approach - Mazuna (Cape Cross)

Saeed Bin Suroor				Godolphin	
PLACINGS: 1-				RPR **90**+	

Starts	1st	2nd	3rd	4th	Win & Pl
1	1	-	-	-	£3,881
	10/14	Donc	1m Cls5 Mdn 2yo gd-sft		£3,881

Runaway nine-length winner of a fillies' maiden at Doncaster in October, staying on strongly over a mile on good to soft ground; looks a fine middle-distance prospect on that evidence and could be an Oaks filly, although isn't certain to cope with a quicker surface.

Belardo (Ire)

3 b c Lope De Vega - Danaskaya (Danehill)

Roger Varian				Godolphin & Prince A A Faisal	
PLACINGS: 14141-				RPR **119**	

Starts	1st	2nd	3rd	4th	Win & Pl
5	3	-	-	2	£281,765
	10/14	NmkR	7f Cls1 Gp1 2yo soft		£255,762
	8/14	Newb	7f Cls1 List 2yo gd-sft		£14,461
	6/14	Yarm	6f Cls5 Mdn 2yo gd-fm		£3,235

Last season's champion two-year-old after winning the Dewhurst Stakes, relishing soft ground and a first-time hood (had been too keen when fourth in the Champagne Stakes); won his maiden on good to firm but yet to prove himself on that going in top company and has a high knee action.

Berkshire (Ire)

4 b c Mount Nelson - Kinnaird (Dr Devious)

Paul Cole				H R H Sultan Ahmad Shah	
PLACINGS: 311/91-				RPR **117**+	

Starts	1st	2nd	3rd	4th	Win & Pl
5	3	-	1	-	£128,222
	10/14	NmkR	1m1f Cls1 Gp3 soft		£36,862
	9/13	NmkR	1m Cls1 Gp2 2yo gd-fm		£56,710
	6/13	Asct	7f Cls1 List 2yo gd-fm		£34,026

Missed nearly all of last season with a colon problem but bounced back to win the Darley

Stakes at Newmarket in October on his first start since the Greenham; had won the Chesham and Royal Lodge Stakes as a juvenile and continues to be held in very high regard by connections.

Biographer

6 b g Montjeu - Reflective (Seeking The Gold)

David Lanigan					B E Nielsen
PLACINGS: 212121/42746/80552-					RPR **114**

Starts		1st	2nd	3rd	4th	Win & Pl
16		5			2	£133,811
	10/12	Asct	1m6f Cls1 List 3yo soft			£19,849
88	8/12	Ffos	1m4f Cls3 76-88 Hcap gd-sft			£6,792
	6/12	Donc	1m4f Cls5 Mdn gd-sft			£2,911

Without a win since 2012 but has run well in several top staying races and produced a career-best effort on final start last season when second to Forgotten Rules in the Long Distance Cup at Ascot; relished heavy ground that day and can bag a big prize when mud is flying.

Breton Rock (Ire)

5 b g Bahamian Bounty - Anna's Rock (Rock Of Gibraltar)

David Simcock					John Cook
PLACINGS: 11/271312/131213-					RPR **116**

Starts		1st	2nd	3rd	4th	Win & Pl
14		7	3	3	-	£183,676
	8/14	Newb	7f Cls1 Gp2 gd-sft			£56,710
	5/14	Hayd	7f Cls1 List soft			£20,983
	4/14	Thsk	7f Cls3 gd-sft			£9,338
97	10/13	Asct	7f Cls2 80-98 App Hcap soft			£32,345
92	9/13	Donc	7f Cls2 81-95 3yo Hcap gd-sft			£12,450
	10/12	Sals	6f Cls2 2yo gd-sft			£7,763
	8/12	Sals	6f Cls5 Mdn Auct 2yo gd-sft			£2,588

Smart 7f specialist who gained biggest win in last season's Hungerford Stakes at Newbury and ran several other good races over the trip; needs cut in the ground and has run only twice on good during his career including only below-par effort last season.

Bronze Angel (Ire)

6 b g Dark Angel - Rihana (Priolo)

Marcus Tregoning					Lady Tennant
PLACINGS: 315/080/75410742113-					RPR **116**

Starts		1st	2nd	3rd	4th	Win & Pl
26		7	2	4	4	£419,500
105	10/14	Asct	1m Cls2 86-110 Hcap heavy			£155,625
99	9/14	NmkR	1m1f Cls2 91-110 Hcap gd-fm			£99,600
94	7/14	York	1m Cls2 85-100 Hcap gd-fm			£16,173
95	9/12	NmkR	1m1f Cls2 90-106 Hcap good			£99,600
87	5/12	Donc	1m Cls4 71-98 3yo Hcap good			£8,410
83	1/12	Ling	1m Cls4 71-98 3yo Hcap stand			£4,205
	12/11	Ling	7f Cls5 Mdn 2yo stand			£3,558

Classy handicapper who enjoyed a fine autumn, winning his second Cambridgeshire and following up on Champions Day; looked below his best when third in a Listed race at Newmarket and worth another chance at that sort of level, although likely to need a strong gallop.

Brooch (USA)

4 b f Empire Maker - Daring Diva (Dansili)

Dermot Weld (Ir)					K Abdullah
PLACINGS: 111-					RPR **105+**

Starts		1st	2nd	3rd	4th	Win & Pl
3		3	-	-	-	£68,987
	9/14	Gowr	1m1½f Gp3 gd-fm			£39,271
	8/14	Klny	1m1½f List good			£21,667
	7/14	Gway	1m1½f Mdn good			£8,050

Has been handled with great patience, not making her debut until last July, but progressed rapidly once on the track, winning three out of three including a strong Group 3; should prove best at around 1m2f but only just got away with good to firm ground last time.

Cable Bay (Ire)

4 b c Invincible Spirit - Rose De France (Diktat)

Charlie Hills			Julie Martin & David R Martin & Partner
PLACINGS: 4124322/0662-			RPR **110**

Starts		1st	2nd	3rd	4th	Win & Pl
11		1	4	1	2	£160,131
	6/13	Leic	6f Cls4 2yo good			£3,881

Finished second in the Dewhurst as a two-year-old but missed the following ten months and took time to find his form last autumn; bounced back to his best when second in the Challenge Stakes to Here Comes When and should win similar races granted an injury-free year.

Cambridge

4 b f Rail Link - Alumni (Selkirk)

Charles Hills					K Abdullah
PLACINGS: 1/7-					RPR **81**

Starts		1st	2nd	3rd	4th	Win & Pl
2		1	-	-	-	£3,234
	10/13	Nott	1m1½f Cls5 Mdn 2yo good			£3,235

Massive plunge horse for the Oaks early last season but flopped when favourite for the Musidora and didn't run again; remains a filly of serious potential (half-sister to Listed winner Dux Scholar) and should find a handicap a formality before stepping up in class again.

Cannock Chase (USA)

4 b c Lemon Drop Kid - Lynnwood Chase (Horse Chestnut)

Sir Michael Stoute					Saeed Suhail
PLACINGS: 2/111-					RPR **111+**

Starts		1st	2nd	3rd	4th	Win & Pl
4		3	1	-	-	£61,452
	6/14	Asct	1m2f Cls1 Gp3 3yo gd-fm			£42,533
89	5/14	Newb	1m2f Cls2 82-92 3yo Hcap gd-fm			£15,563
	4/14	Wind	1m2f Cls5 Mdn 3yo soft			£2,588

Missed second half of last season but had already made a big impression with a hat-trick of wins culminating in Tercentenary Stakes at Royal Ascot; late-maturing type with which his trainer has often excelled in the past so no surprise if he steps up to Group 1 level; should stay 1m4f.

Cape Peron

5 b g Beat Hollow - Free Offer (Generous)

Henry Candy				The Earl Cadogan
PLACINGS: 3/11521/				

Starts	1st	2nd	3rd	4th	Win & Pl
6	3	1	1	-	£62,318
10/13	Chan	1m List soft			£21,138
87 5/13	Donc	1m Cls3 76-87 3yo Hcap gd-sft			£8,410
4/13	Newb	1m Cls4 Mdn 3yo gd-sft			£5,175

Due to return from more than a year off with injury with connections keen to step up to Group level after his progressive form in 2013; finished second in the Betfred Mile on ground quicker than ideal and routed rivals by four lengths in a Listed race at Chantilly on soft.

Cappella Sansevero

3 b c Showcasing - Madam President (Royal Applause)

Ger Lyons (Ir)				Qatar Racing Limited
PLACINGS: 11125314-				RPR 112

Starts	1st	2nd	3rd	4th	Win & Pl
8	4	1	1	1	£131,737
8/14	Curr	6f Gp3 2yo gd-yld			£32,500
5/14	Curr	5f List 2yo sft-hvy			£28,438
5/14	Naas	5f 2yo yld-sft			£8,625
4/14	Dund	5f Mdn Auct 2yo stand			£8,050

Highly tried throughout last season but at least managed to win Group 3 and Listed races; ran several good races in defeat at higher level, most notably when second in Coventry Stakes and close third in Phoenix Stakes; could continue to make mark in decent sprints.

Captain Cat (Ire)

6 b/br g Dylan Thomas - Mother Of Pearl (Sadler's Wells)

Roger Charlton				Seasons Holidays
PLACINGS: /312/0712/211312540-				RPR 117+

Starts	1st	2nd	3rd	4th	Win & Pl
17	5	4	2	1	£259,126
9/14	Hayd	1m Cls1 Gp3 good			£35,727
8/14	Sals	1m Cls1 Gp3 gd-fm			£42,533
4/14	Ling	1m Cls2 stand			£93,375
86 10/13	Kemp	1m Cls3 85-95 Hcap stand			£7,159
5/12	NmkR	1m Cls5 Mdn 3yo gd-fm			£3,235

Progressed well on the all-weather last winter before winning on finals day at Lingfield; returned from a break to confirm improvement back on turf

in the autumn, winning a Group 3 at Haydock and finishing second in Joel Stakes; disappointing in Hong Kong in December.

Captain Joy (Ire)

6 g g Dark Angel - Ardea Brave (Chester House)

Tracey Collins (Ir)				Herb M Stanley
PLACINGS: 15253024-60764805111-2				RPR 109

Starts	1st	2nd	3rd	4th	Win & Pl
29	7	6	2	2	£90,199
1/15	Ling	1m Cls2 Conds stand			£11,971
12/14	Dund	7f Hcap 3yo+ stand			£8,625
10/14	Dund	7f 70-100 Hcap 3yo+ stand			£10,833
3/13	Dund	7f 4yo+ stand			£7,012
12/12	Dund	7f Hcap stand			£7,475
11/12	Dund	7f Hcap 3yo+ stand			£7,475
12/11	Dund	7f Mdn 2yo stand			£5,948

Out of sorts for much of last year following trip to Dubai but bounced back to form when landing a hat-trick on the all-weather from October to January; twice placed in Listed races in 2013 and looks capable of challenging at that level again and perhaps higher.

Celestial Path (Ire)

3 br c Footstepsinthesand - Miss Kittyhawk (Hawk Wing)

Sir Mark Prescott			Gordon Woodall & Prof C Tisdall
PLACINGS: 113-			RPR 111

Starts	1st	2nd	3rd	4th	Win & Pl
3	2	-	1	-	£42,877
9/14	Hayd	1m Cls1 List 2yo good			£14,461
7/14	York	7f Cls4 Auct Mdn 2yo gd-fm			£5,175

Good third in Racing Post Trophy last season having run away with a soft Listed race at Haydock; seems sure to improve on that form having been described as a 'big baby' last term and reportedly found ground too soft at Doncaster, though not certain on pedigree to stay 1m4f.

Charming Thought

3 b c Oasis Dream - Annabelle's Charm (Indian Ridge)

Charlie Appleby				Godolphin
PLACINGS: 2111-				RPR 117

Starts	1st	2nd	3rd	4th	Win & Pl
4	3	1	-	-	£134,010
10/14	NmkR	6f Cls1 Gp1 2yo soft			£123,344
9/14	Leic	6f Cls4 2yo gd-fm			£6,469
9/14	Ling	6f Cls5 Mdn 2yo good			£3,235

Surprise winner of last season's Middle Park Stakes and may have been lucky to run into a below-par

ONE TO FOLLOW

Postponed Suited by fast ground and comfortably bettered York's 1m4f standard time when powering home in last season's Great Voltigeur. A speed figure of 110 suggests he will be a top-class four-year-old with the Coronation Cup and King George among his options. *[Dave Edwards, Topspeed]*

Ivawood but had been progressive prior to that as he completed a hat-trick; dam won over 1m2f so has good prospects of seeing out a mile and could continue to improve.

Christophermarlowe (USA)

3 b c Tapit - Dress Rehearsal (Galileo)

John Gosden   **Michael Tabor**

PLACINGS: **11-**   RPR **97+**

Starts	1st	2nd	3rd	4th	Win & Pl
2	2	-	-	-	£12,596
9/14	Epsm	1m¹/₂f Cls3 2yo good			£8,715
9/14	Sand	1m Cls5 Mdn 2yo good			£3,881

Won both starts last season, overcoming greenness on his debut at Sandown and following up cosily at Epsom; looks a stayer and has plenty of scope; dam won over 1m4f and should be a realistic Derby contender given he has already shown he excels at the course.

Cirrus Des Aigles (Fr) *below left*

9 b g Even Top - Taille De Guepe (Septieme Ciel)

Corine Barande-Barbe (Fr)   **Jean-Claude-Alain Dupouy**

PLACINGS: **2/54251123/421111d54-**   RPR **126**

Starts	1st	2nd	3rd	4th	Win & Pl
61	21	20	6	5	£6,014,622
6/14	Epsm	1m4f Cls1 Gp1 good			£218,901
5/14	Lonc	1m1f Gp1 soft			£119,042
4/14	Lonc	1m2¹/₂f Gp1 v soft			£142,850
10/13	Lonc	1m2f Gp2 soft			£92,683
9/13	MsnL	1m2f Gp3 gd-sft			£32,520
10/12	Lonc	1m2f Gp2 heavy			£95,000
4/12	Lonc	1m2¹/₂f Gp1 heavy			£142,850
3/12	Meyd	1m4f Gp1 good			£1,935,484
10/11	Asct	1m2f Cls1 Gp1 good			£737,230
8/11	Deau	1m4¹/₂f Gp2 v soft			£98,276
8/11	Deau	1m2f Gp3 heavy			£34,483
7/11	Vich	1m2f Gp3 v soft			£34,483
6/11	Lonc	1m2f Gp3 gd-sft			£34,483
10/10	Lonc	1m2f Gp2 v soft			£65,575
9/10	Lonc	1m2f List good			£23,009
10/09	Lonc	1m4f Gp2 gd-sft			£71,942
9/09	Lonc	1m2f Gp3 3yo good			£38,835
8/09	Le L	1m2f List 3yo gd-sft			£26,699
5/09	Lonc	1m2¹/₂f 3yo soft			£27,760
5/09	Lonc	1m2f 3yo good			£14,078
1/09	Cagn	1m 3yo stand			£9,709

Extraordinary gelding who has been a standing dish in top middle-distance races in recent seasons and won three more Group 1 races last season, including a memorable win over Treve in the Prix Ganay; well beaten on last two runs but has bounced back many times before.

Clever Cookie *winning at York, below*

7 b g Primo Valentino - Mystic Memory (Ela-Mana-Mou)

Peter Niven   **Francis Green Racing Ltd**

PLACINGS: **111964-**   RPR **110**

Starts	1st	2nd	3rd	4th	Win & Pl
6	3	-	-	1	£42,862
	5/14	York	1m6f Cls1 List gd-sft		£15,642
88	5/14	York	1m2¹/₂f Cls2 86-100 Hcap soft		£16,173
	4/14	Donc	1m4f Cls5 Mdn soft		£2,588

Bumper and hurdles winner who flourished when switched to the Flat last season; unlucky not to make more of an impact in the Ebor and Doncaster Cup, staying on from too far back both times; trainer eschewed a return to hurdling in order to pursue top staying prizes.

Commemorative

3 ch c Zamindar - Revered (Oasis Dream)

Charlie Hills   **K Abdullah**

PLACINGS: **4117-**   RPR **104**

Starts	1st	2nd	3rd	4th	Win & Pl
4	2	-	-	1	£36,406
	10/14	NmkR	1m Cls1 Gp3 2yo good		£28,355
	9/14	Donc	1m Cls3 Mdn 2yo good		£7,763

Long-striding colt who looked really good when making all in last season's Autumn Stakes at Newmarket; found conditions much too sharp in Breeders' Cup Juvenile Turf, though stayed on well to not be beaten far; should stay at least 1m2f (dam showed best form at that trip).

Connecticut

4 b c New Approach - Craigmill (Slip Anchor)

Luca Cumani   **Sheikh Mohammed Obaid Al Maktoum**

PLACINGS: **311139-**   RPR **110**

Starts	1st	2nd	3rd	4th	Win & Pl
6	3	-	2	-	£38,678
89	7/14	NmkJ	1m4f Cls3 71-90 Hcap gd-fm		£7,763
84	6/14	York	1m2¹/₂f Cls3 76-90 3yo Hcap good		£16,173
	5/14	Newb	1m2f Cls4 Mdn 3yo gd-fm		£6,469

Made good progress last season, winning handicaps at York and Newmarket before a fine third under a big weight in the Melrose when stepped up to 1m6f; disappointing next time at Newmarket but likely type to resume progress having been described as a big baby by trainer last term.

Consort (Ire)

3 gr c Lope De Vega - Mundus Novus (Unbridled's Song)

Sir Michael Stoute

Highclere Thoroughbred Racing (Hardwicke)

PLACINGS: **1-**   RPR **89 +**

Starts	1st	2nd	3rd	4th	Win & Pl
1	1	-	-	-	£5,175
	9/14	NmkR	7f Cls4 Mdn 2yo good		£5,175

Impressive winner of his only start in a maiden at Newmarket, making all and stretching clear to win by nearly three lengths; was a fairly rare first-time-out two-year-old winner for his trainer, which bodes very well for the future; likely to prove best from 1m to 1m2f.

Convey

3 b c Dansili - Insinuate (Mr Prospector)

Sir Michael Stoute   **K Abdullah**

PLACINGS: 1-   RPR **92 + aw**

Starts	1st	2nd	3rd	4th	Win & Pl
1	1	-	-	-	£2,911
	10/14	Kemp	7f Cls5 Mdn 2yo stand		£2,911

Won only start last year in a maiden at Kempton by five lengths, showing a good turn of foot; out of a 1m Listed winner who has produced four other winners (including two with black type from 7f to 1m2f) so should get a mile well and looks an exciting prospect.

Cotai Glory

3 ch c Exceed And Excel - Continua (Elusive Quality)

Charlie Hills   **Ms A A Yap & F Ma**

PLACINGS: 76121U0-   RPR **110**

Starts	1st	2nd	3rd	4th	Win & Pl
7	2	1	-	-	£37,235
	7/14	Gdwd	5f Cls1 Gp3 2yo gd-fm		£28,355
	7/14	Bath	5f Cls5 Mdn 2yo firm		£2,588

Rivalled Tiggy Wiggy for title of fastest juvenile last season, although flopped in Prix de l'Abbaye last time; won Molecomb Stakes and desperately unlucky not to add Flying Childers, jinking right and unseating rider when well clear in final furlong; looked less effective over 6f.

Cougar Mountain (Ire)

4 b c Fastnet Rock - Descant (Nureyev)

Aidan O'Brien (Ir)
     Michael Tabor & Derrick Smith & Mrs John Magnier

PLACINGS: 1590-   RPR **112**

Starts	1st	2nd	3rd	4th	Win & Pl
4	1	-	-	-	£19,469
	6/14	Naas	6f Mdn gd-fm		£5,750

Reportedly held in very high regard at home and sign of that esteem that he ran in three Group 1 races following his maiden win; shaped with most promise when fifth in the July Cup and ran well in the Nunthorpe over a clearly inadequate trip; remains a fascinating prospect.

Cursory Glance (USA)

3 b f Distorted Humor - Time Control (Sadler's Wells)

Roger Varian   **Merry Fox Stud Limited**

PLACINGS: 1121-   RPR **112**

Starts	1st	2nd	3rd	4th	Win & Pl
4	3	1	-	-	£219,858
	9/14	Curr	7f Gp1 2yo gd-fm		£145,000
	6/14	Asct	6f Cls1 Gp3 2yo gd-fm		£39,697
	5/14	Kemp	6f Cls5 Mdn 2yo stand		£2,911

Top-class juvenile filly last season, suffering only defeat to Tiggy Wiggy at York; relished an extra furlong when winning the Moyglare Stud Stakes next time and seems sure to stay a mile; set to miss the 1,000 Guineas with a fetlock injury but could be back for Royal Ascot.

Custom Cut (Ire)

6 b g Notnowcato - Polished Gem (Danehill)

David O'Meara				Gary Douglas & Pat Breslin

PLACINGS: **0126748/32283111118-**   RPR **120**

Starts	1st	2nd	3rd	4th	Win & Pl
37	10	5	4	4	£300,834
	9/14	NmkR	1m Cls1 Gp2 good		£61,814
	8/14	York	1m1f Cls1 Gp3 good		£45,368
	8/14	Leop	1m Gp3 soft		£33,854
	7/14	Pont	1m Cls1 List gd-fm		£25,520
	6/14	Wind	1m¹/₂f Cls1 List gd-sft		£20,983
	4/13	Curr	7f Gp3 gd-yld		£31,707
93	7/12	Curr	7f 80-93 Hcap heavy		£10,833
86	7/12	Naas	7f 66-86 3yo Hcap heavy		£7,475
	6/12	DRoy	7f sft-hvy		£4,600
75	6/12	Cork	7f 57-80 Hcap soft		£5,750

Went from strength to strength after joining David O'Meara last season with five successive victories culminating in the Group 2 Joel Stakes at Newmarket (made all); failed to get home under forcing tactics in Queen Elizabeth II Stakes; worth another crack at a Group 1.

Danzeno

4 b g Denounce - Danzanora (Groom Dancer)

Michael Appleby				A M Wragg

PLACINGS: **81/19122-**   RPR **117**

Starts	1st	2nd	3rd	4th	Win & Pl
7	3	2	-	-	£68,775
	6/14	Newc	6f Cls1 Gp3 gd-fm		£34,026
90	4/14	NmkR	6f 80-99 3yo Hcap good		£12,938
	10/13	Rdcr	6f Cls5 Mdn 2yo soft		£2,911

Sharply progressive sprinter last season; won a Group 3 at Newcastle in June and unlucky to be beaten a head on next two starts having raced too keenly at Doncaster and found soft ground against him at Ascot; always expected to improve with age and could be a Group 1 horse.

Dick Whittington (Ire)

3 b c Rip Van Winkle - Sahara Sky (Danehill)

Aidan O'Brien (Ir)				
		Michael Tabor & Derrick Smith & Mrs John Magnier		

PLACINGS: **221311-**   RPR **114**

Starts	1st	2nd	3rd	4th	Win & Pl
6	3	2	1	-	£154,106
	8/14	Curr	6f Gp1 2yo soft		£96,667
	7/14	Curr	6¹/₂f Gp3 2yo gd-fm		£35,208
	6/14	Navn	6f 2yo gd-fm		£11,375

Among last season's leading juvenile sprinters, battling to narrow victories in the Phoenix and Anglesey Stakes to prove effectiveness on all types of ground; hadn't looked as effective when stepped up to 7f in the Chesham Stakes; should be a force in three-year-old sprints.

Dolniya (Fr)

4 b f Azamour - Daltama (Indian Ridge)

Alain de Royer-Dupre (Fr)				H H Aga Khan

PLACINGS: **211135-**   RPR **117**

Starts	1st	2nd	3rd	4th	Win & Pl
6	3	1	1	-	£263,587
	6/14	StCl	1m4f Gp2 3yo gd-sft		£71,250
	6/14	Comp	1m2f List 3yo soft		£22,917
	5/14	MsnL	1m4¹/₂f 3yo good		£12,083

Fifth in last season's Arc, capping a season of steady progress having won three times and finished third in the Prix Vermeille; should continue to improve with age (out of a winning half-sister to Daylami, who peaked at five) and looks up to Group 1 level.

Due Diligence (USA)

4 b c War Front - Bema (Pulpit)

Aidan O'Brien (Ir)				
		Michael Tabor & Derrick Smith & Mrs John Magnier		

PLACINGS: **14/3112-**   RPR **116**

Starts	1st	2nd	3rd	4th	Win & Pl
6	3	1	1	1	£198,124
	6/14	Naas	6f List 3yo gd-yld		£21,667
97	5/14	Naas	6f 80-97 3yo Hcap yld-sft		£25,000
	8/13	Sara	5¹/₂f 2yo firm		£29,448

Joined Aidan O'Brien from the United States last season and made rapid early progress, winning twice over 6f before finishing second in the Diamond Jubilee Stakes; missed the rest of the campaign through injury but looks sure to be a major player again in Group 1 sprints.

Dutch Connection

3 ch c Dutch Art - Endless Love (Dubai Destination)

Charlie Hills				Mrs Susan Roy

PLACINGS: **32113-**   RPR **108**

Starts	1st	2nd	3rd	4th	Win & Pl
5	2	1	2	-	£83,115
	8/14	York	7f Cls1 Gp3 2yo gd-fm		£45,368
	8/14	Gdwd	7f Cls2 Mdn 2yo gd-fm		£12,938

Made steady progress in maidens last season before making a big leap forward to win the Acomb Stakes at York, although couldn't cope with step up to Group 1 level when third to Gleneagles last time; always looked type to improve at three and should make a useful miler.

Eagle Top

4 ch c Pivotal - Gull Wing (In The Wings)

John Gosden				Lady Bamford

PLACINGS: **1414-**   RPR **119**

Starts	1st	2nd	3rd	4th	Win & Pl
4	2	-	-	2	£177,908
	6/14	Asct	1m4f Cls1 Gp2 3yo gd-fm		£113,789
	4/14	Newb	1m3f Cls4 Mdn 3yo good		£6,469

Very lightly raced colt who finished fourth in last season's King George on only his fourth run and should improve; had looked a Group 1 horse in the making when running away with King Edward VII Stakes; likely to have top 1m4f races on his agenda.

Easter (Ire)

3 b f Galileo - Missvinski (Stravinsky)

Aidan O'Brien (Ir)
Mrs John Magnier & Michael Tabor & Derrick Smith

PLACINGS: 21-				RPR **87**
Starts	1st	2nd	3rd	4th	Win & Pl
2	1	1	-	-	£11,420

10/14	Leop	7f Mdn 2yo yield	£9,488

Did well in two maidens last October, finishing strongly when second at Navan on her debut and looking much better for that experience when making all at Leopardstown; connections have already spoken of her as an Oaks filly.

Ectot

4 b c Hurricane Run - Tonnara (Linamix)

Elie Lellouche (Fr)
Al Shaqab Racing

PLACINGS: 21111/110-				RPR **118+**
Starts	1st	2nd	3rd	4th	Win & Pl
8	6	1	-	-	£306,993

9/14	Lonc	1m4f Gp2 3yo good	£61,750
4/14	Lonc	1m Gp3 3yo good	£33,333
11/13	StCl	1m Gp1 2yo v soft	£116,138
9/13	Lonc	1m Gp3 2yo soft	£32,520
8/13	Deau	1m List 2yo good	£49,593
7/13	Claf	7f 2yo sft-hvy	£9,756

Group 1-winning juvenile who returned with a win over Karakontie in the Prix de Fontainebleau only to miss the Classics through injury; stepped up to 1m4f after absence to land the Prix Niel but pulled too hard in the Arc; worth another chance at top level.

Elm Park

3 b c Phoenix Reach - Lady Brora (Dashing Blade)

Andrew Balding
Qatar Racing Limited

PLACINGS: 31111-				RPR **118**
Starts	1st	2nd	3rd	4th	Win & Pl
5	4	-	1	-	£212,040

10/14	Donc	1m Cls1 Gp1 2yo soft	£122,494
9/14	NmkR	1m Cls1 Gp2 2yo gd-fm	£67,428
8/14	Sals	1m Cls1 List 2yo good	£17,013
8/14	Newb	7f Cls4 Mdn 2yo soft	£4,528

Easy winner of an admittedly soft Racing Post

Trophy on soft ground, making it four wins in a row having also proved himself on quicker going in the Royal Lodge; could have a crack at the 2,000 Guineas but bred for middle-distances and looks more of a Derby horse.

Endless Drama (Ire)

3 b c Lope De Vega - Desert Drama (Green Desert)

Ger Lyons (Ir)
Mrs Annette O'Callaghan

PLACINGS: 1-				RPR **96+**
Starts	1st	2nd	3rd	4th	Win & Pl
1	1	-	-	-	£8,337

10/14	Naas	6f Mdn 2yo gd-yld	£8,338

Stunning winner of a Naas maiden in October, storming five and a half lengths clear of a runner-up who also pulled away from the rest of a fair field; has size and scope and should do well from two to three; set to start in a Guineas trial.

Epicuris

3 b c Rail Link - Argumentative (Observatory)

Criquette Head-Maarek (Fr)
K Abdullah

PLACINGS: 111-				RPR **112**
Starts	1st	2nd	3rd	4th	Win & Pl
3	3	-	-	-	£162,375

11/14	StCl	1m2f Gp1 2yo heavy	£119,042
10/14	Lonc	1m1f Gp3 2yo v soft	£33,333
9/14	Lonc	1m 2yo good	£10,000

Won three out of three last season and made all to win the Group 1 Criterium de Saint-Cloud over 1m2f on heavy ground; has bundles of stamina on that evidence and pedigree suggests he will be equally effective on better ground.

Esoterique (Ire)

5 b m Danehill Dancer - Dievotchka (Dancing Brave)

Andre Fabre (Fr)
Baron Edouard De Rothschild

PLACINGS: 1127/4419144-				RPR **118**
Starts	1st	2nd	3rd	4th	Win & Pl
11	4	1	-	4	£349,161

8/14	Deau	1m Gp1 soft	£142,850
5/14	NmkR	1m1f Cls1 Gp3 gd-fm	£36,862
4/13	Lonc	1m1f Gp3 3yo good	£32,520
4/13	StCl	1m 3yo soft	£10,163

Not the most consistent but a very smart miler on

her day, as she showed with wins in the Prix Rothschild (from Miss France) and Dahlia Stakes (from Integral) last season; finished behind both those fillies when beaten in the Sun Chariot last time; acts on any going.

Estidhkaar (Ire)

3 b c Dark Angel - Danetime Out (Danetime)

Richard Hannon   Hamdan Al Maktoum

PLACINGS: 21114-   RPR **116**

Starts	1st	2nd	3rd	4th	Win & Pl
5	3			1	£117,110

	9/14	Donc	7f Cls1 Gp2 2yo good	£42,533
	7/14	NmkJ	7f Cls1 Gp2 2yo gd-sft	£45,368
	6/14	Newb	6½f Cls4 Mdn 2yo gd-fm	£3,881

Suffered a hairline fracture of his hock when a disappointing favourite in the Dewhurst Stakes and had previously looked a very smart juvenile; bolted up from useful rival Aktabantay at Newmarket and defied a penalty when following up in Champagne Stakes; could be a top miler.

Euro Charline

4 b f Myboycharlie - Eurolink Artemis (Common Grounds)

Marco Botti   Team Valor International

PLACINGS: 1/125311-   RPR **112**

Starts	1st	2nd	3rd	4th	Win & Pl
7	4	1	1	-	£354,646

	8/14	Arlt	1m1½f Gd1 firm	£257,530
	7/14	Asct	1m Cls1 List good	£22,684
78	3/14	Wolv	7f Cls4 66-78 3yo Hcap stand	£5,499
	11/13	Wolv	7f Cls5 Mdn 2yo stand	£2,911

Progressed throughout last season, kicking off with

a win off 78 and culminating in a Grade 1 victory at Arlington; showed best form in between at Ascot, winning a Listed race having finished third in the Coronation Stakes, and could be an ideal type for Royal Ascot again.

Extortionist (Ire) *below, red colours*

4 b c Dandy Man - Dream Date (Oasis Dream)

Olly Stevens   Sheikh Suhaim Al Thani

PLACINGS: 141934/001212307-   RPR **115**

Starts	1st	2nd	3rd	4th	Win & Pl
15	4	2	2	2	£155,857

	7/14	Sand	5f Cls1 Gp3 gd-fm	£35,444
100	6/14	NmkJ	5f Cls2 85-100 3yo Hcap gd-fm	£12,450
	6/13	Asct	5f Cls1 List 2yo good	£34,026
	4/13	Nott	5f Cls5 Mdn 2yo good	£3,235

Enjoyed a rich vein of form on quick ground last summer, winning a Group 3 and coming within half a length of bigger wins at Goodwood and York (in the Nunthorpe); had been slightly disappointing since Windsor Castle win as a juvenile but may not have liked softer ground.

Fadhayyil (Ire)

3 b f Tamayuz - Ziria (Danehill Dancer)

Barry Hills   Hamdan Al Maktoum

PLACINGS: 212-   RPR **108+**

Starts	1st	2nd	3rd	4th	Win & Pl
3	1	2	-	-	£31,705

	9/14	Sals	7f Cls3 Mdn 2yo good	£7,116

Good second to Lucida in Rockfel Stakes on final start when still looking green and seems sure to

progress with time; trainer keen to go straight to 1,000 Guineas, although far from certain to get a mile (out of 5f sprinter and two black-type siblings never won beyond 7f).

Fannaan (USA)

3 ch c Speightstown - Titian Time (Red Ransom)

John Gosden					Hamdan Al Maktoum
PLACINGS: **11-**					RPR **100+**

Starts	1st	2nd	3rd	4th	Win & Pl
2	2	-		-	£11,626
	10/14	NmkR	7f Cls2 2yo soft		£8,715
	9/14	Hayd	6f Cls5 Mdn 2yo good		£2,911

Wasn't stretched to land a conditions race at Newmarket on second start (only serious rival lost chance by pulling hard) but at least built on bright impression made by a winning debut at Haydock; smart prospect and likely to start in a 2,000 Guineas trial.

Fascinating Rock (Ire)

4 b c Fastnet Rock - Miss Polaris (Polar Falcon)

Dermot Weld (Ir)					Newtown Anner Stud Farm Ltd
PLACINGS: **5/11185-**					RPR **110+**

Starts	1st	2nd	3rd	4th	Win & Pl
6	3	-	-	-	£110,233
	5/14	Leop	1m2f Gp3 3yo yld-sft		£50,000
	4/14	Navn	1m2f Gp3 3yo yld-sft		£32,500
	3/14	Leop	1m2f Mdn 3yo sft-hvy		£6,900

Won Ireland's two leading Derby trials last season, the Ballysax and the Derrinstown, but managed only eighth at Epsom and wasn't seen again after finishing

last of five in the Irish Derby; still a decent prospect and may do better back at 1m2f on softer ground.

Faydhan (USA)

3 b/br c War Front - Agreeable Miss (Speightstown)

John Gosden					Hamdan Al Maktoum
PLACINGS: **1-**					RPR **99+**

Starts	1st	2nd	3rd	4th	Win & Pl
1	1	-	-	-	£2,911
	7/14	Hayd	6f Cls5 Mdn 2yo gd-sft		£2,911

Among leading fancies for 2,000 Guineas despite not running since debut win at Haydock in July on good to soft ground; bred to appreciate a much quicker surface and form worked out extraordinarily well (six-length runner-up Dutch Connection won a Group 3).

Fintry (Ire)

4 b f Shamardal - Campsie Fells (Indian Ridge)

Andre Fabre (Fr)					Godolphin Snc
PLACINGS: **1/21113-**					RPR **116**

Starts	1st	2nd	3rd	4th	Win & Pl
6	4	1	1	-	£158,470
	8/14	Sand	1m Cls1 Gp3 gd-sft		£36,862
	6/14	Chan	1m Gp2 3yo good		£61,750
	5/14	Chan	1m List 3yo v soft		£22,917
	9/13	StCl	1m 2yo soft		£9,756

Lightly raced filly who made good progress last season, winning three times over a mile including Group races at Chantilly and Sandown; fair third in the Sun Chariot Stakes on her first crack at a Group 1 and should be able to make her mark at that level.

Flaming Spear (Ire)

3 ch c Lope De Vega - Elshamms (Zafonic)

Kevin Ryan   **Qatar Racing & Essafinaat**

PLACINGS: 1-					RPR **95+**

Starts	1st	2nd	3rd	4th	Win & Pl
1	1	-	-	-	£7,439
	7/14	York	6f Cls3 Auct Mdn 2yo gd-fm.............................£7,439		

Strapping colt who made a hugely impressive debut when winning easily at York in July; missed rest of season after suffering a hairline fracture but reportedly remains on target for a crack at 2,000 Guineas and always looked type to make a better three-year-old anyway.

Flintshire

5 b/br h Dansili - Dance Routine (Sadler's Wells)

Andre Fabre (Fr)   **K Abdullah**

PLACINGS: 121148/242221-					RPR **125**

Starts	1st	2nd	3rd	4th	Win & Pl
12	4	5	-	2	£2,470,475
	12/14	ShTn	1m4f Gp1 gd-fm.............................£732,477		
	7/13	Lonc	1m4f Gp1 3yo good.............................£278,732		
	6/13	Chan	1m4f Gp3 3yo good.............................£32,520		
	5/13	Chan	1m2f 3yo good.............................£10,163		

Ended long winless streak when landing Hong Kong Vase in December but had run several terrific races in defeat all season, most notably when chasing home Treve in the Arc; needs fast ground to produce best and three of four defeats on ground worse than good came when favourite.

Forgotten Rules (below, noseband): Ascot Gold Cup hope

Flying Officer (USA)

5 b g Dynaformer - Vignette (Diesis)

John Gosden   **George Strawbridge**

PLACINGS: 17/1/126-					RPR **111**

Starts	1st	2nd	3rd	4th	Win & Pl
6	3	1	-	-	£46,857
88	4/14	Nott	1m6f Cls1 List soft.............................£22,684		
	6/13	Wind	1m2f Cls3 82-88 3yo Hcap gd-fm.............£7,439		
	9/12	Sand	1m Cls5 Mdn 2yo gd-fm.............................£3,881		

Missed much of last season after winning a Listed race at Nottingham in April, returning at the backend to finish second to Pallasator at Newmarket and sixth in the Long Distance Cup (suffered serious interference); still very lightly raced and could rank considerably higher.

Forever Now

4 b c Galileo - All's Forgotten (Darshaan)

John Gosden   **Lady Bamford**

PLACINGS: 8/21316-					RPR **111**

Starts	1st	2nd	3rd	4th	Win & Pl
6	2	1	1	-	£46,782
	8/14	Gdwd	1m6f Cls1 List good.............................£22,684		
	6/14	Donc	1m4f Cls4 Mdn good.............................£5,175		

Promising young stayer who won a strong Listed race at Goodwood having hacked up in his maiden by eight lengths; just came up short in two biggest tests, including when sixth in the St Leger, but saw out trip well and looks type to progress (still immature last season).

Forgotten Rules (Ire)

5 b g Nayef - Utterly Heaven (Danehill)

Dermot Weld (Ir)   Moyglare Stud Farm

PLACINGS: **11-**   RPR **117+**

Starts	1st	2nd	3rd	4th	Win & Pl
2	2	-	-	-	£189,469

10/14	Asct	2m Cls1 Gp2 heavy	£178,637
8/14	Gway	1m6f soft	£10,833

Defied lack of experience to win Long Distance Cup at Ascot in October on only his third run having won a bumper and a soft Flat race at Galway beforehand; still looked green and seems sure to progress; trainer resisted temptation to go hurdling in order to aim him at Ascot Gold Cup.

Found (Ire)

3 b f Galileo - Red Evie (Intikhab)

Aidan O'Brien (Ir)
Michael Tabor & Derrick Smith & Mrs John Magnier

PLACINGS: **131-**   RPR **116+**

Starts	1st	2nd	3rd	4th	Win & Pl
3	2	-	1	-	£174,837

10/14	Lonc	1m Gp1 2yo good	£142,850
8/14	Curr	1m Mdn 2yo gd-fm	£9,488

Produced an outstanding performance to run away with last season's Prix Marcel Boussac, stepping up on her third in the Moyglare Stud Stakes (had looked green) and relishing return to a mile; could run in the 1,000 Guineas but considered more of an Oaks filly.

Free Eagle (Ire)

4 b c High Chaparral - Polished Gem (Danehill)

Dermot Weld (Ir)   Moyglare Stud Farm

PLACINGS: **12/13-**   RPR **120**

Starts	1st	2nd	3rd	4th	Win & Pl
4	2	1	1	-	£218,051

9/14	Leop	1m2f Gp3 gd-fm	£54,167
8/13	Leop	1m Mdn 2yo good	£8,415

One-time Derby favourite who missed much of last season through injury but made a big impression during the autumn; won by seven lengths on return at Leopardstown and ran a close third in Champion Stakes despite being unsuited by heavy ground; looks a proper Group 1 horse.

Full Mast (USA)

3 b c Mizzen Mast - Yashmak (Danzig)

Criquette Head-Maarek (Fr)   K Abdullah

PLACINGS: **111-**   RPR **112**

Starts	1st	2nd	3rd	4th	Win & Pl
3	3	-	-	-	£210,408

10/14	Lonc	7f Gp1 2yo good	£166,658
9/14	Lonc	7f Gp3 2yo good	£33,333
8/14	Deau	6½f 2yo stand.	£10,417

Won three out of three last year, although needed a stewards' inquiry to keep his unbeaten record when promoted ahead of Gleneagles in the Prix Jean-Luc Lagardere; had been beaten on merit that day but still ran another fine race and could be a leading miler.

G Force (Ire)

4 b c Tamayuz - Flanders (Common Grounds)

David O'Meara   Middleham Park Racing XVIII & Partner

PLACINGS: 2/11325610-   RPR **121**

Starts	1st	2nd	3rd	4th	Win & Pl
9	3	2	1	-	£190,405
	9/14	Hayd	6f Cls1 Gp1 good		£154,818
87	5/14	York	5f Cls3 76-90 3yo Hcap good		£12,938
	4/14	Newc	5f Cls5 Mdn good		£2,588

Had been steadily progressive over 5f last season until making a big leap forward when stepped up a furlong, winning Sprint Cup at Haydock (first time beyond 5f since debut); unsuited by heavy ground next time at Ascot; should again be a leading player in Group 1 sprints.

Geoffrey Chaucer (USA)

4 b c Montjeu - Helsinki (Machiavellian)

Aidan O'Brien (Ir)

Mrs John Magnier & Michael Tabor & Derrick Smith

PLACINGS: 11/300-   RPR **112+**

Starts	1st	2nd	3rd	4th	Win & Pl
5	2	-	1	-	£69,601
	9/13	Curr	1m Gp2 2yo good		£52,846
	7/13	Leop	1m Mdn 2yo gd-fm		£9,256

Badly lost his way last season and wasn't seen after finishing tailed off in the Derby and German Derby; had looked a top middle-distance prospect prior to that, winning both his starts at two and finishing an unlucky third in the Derrinstown; could yet confirm that initial promise.

Giovanni Canaletto (Ire)

3 ch c Galileo - Love Me True (Kingmambo)

Aidan O'Brien (Ir)

Michael Tabor & Derrick Smith & Mrs John Magnier

PLACINGS: 31-   RPR **91+**

Starts	1st	2nd	3rd	4th	Win & Pl
2	1	-	1	-	£10,333
	10/14	Leop	1m Mdn 2yo yld-sft		£9,488

Beaten at 8-11 on his debut last season but took a big step forward next time out when winning at Leopardstown by six and a half lengths, taking time to hit top gear but soon powering clear; full brother to Ruler Of The World and should progress over middle distances.

Gleneagles (Ire)

3 b c Galileo - You'resothrilling (Storm Cat)

Aidan O'Brien (Ir)

Michael Tabor & Mrs John Magnier & Derrick Smith

PLACINGS: 411111d-   RPR **116+**

Starts	1st	2nd	3rd	4th	Win & Pl
6	4	-	1	1	£271,770
	9/14	Curr	7f Gp1 2yo gd-fm		£145,000
	8/14	Curr	7f Gp2 2yo gd-fm		£50,000
	7/14	Leop	7f Gp3 2yo gd-fm		£32,500
	6/14	Curr	7f Mdn 2yo gd-fm		£10,350

Tough and classy juvenile last season; first past the post on all five starts after a losing debut but was denied a Group 1 double when disqualified in the Prix Jean Luc Lagardère (interfered with rivals but clearly the best horse in the race); likely to prove best from a mile to 1m2f.

Gm Hopkins

4 b g Dubawi - Varsity (Lomitas)

John Gosden   R J H Geffen

PLACINGS: 40/11143-   RPR **108+**

Starts	1st	2nd	3rd	4th	Win & Pl
7	3	-	1	2	£35,814
91	9/14	NmkR	1m1f Cls2 75-94 Hcap good		£18,675
87	9/14	Sand	7f Cls3 82-90 3yo Hcap good		£9,338
	4/14	Nott	1m¹/₂f Cls5 Mdn 3yo soft		£3,881

Made a huge impression when winning handicaps at Sandown and Newmarket (Silver Cambridgeshire) last season, looking a surefire Pattern horse in the making; failed to justify favouritism next twice after 9lb rise but may not have been suited by slight drop in trip.

Golden Horn

3 b c Cape Cross - Fleche D'Or (Dubai Destination)

John Gosden   A E Oppenheimer

PLACINGS: 1-   RPR **83+**

Starts	1st	2nd	3rd	4th	Win & Pl
1	1	-	-	-	£6,469
	10/14	Nott	1m¹/₂f Cls4 Mdn 2yo gd-sft		£6,469

Very well-bred colt (half-brother to 1m2f Listed winner Eastern Belle out of an unraced half-sister to two Group winners at up to 1m3½f) who won his only start last year despite being slowly away and outpaced; should come into his own over middle distances.

Gordon Lord Byron (Ire)

7 b g Byron - Boa Estrela (Intikhab)

Tom Hogan (Ir)   **Dr Cyrus Poonawalla & Morgan J Cahalan**

PLACINGS: 42311274/1678223214-   **RPR 121**

Starts	1st	2nd	3rd	4th	Win & Pl
44	11	11	7	5	£1,552,957

	10/14	Asct	6f Cls1 Gp2 heavy		£207,856
	3/14	Rose	7¹/₂f Gp1 soft		£325,269
	9/13	Hayd	6f Cls1 Gp1 gd-sft		£141,775
	8/13	Leop	1m Gp3 good		£31,707
	3/13	Dund	6f stand		£8,415
	10/12	Lonc	7f Gp1 heavy		£142,850
	8/12	York	7f Cls1 List gd-sft		£28,355
	5/12	Cork	6f gd-sft		£8,625
90	5/12	Tipp	5f 70-96 Hcap heavy		£7,475
78	11/11	Dund	6f 77-95 Hcap stand		£7,733
	10/11	Dund	6f Mdn stand		£4,759

Versatile and evergreen performer who has won Group 1 races in each of the last three years from 6f to 7¹/₂f; has gained all biggest wins on good to soft ground or worse, though also finished second in Haydock Sprint Cup and Prix de la Foret on good last season.

Gospel Choir *pictured below*

6 ch g Galileo - Chorist (Pivotal)

Sir Michael Stoute   **Cheveley Park Stud**

PLACINGS: 3/1117/715/411-   **RPR 116**

Starts	1st	2nd	3rd	4th	Win & Pl
11	6	-	1	1	£195,318

	5/14	York	1m6f Cls1 Gp2 good		£79,394
	5/14	NmkR	1m4f Cls1 Gp2 gd-fm		£56,710
97	9/13	Gdwd	1m4f Cls2 87-97 Hcap good		£12,938
90	8/12	Hayd	1m4f Cls2 77-96 3yo Hcap gd-fm		£31,125
84	7/12	Asct	1m4f Cls4 66-84 3yo Hcap gd-sft		£6,469
	7/12	Sals	1m2f Cls5 Mdn gd-fm		£2,911

Missed much of last season but had already taken step up to higher grade in his stride with wins in Jockey Club Stakes and Yorkshire Cup; more likely to run in top middle-distance races than staying contests (had Hardwicke Stakes and King George as aims prior to setback).

Here Comes When (Ire)

5 b g Danehill Dancer - Quad's Melody (Spinning World)

Andrew Balding   **Mrs Fitri Hay**

PLACINGS: 14/2140/15011-   **RPR 118**

Starts	1st	2nd	3rd	4th	Win & Pl
11	5	1	-	2	£133,616

	10/14	NmkR	7f Cls1 Gp2 soft		£56,710
	9/14	Badn	1m Gp2 soft		£33,333
95	5/14	Ches	7¹/₂f Cls2 90-103 Hcap soft		£15,753
89	5/13	Ches	7¹/₂f Cls2 86-100 3yo Hcap good		£15,753
	7/12	Sals	7f Cls4 Mdn 2yo gd-fm		£4,399

Flopped for second successive year at Royal Ascot last season (only runs on good to firm ground since two-year-old days) but bounced back on soft in the autumn with two Group 2 wins, most notably in the Challenge Stakes at Newmarket; could be a top miler with some cut.

High Celebrity (Fr)

3 b f Invincible Spirit - High Surf (Storm Cat)

Andre Fabre (Fr)   **Ecurie Victoria Dreams**

PLACINGS: 1213-   **RPR 111**

Starts	1st	2nd	3rd	4th	Win & Pl
4	2	1	1	-	£83,277

	9/14	Chan	5¹/₂f Gp3 2yo gd-sft		£33,333
	6/14	Chan	7f 2yo good		£10,417

Had nothing go right in two trips to Newmarket last season, struggling to pick up on soft ground in

the Duchess of Cambridge Stakes and failing to settle in the Cheveley Park; proved her class with an impressive Group 3 win in between and trainer still feels she's a Group 1 filly.

High Jinx (Ire)

7 b g High Chaparral - Leonara (Surumu)

James Fanshawe   **Mr & Mrs W J Williams**

PLACINGS: **412222/4250/3521312-**   RPR **113**

Starts	1st	2nd	3rd	4th	Win & Pl
21	4	7	4	3	£447,973
	10/14	Lonc	2m4f Gp1 good		£142,850
	7/14	MsnL	1m7¹/₂f List good		£21,667
92	6/12	NmkJ	1m4f Cls2 87-102 Hcap gd-sft		£32,345
	6/11	Donc	1m4f Cls5 Mdn gd-sft		£2,526

Bounced back to his best last season after a year in the doldrums and finally nailed a major staying prize (has now been second five times in total at Group 1 or 2 level) when winning the Prix du Cadran over 2m4f; likely to be knocking on the door again.

Highland Reel (Ire)

3 b c Galileo - Hveger (Danehill)

Aidan O'Brien (Ir)
Derrick Smith & Mrs John Magnier & Michael Tabor

PLACINGS: **211-**   RPR **110+**

Starts	1st	2nd	3rd	4th	Win & Pl
3	2	1	-	-	£55,905
	7/14	Gdwd	7f Cls1 Gp2 2yo gd-fm		£45,368
	7/14	Gowr	1m Mdn 2yo gd-fm		£8,338

Impressive winner of last season's Vintage Stakes at Goodwood; form worked out badly but had already won his maiden by 12 lengths and connections hold him in high regard; likely to be kept to a mile with the 2,000 Guineas and St James's Palace Stakes likely targets.

Hillstar

5 b h Danehill Dancer - Crystal Star (Mark Of Esteem)

Sir Michael Stoute   **Sir Evelyn De Rothschild**

PLACINGS: **41/221346/0222211-**   RPR **117**

Starts	1st	2nd	3rd	4th	Win & Pl
15	4	6	1	2	£755,528
	10/14	Wood	1m4f Gd1 good		£340,909
	9/14	Newb	1m3f Cls3 Gp3 soft		£34,026
	6/13	Asct	1m4f Cls1 Gp2 3yo gd-fm		£99,243
	10/12	Leic	7f Cls4 Mdn 2yo soft		£4,334

Hugely consistent last year and unlucky to finish second four times before gaining deserved reward

in the autumn, winning Canadian International at Woodbine and a Group 3 at Newbury; needs to find just a bit more to make mark at Group 1 level in Europe.

Hors De Combat

4 ch g Mount Nelson - Maid For Winning (Gone West)

James Fanshawe   **Chris Van Hoorn**

PLACINGS: **12/513253-**   RPR **113**

Starts	1st	2nd	3rd	4th	Win & Pl
8	2	2	2		£56,234
	5/14	NmkR	1m Cls2 84-97 3yo Hcap gd-fm		£12,938
91	8/13	NmkJ	7f Cls5 Auct Mdn 2yo gd-fm		£3,235

Progressed out of handicaps early last season (third in the Britannia Stakes at Royal Ascot) and did well to be placed a couple of times at Group level; looks best suited by quick ground; remains open to further improvement and could make a mark in good mile races.

Hot Streak (Ire)

4 ch c Iffraaj - Ashirah (Housebuster)

Kevin Ryan   **Qatar Racing Limited**

PLACINGS: **115312/3137500-**   RPR **116**

Starts	1st	2nd	3rd	4th	Win & Pl
13	4	1	3	-	£221,889
	5/14	Hayd	5f Cls1 Gp2 soft		£56,710
	10/13	Asct	5f Cls1 Gp3 gd-sft		£22,684
	8/13	York	5f Cls1 List 2yo soft		£28,355
	7/13	York	6f Cls4 Auct Mdn 2yo gd-fm		£6,469

Close second in the Middle Park as a juvenile and built on that promise with some excellent performances last season, winning Temple Stakes and finishing within two lengths in King's Stand and Nunthorpe Stakes; well down the field on final two starts but remains a top prospect.

Integral

5 b m Dalakhani - Echelon (Danehill)

Sir Michael Stoute   **Cheveley Park Stud**

PLACINGS: **11712/211317-**   RPR **119**

Starts	1st	2nd	3rd	4th	Win & Pl
11	6	2	1	-	£441,704
	10/14	NmkR	1m Cls1 Gp1 good		£113,420
	7/14	NmkJ	1m Cls1 Gp1 soft		£113,420
	6/14	Asct	1m Cls1 Gp2 gd-fm		£82,882
	8/13	Sand	1m Cls1 Gp3 gd-fm		£23,463
	7/13	Sand	1m Cls1 List 3yo gd-fm		£20,983
	5/13	Gdwd	1m Cls5 Mdn good		£3,235

Came of age last season with Group 1 wins in

Falmouth Stakes (didn't need to be at her best on soft ground) and Sun Chariot Stakes (made all and beat strong field); still quite lightly raced and family have tended to progress with age so may still have plenty more to offer.

Intrinsic

5 b h Oasis Dream - Infallible (Pivotal)

Robert Cowell				Malih Lahej Al Basti	
PLACINGS: 8631/11180-				RPR **106+**	

Starts	1st	2nd	3rd	4th	Win & Pl
9	4	-	1	-	£87,302
95	8/14	Gdwd	6f Cls2 94-108 Hcap gd-fm		£62,250
89	5/14	Gdwd	6f Cls2 81-98 Hcap soft		£15,563
80	5/14	Asct	6f Cls4 67-80 Hcap gd-sft		£6,469
	10/13	Newc	6f Cls5 Mdn gd-fm		£2,588

Hugely impressive winner of last season's Stewards' Cup, comfortably completing a hat-trick (on various going) as he worked his way through handicap ranks; disappointed twice subsequently but scoped dirty after first poor run and well worth more chances at a higher level.

Ivawood (Ire)

3 b c Zebedee - Keenes Royale (Red Ransom)

Richard Hannon				Carmichael Jennings	
PLACINGS: 1112-				RPR **117**	

Starts	1st	2nd	3rd	4th	Win & Pl
4	3	1	-	-	£141,379
	7/14	Gdwd	6f Cls1 Gp2 2yo gd-fm		£45,368
	7/14	NmkJ	6f Cls1 Gp2 2yo gd-fm		£45,368
	6/14	Sand	5f Cls5 Mdn 2yo good		£3,881

Won three out of four last season with only defeat coming by a nose in Middle Park Stakes; looked just below his best on soft ground that day having shown blinding speed to win Group 2 races at Newmarket and Goodwood; likely to run in 2,000 Guineas but may not stay a mile.

Jack Naylor

3 b f Champs Elysees - Fashionable (Nashwan)

Jessica Harrington (Ir)				Gerard Byrne	
PLACINGS: 521113-				RPR **107**	

Starts	1st	2nd	3rd	4th	Win & Pl
6	3	1	1	-	£97,500
	8/14	Curr	1m List 2yo good		£27,083
	7/14	Leop	7f Cls1 Gp3 2yo gd-fm		£32,500
	7/14	Rosc	7f Mdn Auct 2yo gd-fm		£7,475

Did well last season when beating Agnes Stewart in a 7f Group 3 at Leopardstown and then defying a penalty in a strong Listed race; lacked class of impressive Found when only third in Prix Marcel Boussac but should leave that form behind when stepped up in trip this season.

ONE TO FOLLOW

Golden Spun Has joined David O'Meara who has done exceptionally well with recruits from Brian Smart. *[Simon Turner, Racing Post Ratings]*

Jamaica (Ire)

3 gr c Galileo - Dialafara (Anabaa)

Aidan O'Brien (Ir)
Mrs John Magnier & Michael Tabor & Derrick Smith

PLACINGS: 314-				RPR **101**	

Starts	1st	2nd	3rd	4th	Win & Pl
3	1	-	1	1	£14,825
	7/14	Gway	7f Mdn 2yo good		£9,488

Big Derby mover during the winter having won a Galway maiden, but managed only fourth in the Acomb Stakes last season; may have found good to firm ground too quick for him that day and market vibes suggest he will prove a good deal better over middle distances.

Jellicle Ball (Ire)

3 b f Invincible Spirit - Dance Troupe (Rainbow Quest)

John Gosden				Lord Lloyd-Webber	
PLACINGS: 1-				RPR **83+aw**	

Starts	1st	2nd	3rd	4th	Win & Pl
1	1	-	-	-	£3,752
	10/14	Kemp	7f Cls4 Mdn 2yo stand		£3,752

280,000gns filly who won well on her only start at Kempton in October despite looking green; became her dam's fourth winning foal out of four and all three others won over at least 1m2f (including one at Group 3 level) but sire suggests she could also make an impact at a mile.

John F Kennedy (Ire)

3 b c Galileo - Rumplestiltskin (Danehill)

Aidan O'Brien (Ir)
Mrs John Magnier & Michael Tabor & Flaxman Stables

PLACINGS: 211-				RPR **113+**	

Starts	1st	2nd	3rd	4th	Win & Pl
3	2	1	-	-	£61,687
	9/14	Leop	1m Gp3 2yo gd-fm		£50,000
	8/14	Curr	1m Mdn 2yo yield		£9,488

Exciting colt who was too green to justify odds-on favouritism on his debut but made amends by winning twice subsequently, most notably in a Group 3 at Leopardstown; looks a middle-distance horse in the making and likely to start in the Ballysax Stakes en route to Epsom.

Just The Judge (Ire)

5 b/br m Lawman - Faraday Light (Rainbow Quest)

Charlie Hills				Qatar Racing Limited & Sangster Family	
PLACINGS: 111/21306/533313-				RPR **111**	

Starts	1st	2nd	3rd	4th	Win & Pl
14	5	1	5	-	£685,490
	10/14	Wood	1m2f Gd1 good		£170,455
	5/13	Curr	1m Gp1 3yo gd-fm		£141,463
	10/12	NmkR	7f Cls1 Gp2 2yo gd-sft		£34,026
	8/12	Newb	7f Cls1 List 2yo gd-fm		£13,043
	6/12	Newb	7f Cls4 Mdn 2yo gd-sft		£3,558

High-class mare who has won Group/Grade 1

races in each of the last two seasons while finishing placed in five others; seemed to benefit from step up to 1m2f last season, winning at the top level over the trip in Canada, and should have many more opportunities in similar races.

Justice Day (Ire)

4 b c Acclamation - Rock Exhibition (Rock Of Gibraltar)

David Elsworth					Robert Ng
PLACINGS: 21295213/4440105217-					RPR **111**

Starts	1st	2nd	3rd	4th	Win & Pl
19	5	4	1	3	£120,900

10/14	Asct	5f Cls1 List gd-sft		£25,520
7/14	Hayd	6f Cls2 gd-sft		£14,940
10/13	Sals	6f Cls2 2yo heavy		£9,704
5/13	NmkR	6f Cls4 2yo good		£5,175
4/13	Newb	5f Cls4 Mdn 2yo gd-sft		£4,528

Finished third in the Middle Park as a two-year-old and progressed well last year, including a Listed victory at Ascot; suited by plenty of cut that day so may head to France in search of similar ground; trainer feels he's best at 5f but has also won three times over 6f.

Justice Good (Ire)

3 b c Acclamation - Qui Moi (Swain)

David Elsworth					Robert Ng
PLACINGS: 61114-					RPR **105**

Starts	1st	2nd	3rd	4th	Win & Pl
5	3	-	-	1	£20,009

6/14	Wind	5f Cls4 2yo good		£6,469
5/14	NmkR	6f Cls4 2yo gd-fm		£4,197
4/14	Wind	5f Cls5 Mdn 2yo soft		£2,911

Won three times (including a dead-heat) early last

season before good fourth in Coventry Stakes, showing great speed to make much of the running; missed rest of season through injury but reported to have wintered well; being aimed at 2,000 Guineas but looks more of a sprinter.

Karakontie (Jpn)

4 b c Bernstein - Sun Is Up (Sunday Silence)

Jonathan Pease (Fr)					Niarchos Family
PLACINGS: 1211/21801-					RPR **120**

Starts	1st	2nd	3rd	4th	Win & Pl
9	5	2	-	-	£1,151,688

11/14	SnAt	1m Gd1 firm		£662,651
5/14	Lonc	1m Gp1 3yo gd-sft		£261,892
10/13	Lonc	7f Gp1 2yo soft		£162,593
9/13	Lonc	7f Gp3 2yo good		£32,520
7/13	Comp	7f 2yo v soft		£9,756

Triple Group 1 winner who produced his best performance when landing last season's Breeders' Cup Mile on firm ground, proving effectiveness on all types of going (previous two major wins on much softer); looks sure to be a big player in more top mile races.

Kingston Hill *pictured below*

4 rg c Mastercraftsman - Audacieuse (Rainbow Quest)

Roger Varian					Paul Smith
PLACINGS: 111/82414-					RPR **123**

Starts	1st	2nd	3rd	4th	Win & Pl
8	4	1	-	2	£1,104,278

9/14	Donc	1m6¹/₂f Cls1 Gp1 3yo good		£368,615
10/13	Donc	1m Cls1 Gp1 2yo soft		£149,714
10/13	NmkR	1m Cls1 Gp3 2yo gd-sft		£22,684
9/13	Newb	7f Cls4 Mdn 2yo soft		£4,528

Won last year's St Leger to add to his Racing Post Trophy victory as a juvenile; also showed top-class form in both runs over 1m4f, finishing second in the Derby and fourth in the Arc, and should be a major force over that trip again; has missed races in the past due to quick ground.

Kiyoshi

4 b f Dubawi - Mocca (Sri Pekan)

Charles Hills					Qatar Racing Limited
PLACINGS: 4112d3/062415-					RPR **111 +**

Starts	1st	2nd	3rd	4th	Win & Pl
11	3	1	2	2	£138,968

9/14	Donc	7f Cls1 Gp3 good		£35,520
6/13	Asct	6f Cls1 Gp3 2yo gd-fm		£39,697
5/13	Gdwd	6f Cls5 Mdn 2yo gd-fm		£3,881

Top-class juvenile in 2013 (won Albany Stakes and twice placed at Group 1 level) but was held up by sickness last season; twice unsuited by soft ground

on return and never convinced when tried over a mile but showed she retains all her class with impressive Group 3 win over 7f.

Kodi Bear (Ire)
3 b c Kodiac - Hawattef (Mujtahid)

Clive Cox					Mrs Olive Shaw
PLACINGS: 2512-					RPR **114**

Starts	1st	2nd	3rd	4th	Win & Pl
4	1	2	-	-	£119,131
	7/14	Asct	7f Cls1 List 2yo good £17,013		

Relished step up to 7f when winning at Ascot last July before being put away for Dewhurst Stakes and nearly rewarded connections' patience when fine second to Belardo at Newmarket; should appreciate going further again and looks a dark horse for 2,000 Guineas.

Kool Kompany (Ire)
3 br c Jeremy - Absolutely Cool (Indian Ridge)

Richard Hannon					Kool Kompany Partnership
PLACINGS: 111011265-					RPR **112**

Starts	1st	2nd	3rd	4th	Win & Pl
9	5	1	-	-	£202,702
	7/14	MsnL	5½f Gp2 2yo v soft £61,750		
	6/14	Curr	6f Gp2 2yo gd-fm £50,000		
	6/14	Naas	6f List 2yo gd-yld £32,500		
	5/14	Wind	5f Cls2 2yo gd-fm £9,704		
	4/14	Leic	5f Cls5 Auct Mdn 2yo good £3,235		

Very smart sprinting juvenile early last season, winning Railway Stakes and Prix Robert Papin on contrasting ground before close second in Phoenix Stakes; badly drawn next time in sales race at York

and failed to fire after two-month break when fifth in Middle Park.

Lady Correspondent (USA)
3 b f War Front - Fanzine (Cozzene)

John Gosden					K Abdullah
PLACINGS: 1-					RPR **78+**

Starts	1st	2nd	3rd	4th	Win & Pl
1	1	-	-	-	£5,175
	9/14	NmkR	7f Cls4 Mdn 2yo gd-fm £5,175		

Won only start in a Newmarket maiden last season and expected to go on to better things by connections; likely to prove best over a mile (out of unraced sister to top-class miler Mizzen Mast), although plenty of sire's progeny get slightly further and a half-sister won twice over 1m4f.

Latharnach (USA)
3 b c Iffraaj - Firth Of Lorne (Danehill)

Charlie Appleby					Godolphin
PLACINGS: 411-					RPR **97+**

Starts	1st	2nd	3rd	4th	Win & Pl
3	2	-	-	1	£10,831
	9/14	Sand	7f Cls3 2yo good £6,469		
	7/14	Sand	7f Cls5 Mdn 2yo gd-fm £3,881		

Won his maiden over 7f at Sandown last season and followed up in a novice race over course and distance, albeit when gifted a soft lead; has plenty of size and looks type to progress; should prove best over a mile (five half-siblings all won over that trip).

Lightning Moon (Ire)
4 b c Shamardal - Catch The Moon (Peintre Celebre)

Ed Walker | **M Betamar**

PLACINGS: **111-** | RPR **114**

Starts	1st	2nd	3rd	4th	Win & Pl
3	3	-	-	-	£49,400
	10/14	Asct	6f Cls1 Gp3 soft £39,697		
82	5/14	Hayd	6f Cls4 70-84 3yo Hcap gd-sft.......................... £6,469		
	5/14	Sals	6f Cls5 Mdn soft £3,235		

Hugely exciting sprinter who has won all three starts, most notably when beating Danzeno by a head in a Group 3 at Ascot; may well be Group 1 class but trainer reports he can get jarred up due to his size and has yet to run him on good ground; should also stay 7f.

Lightning Thunder
4 b f Dutch Art - Sweet Coincidence (Mujahid)

Olly Stevens | **Mohd Al Kubasi & Pearl Bloodstock Ltd**

PLACINGS: **1124/2294-** | RPR **110**

Starts	1st	2nd	3rd	4th	Win & Pl
8	2	3	-	2	£172,847
	9/13	Donc	6f Cls2 2yo gd-sft.. £12,450		
	8/13	Newb	6f Cls4 Mdn 2yo good £4,528		

Without a win since September 2013 but built on strong juvenile form when finishing second in 1,000 Guineas at Newmarket and the Curragh last season; suffered a hard race on soft ground in the latter and flopped twice subsequently but should have benefited from a break.

Limato (Ire)
3 b g Tagula - Come April (Singspiel)

Henry Candy | **Paul G Jacobs**

PLACINGS: **1111-** | RPR **116+**

Starts	1st	2nd	3rd	4th	Win & Pl
4	4	-	-	-	£140,493
	10/14	Rdcr	6f Cls1 List 2yo good £117,220		
	7/14	Newb	6f Cls1 List 2yo gd-fm.................................... £14,461		
	6/14	Kemp	6f Cls3 2yo stand £6,225		
	6/14	Kemp	6f Cls5 Mdn 2yo stand.................................... £2,588		

Untried above Listed level but ran to form worthy of a much higher grade when claiming scalp of Cotai Glory at Newbury and decimating a strong field in Two-Year-Old Trophy at Redcar; looks a pure sprinter and a likely type for new Group 1 three-year-old sprint at Royal Ascot.

Louis The Pious
7 b/br g Holy Roman Emperor - Whole Grain (Polish Precedent)

David O'Meara | **F Gillespie**

PLACINGS: **60170209/7201707135-** | RPR **114**

Starts	1st	2nd	3rd	4th	Win & Pl
38	7	6	4	2	£283,032
104	9/14	Ayr	6f Cls2 96-110 Hcap gd-fm.......................... £99,600		
99	6/14	Asct	7f Cls2 92-105 Hcap gd-fm.......................... £62,250		
	7/13	Hayd	6f Cls2 gd-fm £15,563		
83	7/11	Newc	6f Cls3 71-84 3yo Hcap gd-sft........................ £5,175		
80	7/11	Ches	6f Cls4 61-80 3yo Hcap good.......................... £5,175		
74	6/11	Pont	6f Cls3 72-82 3yo Hcap gd-fm £6,670		
	5/11	Haml	6f Cls5 Mdn good £2,590		

Did remarkably well to win two big handicaps last season, landing the Buckingham Palace Stakes

over 7f and Ayr Gold Cup over 6f (both on good to firm); fair third on Pattern debut on soft ground and could do better at that level back on a quicker surface.

Lucida (Ire)

3 b f Shamardal - Lura (Street Cry)

Jim Bolger (Ir)					Godolphin
PLACINGS: 12215-					**RPR 111 +**

Starts	1st	2nd	3rd	4th	Win & Pl
5	2	2	-	-	£140,093
	9/14	NmkR	7f Cls1 Gp2 2yo good		£61,814
	8/14	Naas	6f 2yo yield		£8,625

Generally consistent in top juvenile fillies' races last season, failing to run to form just once when perhaps finding ground too soft in Fillies' Mile; had previously coped well with Rowley Mile when winning Rockfel Stakes following seconds in Moyglare Stud and Debutante Stakes.

Lucky Kristale

4 b f Lucky Story - Pikaboo (Pivotal)

George Margarson					Graham Lodge Partnership
PLACINGS: 11611/008-					**RPR 101**

Starts	1st	2nd	3rd	4th	Win & Pl
8	4	-	-	-	£137,847
	8/13	York	6f Cls1 Gp2 2yo gd-fm		£85,065
	7/13	NmkJ	6f Cls1 Gp2 2yo gd-fm		£45,368
	5/13	Yarm	6f Cls5 2yo gd-fm		£3,235
	5/13	NmkR	6f Cls5 Mdn Auct 2yo good		£3,235

Won the Duchess of Cambridge and Lowther Stakes as a two-year-old but struggled last season over unsuitable trips; twice flopped over a mile and even failed to last 7f in a Group 3 at Doncaster having quickened to lead; should do better being campaigned as a sprinter.

Maarek

8 b g Pivotal - Ruby Rocket (Indian Rocket)

Evanna McCutcheon (Ir)					Lisbunny Syndicate
PLACINGS: 15290110/7212580040-					**RPR 118**

Starts	1st	2nd	3rd	4th	Win & Pl
44	12	7	2	5	£646,422
	5/14	Curr	6f Cls1 Gp2 soft		£56,710
	10/13	Lonc	5f Gp1 soft		£162,593
	9/13	Newb	5f Cls1 Gp3 soft		£34,026
	4/13	Naas	5f List soft		£21,138
	10/12	Asct	6f Cls1 Gp2 soft		£141,775
	9/12	Curr	6f Gp3 yield		£31,146
	6/12	Newc	6f Cls1 Gp3 heavy		£31,191
102	5/12	NmkR	6f Cls2 82-104 Hcap gd-sft		£27,390
97	4/12	Naas	6f 73-97 Hcap gd-yld		£10,833
89	9/11	Curr	6f 79-103 Hcap heavy		£25,216
79	6/11	Curr	5f 61-85 Hcap soft		£6,246
69	4/11	Navn	6f 47-70 Hcap gd-yld		£4,759

Has gained last five wins on soft ground and has proved himself a top-class sprinter in such conditions with those victories including 2012 Champions Sprint at Ascot and 2013 Prix de l'Abbaye; added Duke of York Stakes last year and close fourth back in big Ascot sprint.

Madame Chiang

4 b f Archipenko - Robe Chinoise (Robellino)

David Simcock					Miss K Rausing
PLACINGS: 1/1061-					**RPR 115**

Starts	1st	2nd	3rd	4th	Win & Pl
5	3	-	-	-	£392,792
	10/14	Asct	1m4f Cls1 Gp1 heavy		£344,513
	5/14	York	1m2½f Cls1 Gp3 3yo soft		£45,368
	10/13	Yarm	1m Cls5 Mdn 2yo soft		£2,911

Has won three out of three on soft or heavy ground, most notably when staying on relentlessly in particularly gruelling conditions in a Group 1 on Champions Day at Ascot; fair sixth in Prix Vermeille on good ground having been outpaced; seems sure to stay further.

Malabar

3 b f Raven's Pass - Whirly Bird (Nashwan)

Mick Channon					Jon And Julia Aisbitt
PLACINGS: 241144-					**RPR 108**

Starts	1st	2nd	3rd	4th	Win & Pl
6	2	1	-	3	£55,546
	8/14	Gdwd	7f Cls1 Gp3 2yo good		£22,684
	7/14	Asct	7f Cls4 Mdn 2yo gd-fm		£6,469

Impressive Group 3 winner at Goodwood last season and caught the eye in two runs at Group 1 level subsequently, finishing strongly in fourth both times; had been unable to get a run in Prix Marcel Boussac and capable of much better, perhaps even in 1,000 Guineas.

Marsh Hawk

3 b f Invincible Spirit - Asaawir (Royal Applause)

Richard Hannon					Rockcliffe Stud
PLACINGS: 1214-					**RPR 105**

Starts	1st	2nd	3rd	4th	Win & Pl
4	2	1	-	1	£35,574
	9/14	Newb	7f Cls2 2yo gd-sft		£9,960
	8/14	NmkJ	7f Cls4 Mdn 2yo soft		£3,881

Didn't quite live up to promise of seven-length debut win last season, winning only a conditions race at Newbury subsequently, though found drop in trip against her when just beaten at Salisbury and didn't fare badly when fourth in Fillies' Mile; still an interesting prospect.

Marzocco (USA)

4 b/br g Kitten's Joy - Dynamia (Dynaformer)

John Gosden					Godolphin
PLACINGS: 1/22354528-					**RPR 112**

Starts	1st	2nd	3rd	4th	Win & Pl
9	3	3	1	1	£77,757
	10/13	Kemp	1m Cls5 Mdn 2yo stand		£2,911

Good staying prospect who was unlucky not to win last season, twice being narrowly beaten in Listed races; was highly tried otherwise with two fifth-place finishes at Group 1 level (including the St

Leger) and proved stamina when third in the Queen's Vase over 2m.

Mecca's Angel (Ire)
4 gr f Dark Angel - Folga (Atraf)

Michael Dods   **David T J Metcalfe**

PLACINGS: **411224/11511-**   RPR **115**

Starts		1st	2nd	3rd	4th	Win & Pl
11		6	2	-	2	£115,860
	9/14	Newb	5f Cls1 Gp3 soft			£34,026
	9/14	Donc	5f Cls1 List good			£23,680
	5/14	Haml	5f Cls2 3yo gd-sft			£16,173
95	4/14	Thsk	5f Cls3 76-95 3yo Hcap gd-sft			£7,439
78	7/13	Sthl	5f Cls6 57-78 2yo Hcap stand			£1,941
	6/13	Hayd	5f Cls5 Mdn 2yo good			£2,911

Very speedy filly who won four out of five last season with sole defeat coming on only run beyond 5f (has failed to last home on both starts over further); took step up to Group 3 level in her stride

at Newbury last time and capable of ranking higher; loves soft ground.

Miss France (Ire)
4 b f Dansili - Miss Tahiti (Tirol)

Andre Fabre (Fr)   **Ballymore Thoroughbred Ltd**

PLACINGS: **911/61522-**   RPR **117**

Starts		1st	2nd	3rd	4th	Win & Pl
8		3	2	-	-	£393,156
	5/14	NmkR	1m Cls1 Gp1 3yo gd-fm			£246,618
	9/13	NmkR	7f Cls1 Gp3 2yo gd-fm			£22,684
	8/13	Chan	1m 2yo good			£11,789

Narrow winner of last season's 1,000 Guineas and improved on that form even in defeat when going close in the Prix Rothschild and Sun Chariot Stakes; worth another chance over further after an unlucky fifth in the Prix de Diane (stayed on having been blocked in her run).

Moheet (Ire) *pictured below*

3 b c High Chaparral - Abunai (Pivotal)

Richard Hannon   **Al Shaqab Racing**

PLACINGS: **1-**   RPR **87 +**

Starts	1st	2nd	3rd	4th	Win & Pl
1	1	-	-	-	£4,204
10/14	Sals	1m Cls4 Mdn 2yo good			£4,205

One of the stars of the Craven breeze-ups last year, selling for 800,000gns, and duly made a hugely promising debut at Salisbury in October when winning his maiden by seven lengths; pedigree has a mix of speed and stamina; looks a fine prospect.

Mount Athos (Ire)

8 b g Montjeu - Ionian Sea (Slip Anchor)

Marco Botti   Dr Marwan Koukash

PLACINGS: **84/11150/158239/381-**   RPR **114**

Starts		1st	2nd	3rd	4th	Win & Pl
31		9	1	3	5	£642,776
	5/14	Newb	1m5½f Cls1 List gd-fm			£20,983
	5/13	Ches	1m5½f Cls1 Gp3 gd-sft			£42,533
	8/12	Newb	1m5½f Cls1 Gp3 gd-fm			£31,191
108	7/12	York	1m6f Cls1 List 94-108 Hcap good			£19,536
103	5/12	NmkR	1m6f Cls2 82-103 Hcap gd-fm			£18,675
94	4/11	Dund	1m4f 74-95 Hcap stand			£11,207
84	8/10	York	1m6f Cls2 83-104 3yo Hcap gd-fm			£42,094
70	7/10	Folk	1m4f Cls5 51-70 3yo Hcap gd-fm			£2,730
64	7/10	Hayd	1m2½f Cls5 58-70 Hcap gd-fm			£2,590

Won a Listed race at Newbury last May only to miss rest of the season through injury; has also won Ormonde and Geoffrey Freer Stakes in previous two seasons and deserves more chances over longer trips having finished third and fifth in the Melbourne Cup over 2m.

Mount Logan (Ire)

4 ch c New Approach - Vistaria (Distant View)

Luca Cumani   Sheikh Mohammed Obaid Al Maktoum

PLACINGS: **417/13310-**   RPR **108**

Starts		1st	2nd	3rd	4th	Win & Pl
8		3	-	2	1	£38,367
96	9/14	Donc	1m4f Cls2 89-103 Hcap good			£16,173
85	6/14	Gdwd	1m2f Cls3 78-87 3yo Hcap good			£7,763
	9/13	Yarm	1m Cls5 Mdn 2yo good			£2,911

Progressed with every run in some good middle-distance handicaps last season, finally grabbing a deserved win at Doncaster; flopped in November Handicap on final start, though several runners failed to cope with desperate ground; remains open to further improvement.

Move In Time

7 ch g Monsieur Bond - Tibesti (Machiavellian)

David O'Meara   A Turton, J Blackburn & R Bond

PLACINGS: **90/1132740/40612221-**   RPR **115**

Starts		1st	2nd	3rd	4th	Win & Pl
40		7	7	5	5	£355,936
	10/14	Lonc	5f Gp1 good			£166,658
	7/14	NmkJ	5f Cls3 gd-fm			£8,715
95	4/13	Donc	5f Cls2 87-109 Hcap good			£31,505
85	3/13	Muss	5f Cls4 67-85 Hcap gd-sft			£5,175
	10/11	Asct	5f Cls1 List good			£19,849
	5/11	Bevl	5f Cls4 3yo gd-fm			£5,296
	5/10	Newc	6f Cls5 Auct Mdn 2yo good			£2,590

Surprise winner of last season's Prix de l'Abbaye at Longchamp; had twice finished second at the track and has struggled to run to that form at home, though his form had been progressive prior to that and wasn't out of the first two in last five runs.

Moviesta (USA)

5 b g Hard Spun - Miss Brickyard (A.P. Indy)

Bryan Smart   Redknapp, Salthouse & Fiddes

PLACINGS: **321/8112210/5083403-**   RPR **115+**

Starts		1st	2nd	3rd	4th	Win & Pl
17		4	3	3	1	£174,871
	8/13	Gdwd	5f Cls1 Gp2 good			£56,710
87	4/13	York	5f Cls3 76-90 3yo Hcap soft			£9,704
83	4/13	Donc	6f Cls3 75-88 3yo Hcap gd-fm			£7,439
	9/12	Wolv	5f Cls5 Mdn 2yo stand			£2,264

Without a win since a Group 2 at Glorious Goodwood in 2013 but bounced back to form towards end of last season when going close in several top sprints, most notably when an unlucky third in Prix de l'Abbaye (checked in run and just failed to get up); best on quick ground.

Muhaarar

3 b c Oasis Dream - Tahrir (Linamix)

Charlie Hills   Hamdan Al Maktoum

PLACINGS: **13313-**   RPR **113**

Starts		1st	2nd	3rd	4th	Win & Pl
5		2	-	3	-	£151,240
	8/14	York	6f Cls1 Gp2 2yo good			£113,420
	5/14	Donc	5½f Cls5 Mdn 2yo soft			£2,588

Smart sprinting juvenile last season; scraped home to win Gimcrack Stakes at York before a good third in Middle Park; hadn't appeared to stay 7f when stepped up to that trip at Ascot but may be given a chance to prove himself over a mile in 2,000 Guineas.

Muraaqaba

3 b f Dubawi - Nufoos (Zafonic)

Mark Johnston   Hamdan Al Maktoum

PLACINGS: **1412-**   RPR **105**

Starts		1st	2nd	3rd	4th	Win & Pl
4		2	1	-	1	£50,613
	8/14	NmkJ	7f Cls1 Gp3 2yo soft			£28,355
	6/14	NmkJ	6f Cls4 Mdn 2yo gd-fm			£4,528

Relished going up in trip last season, winning Sweet Solera Stakes on soft ground and seeing out a mile well when good second to Agnes Stewart in May Hill having been outpaced when fourth in Princess Margaret; may well get 1m2f but unlikely to stay further on pedigree.

Music Master

5 b h Piccolo - Twilight Mistress (Bin Ajwaad)

Henry Candy   Godfrey Wilson

PLACINGS: **4/125282/16413-**   RPR **115+**

Starts		1st	2nd	3rd	4th	Win & Pl
12		3	3	1	2	£132,136
	7/14	Newb	6f Cls1 Gp3 good			£34,026
	4/14	Wwck	6f Cls3 good			£7,763
	4/13	NmkR	7f Cls4 Mdn 3yo good			£4,852

Spent much of 2013 racing over 7f but has flourished since dropped to sprint trips, winning a Group 3 at Newbury last season and making the frame in the Diamond Jubilee Stakes and Haydock

Sprint Cup; may also be worth a try over 5f; best on quick ground.

Mustajeeb

4 ch c Nayef - Rifqah (Elusive Quality)

Dermot Weld (Ir)				Hamdan Al Maktoum

PLACINGS: 412/13126-   RPR **121 +**

Starts	1st	2nd	3rd	4th	Win & Pl
8	3	2	1	1	£155,825

	6/14	Asct	7f Cls1 Gp3 3yo good £42,533
	5/14	Leop	1m Gp3 yld-sft £33,854
	7/13	Gway	7f Mdn 2yo yield £9,256

Good winner of last season's Jersey Stakes at Royal Ascot, relishing quicker ground having been well beaten on soft in Irish 2,000 Guineas; yet to prove quite as effective over a mile and just seemed outstayed in a Group 2 at Leopardstown next time; should have more to offer.

Mutakayyef

4 ch c Sea The Stars - Infallible (Pivotal)

William Haggas				Hamdan Al Maktoum

PLACINGS: 2/221223-   RPR **116**

Starts	1st	2nd	3rd	4th	Win & Pl
7	1	5	1		£49,257

| | 5/14 | Sand | 1m2f Cls5 Mdn 3-4yo soft .... £3,881 |

Has only a maiden win to his name in seven runs but ran several big races in defeat last season; finished second to Cannock Chase at Royal Ascot and Berkshire in Darley Stakes on first run after four-month absence with ringworm; failed to settle off slow gallop next time.

Muthmir (Ire)

5 b g Invincible Spirit - Fairy Of The Night (Danehill)

William Haggas				Hamdan Al Maktoum

PLACINGS: 4215/2151-   RPR **115 +**

Starts	1st	2nd	3rd	4th	Win & Pl
8	3	2		1	£78,131

100	9/14	Donc	5½f Cls2 93-103 Hcap good £37,350
93	7/14	York	6f Cls2 87-104 Hcap gd-fm £31,125
	7/13	Donc	6f Cls5 Mdn gd-fm £2,588

Ran away with last season's Portland at Doncaster, atoning for managing only fifth when heavily backed for Stewards' Cup (race came too soon just a week after winning at York); missed subsequent targets due to preference for quick ground; looks well up to Group class.

Muwaary

4 b/br c Oasis Dream - Wissal (Woodman)

John Gosden				Hamdan Al Maktoum

PLACINGS: 1/1425-   RPR **115 +**

Starts	1st	2nd	3rd	4th	Win & Pl
5	2	1		1	£68,184

| 82 | 4/14 | Newb | 7f Cls2 78-95 Hcap gd-sft .... £11,828 |
| | 7/13 | Newb | 7f Cls4 Mdn 2yo gd-fm .... £4,528 |

Highly tried last season and ran big races when second in Jersey Stakes and fourth in French 2,000 Guineas (raced keenly both times) before pulling far too hard when fifth in Prix Jean Prat; has still run only five times and could be a Group 1 miler if learning to settle better.

Naadirr (Ire)

4 b c Oasis Dream - Beach Bunny (High Chaparral)

Marco Botti			Sheikh Mohammed Bin Khalifa Al Maktoum

PLACINGS: 91/322441-   RPR **112**

Starts	1st	2nd	3rd	4th	Win & Pl
8	2	1	2	2	£65,688

| | 9/14 | York | 6f Cls1 List gd-fm.................................... £20,983 |
| | 11/13 | Kemp | 7f Cls5 Mdn 2yo stand................................. £2,911 |

Highly tried last season having won only a maiden as a two-year-old and ran well in Group 3 and Listed company before finally winning again in a Listed race at York; good prospect but probably needs quick ground (hasn't raced on worse than good since disappointing on debut).

Nafaqa (Ire)

3 b c Sir Percy - Maghya (Mujahid)

Barry Hills				Hamdan Al Maktoum

PLACINGS: 4112-   RPR **109**

Starts	1st	2nd	3rd	4th	Win & Pl
4	2	1	-	1	£50,560

| | 9/14 | Donc | 7f Cls1 List 2yo good .... £15,312 |
| | 7/14 | Newb | 7f Cls4 Mdn 2yo gd-fm .... £6,469 |

Always likely to come into his own as a middle-distance horse in time and showed plenty of promise last season, most notably when overcoming greenness to win a strong Listed race at Doncaster on penultimate start; ran Elm Park close in Royal Lodge on final outing.

New Providence

3 ch f Bahamian Bounty - Bayja (Giant's Causeway)

Hugo Palmer				Chris Humber

PLACINGS: 113213-   RPR **103**

Starts	1st	2nd	3rd	4th	Win & Pl
6	3	1	2	-	£110,450

	9/14	Sals	6f Cls1 Gp3 2yo good £24,102
75	7/14	Donc	6f Cls4 63-78 2yo Hcap gd-fm £3,881
	6/14	Ling	5f Cls5 Mdn 2yo good £2,911

Just outstayed Marsh Hawk when winning a Group 3 over 6f at Salisbury last season and saw out extra furlong well enough when a fair third in the Rockfel Stakes behind Lucida; still seen as a 1,000 Guineas candidate by connections and could start in the Fred Darling.

Night Of Thunder (Ire)

4 ch c Dubawi - Forest Storm (Galileo)

Richard Hannon — **Godolphin**

PLACINGS: 11/212832- RPR **124**

Starts	1st	2nd	3rd	4th	Win & Pl
8	3	3	1	-	£650,388
5/14	NmkR	1m Cls1 Gp1 3yo gd-fm			£255,195
10/13	Donc	6f Cls1 List 2yo soft			£15,836
10/13	Gdwd	6f Cls5 Mdn Auct 2yo soft			£3,235

Shock winner of 2,000 Guineas last season when producing a powerful late burst to run down Kingman; unlucky not to win again at top level, twice getting beaten half a length by Charm Spirit having struggled to get a run, most notably in QEII; well beaten on only run over 1m2f.

Ol' Man River (Ire)

3 b c Montjeu - Finsceal Beo (Mr Greeley)

Aidan O'Brien (Ir) — **Mrs John Magnier & Michael Tabor & Derrick Smith**

PLACINGS: 11- RPR **114+**

Starts	1st	2nd	3rd	4th	Win & Pl
2	2	-	-	-	£63,654
9/14	Curr	1m Gp2 2yo gd-fm			£54,167
8/14	Curr	1m Mdn 2yo good			£9,488

Always held in very high regard last season and justified short odds to win both of his races over a mile, including an easy win in the Beresford Stakes; yet to be seriously tested but looks a Group 1 horse and likely to be a leading Derby contender, possibly taking in the 2,000 Guineas first.

Order Of St George (Ire)

3 b c Galileo - Another Storm (Gone West)

Aidan O'Brien (Ir) — **Michael Tabor & Derrick Smith & Mrs John Magnier**

PLACINGS: 42152- RPR **102**

Starts	1st	2nd	3rd	4th	Win & Pl
5	1	2	-	1	£19,965
8/14	Leop	1m Mdn 2yo soft			£9,488

Won a Leopardstown maiden by eight and a half lengths on soft ground last season; slightly disappointing he couldn't make more impact when twice stepped up in grade, though still ran well in second behind Parish Boy over 1m1f; might prove better in time, especially back on soft.

Osaila (Ire)

3 b f Danehill Dancer - Mennetou (Entrepreneur)

Richard Hannon — **Al Shaqab Racing**

PLACINGS: 2511513- RPR **108**

Starts	1st	2nd	3rd	4th	Win & Pl
7	3	1	1	-	£271,109
10/14	NmkR	7f Cls2 2yo gd-fm			£168,199
7/14	Asct	6f Cls1 Gp3 2yo good			£28,355
7/14	Donc	6f Cls4 2yo gd-fm			£6,469

Smart filly who had a productive campaign last season, winning Princess Margaret Stakes and a valuable sales race at Newmarket; twice ran well at Group 1 level, finishing fifth (beaten a length and a half) in Moyglare Stud and third in Breeders' Cup Juvenile Fillies Turf.

Pallasator

6 b g Motivator - Ela Athena (Ezzoud)

Sir Mark Prescott   Qatar Racing Limited

PLACINGS: 4/111/35/214713-   RPR **115**

Starts	1st	2nd	3rd	4th	Win & Pl
12	5	1	2	2	£130,518

	9/14	NmkR	2m Cls1 List good	....£22,684
103	7/14	Asct	1m4f Cls2 89-103 Hcap gd-fm	..............£18,675
91	9/12	Hayd	1m6f Cls3 81-91 3yo Hcap heavy	................£6,663
85	9/12	Kemp	1m4f Cls4 75-86 3yo Hcap stand	...............£4,075
	7/12	Leic	1m2f Cls6 Auct Mdn 3-4yo good	..................£1,941

Steadily progressive in recent seasons and graduated to Pattern company after a good effort when fourth under a big weight in the Ebor; finished a game third in the Long Distance Cup at Ascot after landing a Listed race at Newmarket; huge horse who should improve again.

Panama Hat *pictured below*

4 ch g Medicean - Street Style (Rock Of Gibraltar)

Andy Oliver (Ir)   Team Valor

PLACINGS: 99790/02111112-   RPR **116**

Starts	1st	2nd	3rd	4th	Win & Pl
13	5	2	-	-	£70,870

96	8/14	Dund	1m2½f 79-96 Hcap stand	.............................£25,000
85	7/14	Naas	1m2f 65-85 Hcap gd-fm	................................£5,750
75	7/14	Rosc	1m4f 59-75 3yo Hcap gd-fm	.........................£5,463
70	7/14	Fair	1m2f 52-71 3yo Hcap gd-fm	.........................£4,888
60	6/14	Leop	1m2f 48-69 Hcap gd-fm	................................£4,888

One of the success stories of last season when he won five handicaps in a row, taking him to a rating of 108 from a starting point of just 60; nearly defied the higher mark when second on Irish Champions Weekend at the Curragh; ready for Pattern level from 1m2f to 1m4f.

Parish Boy

3 gr c New Approach - Requesting (Rainbow Quest)

Jim Bolger (Ir)   Godolphin

PLACINGS: 511-   RPR **103**

Starts	1st	2nd	3rd	4th	Win & Pl
3	2	-	-	-	£31,087
	10/14 Leop	1m1f List 2yo yield			£22,750
	8/14 Naas	7f Mdn 2yo yield			£8,338

Twice beat smart rival Order Of St George last season, most notably when stepping up to 1m1f in a Listed race at Leopardstown at the end of October; seems sure to be a middle-distance performer in time, though trainer feels he could also make his mark over a mile first.

Pearl Secret

6 ch h Compton Place - Our Little Secret (Rossini)

David Barron   Qatar Racing Limited

PLACINGS: 1/1119/3/1820150-   RPR **117**

Starts	1st	2nd	3rd	4th	Win & Pl
13	6	1	1	-	£142,567
	8/14 Bevl	5f Cls1 List gd-fm			£23,680
	4/14 Nott	5f Cls3 soft			£7,470
	6/12 Sand	5f Cls1 List 3yo soft			£18,514
	5/12 York	5f Cls2 3yo good			£12,938
85	4/12 Donc	5f Cls3 76-87 3yo Hcap heavy			£6,792
	10/11 York	5½f Cls3 Mdn 2yo good			£6,469

High-class sprinter who won Beverley Bullet on good to firm ground last season but is much better on soft and never got suitable conditions following close second in Temple Stakes; fair fifth in Haydock Sprint Cup on only start over 6f; still unexposed and can do better.

Pether's Moon (Ire)

5 b h Dylan Thomas - Softly Tread (Tirol)

Richard Hannon   John Manley

PLACINGS: 2/1202131/223319117-   RPR **117**

Starts	1st	2nd	3rd	4th	Win & Pl
18	6	5	3	-	£348,068
	10/14 Asct	1m4f Cls1 Gp3 soft			£34,026
	9/14 Veli	1m4f Gp2 v soft			£150,000
	8/14 Gdwd	1m4f Cls1 Gp3 gd-fm			£34,026
	11/13 Kemp	1m4f Cls1 List stand			£20,983
95	8/13 Gdwd	1m4f Cls2 82-99 3yo Hcap good			£31,125
	4/13 Kemp	1m Cls5 Mdn 3yo stand			£3,881

Kept very busy last season and maintained his form remarkably well, producing arguably his best performance in the Cumberland Lodge Stakes on his penultimate start when landing a third Group victory; no surprise to see him win more good races over 1m4f.

ONE TO FOLLOW

Cosmic Statesman Showed enough in four starts last year to suggest he can more than pay his way and uphold his family's tradition. *[Simon Turner, Racing Post Ratings]*

Pique Sous (Fr)

8 gr g Martaline - Six Fois Sept (Epervier Bleu)

Willie Mullins (Ir)   Supreme Horse Racing Club

PLACINGS: 1321/51-   RPR **101+**

Starts	1st	2nd	3rd	4th	Win & Pl
6	3	1	1	-	£73,463
	6/14 Asct	2m5½f Cls2 gd-fm			£37,350
88	9/13 Leop	1m6f 78-97 Hcap good			£29,268
	2/13 Dund	2m Mdn stand			£4,488

Grade 2-winning hurdler who has been switched to the Flat in last two seasons, albeit still in very few races due to suffering from colic; impressive winner of Queen Alexandra Stakes last season despite racing very keenly; looks capable of better and could be a Group horse.

Pleascach (Ire)

3 b f Teofilo - Toirneach (Thunder Gulch)

Jim Bolger (Ir)   Mrs J S Bolger

PLACINGS: 41-   RPR **90+**

Starts	1st	2nd	3rd	4th	Win & Pl
2	1			1	£11,112
	7/14 Leop	7f Mdn 2yo gd-fm			£9,488

Shaped well on her debut in a very competitive Group 3 at the Curragh, finishing fourth, and confirmed that promise when beating a smart rival (twice Listed-placed) in her maiden; relished an extra furlong that day and bred to thrive over middle distances (dam won over 1m2f).

Postponed (Ire)

4 b c Dubawi - Ever Rigg (Dubai Destination)

Luca Cumani   Sheikh Mohammed Obaid Al Maktoum

PLACINGS: 512/34311-   RPR **121+**

Starts	1st	2nd	3rd	4th	Win & Pl
8	3	1	2	1	£238,568
	8/14 York	1m4f Cls1 Gp2 3yo gd-fm			£85,065
	7/14 Haml	1m3f Cls1 List 3yo gd-fm			£22,684
	8/13 Yarm	7f Cls5 Mdn 2yo gd-fm			£2,911

Improved throughout last season, stepping up in trip throughout, and signed off with a hugely impressive victory in Great Voltigeur Stakes at York; was well fancied for St Leger subsequently but put away with this season in mind; should be a force in top races over 1m4f.

Provenance

4 b f Galileo - Echelon (Danehill)

Sir Michael Stoute   Cheveley Park Stud

PLACINGS: 131135-   RPR **104+**

Starts	1st	2nd	3rd	4th	Win & Pl
6	3	-	2	-	£25,556
90	8/14 Hayd	1m Cls3 80-93 3yo Hcap good			£8,086
84	7/14 Sand	7f Cls3 75-87 3yo Hcap good			£7,470
	5/14 Kemp	1m Cls5 Mdn 3yo stand			£3,881

Won a couple of good handicaps last season and unlucky not to do better when third in a Listed race at Newmarket (finished lame); disappointed when upped to 1m2f next time; likely to have more to offer given how much half-sister Integral improved from three to four.

Queen Nefertiti (Ire)
3 b f Galileo - Chintz (Danehill Dancer)
David Wachman
          Michael Tabor & Mrs John Magnier & Derrick Smith

PLACINGS: 1-					RPR 93+
Starts	1st	2nd	3rd	4th	Win & Pl
1	1	-	-	-	£9,487
	6/14	Leop	7f Mdn 2yo good		£9,488

Hugely impressive winner of her sole start in a Curragh maiden last June, storming home by four and a half lengths, and form worked out exceptionally well (runner-up twice placed at Listed level and fourth won a Group 3 next time); pedigree suggests she could do well over a variety of trips.

Raydara (Ire)
3 b/br f Rock Of Gibraltar - Raydiya (Marju)
Michael Halford (Ir)   **H H Aga Khan**

PLACINGS: 2141-					RPR 110+
Starts	1st	2nd	3rd	4th	Win & Pl
4	2	1	-	1	£68,216
	8/14	Curr	7f Gp2 2yo gd-fm		£54,167
	7/14	Leop	7f Mdn Auct 2yo gd-fm		£10,350

Looked a potentially high-class filly when beating Lucida to win Debutante Stakes last season, benefiting from switch to hold-up tactics having been ridden too forcefully when below-par on previous start; thought to be heavily reliant on quick ground (yet to run on worse than good to firm).

Reckless Abandon
5 b h Exchange Rate - Sant Elena (Efisio)
Charlie Appleby   **Godolphin**

PLACINGS: 11111/355/320-					RPR 113
Starts	1st	2nd	3rd	4th	Win & Pl
11	5	1	2	-	£399,414
	10/12	NmkR	6f Cls1 Gp1 2yo gd-sft		£85,065
	8/12	Deau	6f Gp1 2yo good		£166,658
	7/12	MsnL	5½f Gp2 2yo good		£61,750
	6/12	Asct	5f Cls1 Gp2 2yo gd-sft		£42,533
	5/12	Donc	5f Cls5 Mdn Auct 2yo good		£2,911

Top-class two-year-old in 2012 (unbeaten dual

Group 1 winner) who ran some decent races at three before initially being retired; belatedly returned to the track last season and was placed in two Listed sprints; could do better with a proper preparation under his belt.

Remote
5 b h Dansili - Zenda (Zamindar)
John Gosden   **K Abdullah**

PLACINGS: 3111/					
Starts	1st	2nd	3rd	4th	Win & Pl
4	3	-	1	-	£62,516
	6/13	Asct	1m2f Cls1 Gp3 3yo gd-fm		£42,533
89	6/13	Donc	1m Cls2 85-103 3yo Hcap good		£12,938
	5/13	Newb	1m2f Cls4 Mdn 3yo gd-fm		£6,469

Hasn't run since June 2013 due to injury but has been kept in training and remains a horse of Group 1 potential; had won three out of four as a three-year-old prior to setback, culminating in a Group 3 at Royal Ascot; trainer believes 1m2f is his optimum trip.

Ribbons
5 ch m Manduro - Sister Act (Marju)
James Fanshawe   **Elite Racing Club**

PLACINGS: 1/1113/1212-					RPR 114
Starts	1st	2nd	3rd	4th	Win & Pl
9	6	2	1	-	£256,172
	8/14	Deau	1m2f Gp1 v soft		£119,042
	4/14	Kemp	1m Cls1 List stand		£20,983
86	7/13	Gdwd	1m1f Cls3 76-95 Hcap gd-sft		£10,894
79	6/13	NmkJ	1m Cls4 67-79 Hcap good		£6,469
75	5/13	Gdwd	1m Cls4 73-83 Hcap good		£6,469
	11/12	Kemp	1m Cls5 Mdn 2yo stand		£3,170

Stepped sharply up in grade last autumn but rose to the challenge when winning the Prix Jean Romanet at Deauville and finishing second in the Prix de l'Opera; remains lightly raced and has scope for further improvement; should be a force in Group 1 races for fillies and mares.

Richard Pankhurst
3 ch c Raven's Pass - Mainstay (Elmaamul)
John Gosden   **Godolphin**

PLACINGS: 41-					RPR 114+
Starts	1st	2nd	3rd	4th	Win & Pl
2	1	-	-	1	£34,362
	6/14	Asct	7f Cls1 List 2yo gd-fm		£34,026

Hasn't run since Royal Ascot but had already made

mark on this season's 2,000 Guineas market when storming to an impressive win in the Chesham Stakes from subsequent Group 1 winner Dick Whittington; since bought by Godolphin; likely to prove best at around a mile.

Rizeena (Ire) *pictured below right*

4 b f Iffraaj - Serena's Storm (Statue Of Liberty)

Clive Brittain		Sheikh Rashid Bin Dalmook Al Maktoum			
PLACINGS: 51112312/71242-					RPR **113**

Starts	1st	2nd	3rd	4th	Win & Pl
13	5	4	1	1	£603,290
	6/14	Asct	1m Cls1 Gp1 3yo gd-fm		£212,663
	9/13	Curr	7f Gp1 2yo gd-fm		£106,098
	6/13	Asct	5f Cls1 Gp2 2yo gd-fm		£56,710
	5/13	Sand	5f Cls1 List 2yo gd-sft		£14,461
	5/13	Asct	5f Cls4 Mdn 2yo gd-fm		£5,175

Group 1 winner in each of last two seasons, landing last season's Coronation Stakes at Royal Ascot to add to Moyglare victory as a two-year-old; went on to finish second in Falmouth Stakes and Matron Stakes; should continue to be a force in top fillies' mile races.

Romsdal

4 ch c Halling - Pure Song (Singspiel)

John Gosden		HRH Princess Haya Of Jordan			
PLACINGS: 312372-					RPR **118**

Starts	1st	2nd	3rd	4th	Win & Pl
6	1	2	2	-	£306,784
	4/14	Kemp	1m3f Cls6 Auct Mdn 3-5yo stand		£1,941

Finished in the places in two Classics last season, coming third in the Derby and then getting much

closer to Kingston Hill when nailed close home in the St Leger; was a late developer (didn't make his debut until last March) so may well continue to improve.

Royal Razalma (Ire)

3 ch f Lope De Vega - Twiggy's Sister (Flying Spur)

Jonathan Portman		David & Gwyn Joseph			
PLACINGS: 021541-					RPR **104**

Starts	1st	2nd	3rd	4th	Win & Pl
6	2	1	-	1	£63,435
	10/14	NmkR	5f Cls1 Gp3 2yo soft		£45,368
	7/14	Gdwd	6f Cls2 Mdn 2yo gd-fm		£12,938

Won at 16-1 when dropped to 5f for first time in last season's Cornwallis Stakes, relishing shorter trip having shown plenty of promise but not quite seen out a couple of good races over 6f; remains unexposed over minimum trip and should make a useful sprinter.

Second Step (Ire)

4 b g Dalakhani - My Dark Rosaleen (Sadler's Wells)

Luca Cumani		Merry Fox Stud Limited			
PLACINGS: 2/11371-					RPR **103**

Starts	1st	2nd	3rd	4th	Win & Pl
6	3	1	1	-	£35,117
	10/14	Curr	1m4f List yield.		£21,667
85	7/14	Newb	1m4f Cls4 76-85 3yo Hcap good		£4,690
	5/14	Newb	1m2f Cls5 Mdn 3yo gd-sft		£3,235

Progressive middle-distance performer last season; won a handicap at Newbury and ran well in much stronger contests at Goodwood and Ascot (given too much to do both times) before breaking

through at Listed level at the Curragh; could improve again into a Group horse.

Secret Gesture

5 b m Galileo - Shastye (Danehill)

Ralph Beckett   **Qatar Racing Ltd & Newsells Park Stud**

PLACINGS: 21/12239/21235-   RPR **111**

Starts	1st	2nd	3rd	4th	Win & Pl
12	3	5	2	-	£356,945
	6/14 Nott	1m2f Cls1 List gd-fm			£22,684
	5/13 Ling	1m3¹/₂f Cls1 List 3yo gd-sft			£22,684
	10/12 Newb	1m Cls4 Mdn 2yo heavy			£4,399

High-class mare who has found a Group win elusive despite running well in several top races and finishing placed six times; didn't seem to quite see out 1m4f as a three-year-old so stuck to 1m2f last season but was staying on in every race and may benefit from return to further.

Sheikhzayedroad

6 b g Dubawi - Royal Secrets (Highest Honor)

David Simcock   **Mohammed Jaber**

PLACINGS: 35/121239/136921116-   ·   RPR **115**

Starts	1st	2nd	3rd	4th	Win & Pl
22	8	3	4	1	£327,431
	9/14 Wood	1m4f Gd1 good			£102,273
	7/14 York	1m2¹/₂f Cls1 Gp2 gd-fm			£56,710
	6/14 NmkJ	1m4f Cls1 List gd-sft			£20,983
106	1/14 Meyd	1m2f 100-109 Hcap good			£43,373
92	6/13 Epsm	1m4f Cls2 76-92 Hcap good			£15,563
84	4/13 Donc	1m2¹/₂f Cls3 82-89 Hcap good			£7,763
76	7/12 Brig	1m2f Cls4 66-79 Hcap gd-sft			£4,075
	5/12 Haml	1m¹/₂f Cls5 Mdn 3-5yo gd-sft			£3,235

Late developer who really blossomed last summer with a hat-trick of victories culminating in the Canadian International; had gained biggest win in Britain in the York Stakes (got up despite hanging on good to firm ground) and should prove even better on softer.

Shifting Power

4 ch c Compton Place - Profit Alert (Alzao)

Richard Hannon   **Ms Elaine Chivers & Potensis Ltd**

PLACINGS: 11/14225-   RPR **117**

Starts	1st	2nd	3rd	4th	Win & Pl
7	3	2	-	1	£178,179
105	4/14 NmkR	7f Cls1 List 100-111 3yo Hcap good			£20,983
	8/13 NmkJ	7f Cls4 2yo good			£4,528
	7/13 Sand	7f Cls5 Mdn Auct 2yo gd-fm			£3,235

Just below top milers last season but ran several fine races in defeat, finishing fourth in the 2,000 Guineas and second in the Irish version and Prix Jean Prat; ought to benefit from a drop in grade before another crack at top level.

Sir Isaac Newton

3 b c Galileo - Shastye (Danehill)

Aidan O'Brien (Ir)

    Derrick Smith & Mrs John Magnier & Michael Tabor

PLACINGS: 2-   RPR **90+**

Starts	1st	2nd	3rd	4th	Win & Pl
1	-	1	-	-	£2,200

Cost 3.6m gns as a yearling and impressed even in defeat on his only start last year, finishing second to the smart Zawraq (pair seven lengths clear) when Aidan O'Brien said he had left plenty to work

on; no surprise to see him develop into a top middle-distance performer.

Sky Hunter

5 b g Motivator - Pearl Kite (Silver Hawk)

Saeed Bin Suroor					Godolphin
PLACINGS: 1/1131/461d1-					RPR **117**

Starts	1st	2nd	3rd	4th	Win & Pl
9	5	-	1	1	£235,233

10/14	Newb	1m4f Cls1 Gp3 soft	£34,026
7/13	Vich	1m4f List 3yo gd-sft	£22,358
5/13	MsnL	1m2¹/₂f 3yo good	£13,821
4/13	Lonc	1m2f 3yo good	£11,789
11/12	MsnL	1m2f 2yo heavy	£10,000

Former Prix du Jockey Club third who switched to Godolphin last season and recovered best form during the autumn after gelding operation; particularly impressive when winning a Group 3 at Newbury by nine lengths, relishing soft ground; could be a Group 1 horse this year.

Smuggler's Cove (Ire)

3 b c Fastnet Rock - Chenchikova (Sadler's Wells)

Aidan O'Brien (Ir)					
Derrick Smith & Mrs John Magnier & Michael Tabor					
PLACINGS: 5113-					RPR **108**

Starts	1st	2nd	3rd	4th	Win & Pl
4	2	-	1	-	£83,456

10/14	Dund	7f List 2yo stand	£25,729
9/14	List	7f Mdn 2yo good	£9,200

Won a Listed race at Dundalk in October by seven lengths, looking very impressive despite form having little substance; well-beaten third in the Dewhurst but had excuses (came just seven days after Dundalk and may not have liked soft ground) and remains a good prospect.

Snow Sky

4 b c Nayef - Winter Silence (Dansili)

Sir Michael Stoute					K Abdullah
PLACINGS: 3418/2141237-					RPR **117+**

Starts	1st	2nd	3rd	4th	Win & Pl
11	3	2	2	2	£222,817

7/14	Gdwd	1m4f Cls1 Gp3 3yo gd-fm	£45,368
5/14	Ling	1m3¹/₂f Cls1 List 3yo good	£56,710
10/13	Sals	1m Cls4 Mdn 2yo heavy	£4,205

Won the Gordon Stakes and Lingfield Derby Trial last season but just came up short in stronger races, finishing placed in the St Leger (saw out longer trip well) and Great Voltigeur Stakes; already quite heavily raced but has long been regarded as type to progress with age.

Sole Power

8 b g Kyllachy - Demerger (Distant View)

Edward Lynam (Ir)					Mrs S Power
PLACINGS: /241415362/47111489-					RPR **120**

Starts	1st	2nd	3rd	4th	Win & Pl
45	10	7	6	6	£1,540,340

8/14	York	5f Cls1 Gp1 good	£150,282
6/14	Asct	5f Cls1 Gp1 good	£212,663
5/14	NmkR	5f Cls1 Gp3 gd-fm	£36,862
6/13	Asct	5f Cls1 Gp1 good	£198,485
5/13	NmkR	5f Cls1 Gp3 gd-fm	£34,026
9/12	Donc	5f Cls1 List good	£23,680
5/11	Hayd	5f Cls1 Gp2 gd-fm	£45,416
8/10	York	5f Cls1 Gp1 gd-fm	£136,248
4/10	Dund	5f stand	£10,075
11/09	Dund	5f Mdn 2yo stand	£9,057

Outstanding sprinter of recent seasons who seems

to have got better and better with age; achieved King's Stand and Nunthorpe Stakes double for first time last season (second win in all in both races); only fourth in Haydock Sprint Cup and seems less effective over 6f.

Solow

5 gr g Singspiel - High Maintenance (Highest Honor)

Freddy Head (Fr)   Wertheimer & Frere

PLACINGS: **32/241/116111-**   RPR **119+**

Starts	1st	2nd	3rd	4th	Win & Pl
11	6	2	1	1	£196,857
	10/14	Lonc	1m Gp2 good		£95,000
	8/14	Deau	1m Gp3 v soft		£33,333
	8/14	Claf	1m1f heavy		£18,750
	5/14	StCl	1m2¹/₂f soft		£13,750
	4/14	Lonc	1m2f 4yo good		£11,667
	6/13	Lonc	1m4f 3yo gd-sft		£9,756

Won five out of six races last season, with only defeat coming when stepped up to 1m7f; took form to a new level subsequently when dropped all the way back to a mile, winning the Prix Daniel Wildenstein having landed a Group 3 by five lengths; looks set for top mile races.

Star Of Seville

3 b f Duke Of Marmalade - Stage Presence (Selkirk)

John Gosden   Lady Bamford

PLACINGS: **31-**   RPR **85**

Starts	1st	2nd	3rd	4th	Win & Pl
2	1	-	1	-	£4,651
	10/14	Donc	1m Cls5 Mdn 2yo gd-sft		£3,881

Impressive six-length winner of a fillies' maiden at Doncaster in October, making all and seeing out

the mile strongly; had also travelled notably well when third on her debut; likely to come into her own over middle distances and has already attracted plenty of support for the Oaks.

Stepper Point *pictured below left*

6 b g Kyllachy - Sacre Coeur (Compton Place)

William Muir   C L A Edginton

PLACINGS: **8331140/15434264219-**   RPR **117+**

Starts	1st	2nd	3rd	4th	Win & Pl
38	7	4	3	5	£354,966
	9/14	Curr	5f Gp3 gd-fm		£54,167
	3/14	Ling	5f Cls1 List stand		£25,520
	8/13	Bevl	5f Cls1 List gd-fm		£23,680
	8/13	Nott	5f Cls3 good		£8,715
	10/11	Lonc	5f List 2yo gd-sft		£23,707
73	8/11	Wwck	5¹/₂f Cls5 52-74 2yo Hcap good		£2,264
68	8/11	Gdwd	5f Cls5 53-70 2yo Hcap good		£2,588

Developed into a genuine Group 1 sprinter last season, beating all bar Sole Power in the King's Stand and Nunthorpe Stakes; has a poor strike-rate for a horse of that ability but finally broke through at Group level at 20th attempt when blitzing rivals at the Curragh in September.

Stomachion (Ire)

5 b g Duke Of Marmalade - Insight (Sadler's Wells)

Sir Michael Stoute   Niarchos Family

PLACINGS: **73511/4128510-**   RPR **103**

Starts	1st	2nd	3rd	4th	Win & Pl
12	4	1	1	1	£49,116
92	9/14	Donc	1m6¹/₂f Cls2 87-102 Hcap gd-sft		£25,876
84	5/14	NmkJ	1m2f Cls3 77-92 Hcap gd-fm		£9,704
74	10/13	Yarm	1m3¹/₂f Cls5 62-74 Hcap soft		£2,588
68	10/13	Sals	1m2f Cls5 56-68 3yo Hcap heavy		£2,749

Relished step up to staying distances when winning

the Mallard Handicap at Doncaster last season having seen progress stall over shorter; only seventh when favourite for Irish November Handicap next time but looks capable of better and should be a force in good staying races.

Strath Burn

3 b c Equiano - Irish Light (Irish River)

Charles Hills   Qatar Racing & Meikle Ben Stables Ltd

PLACINGS: **1d242-**   RPR **107**

Starts	1st	2nd	3rd	4th	Win & Pl
4	-	2	-	1	£45,053

Highly tried following impressive debut last season (subsequently disqualified for a prohibited substance) and ran fine races to finish second in

the Prix Robert Papin and Cornwallis Stakes; lost his action on desperate ground at Newbury but proven on soft otherwise.

Sympathy (USA)

3 b f Henrythenavigator - Sweet Temper (Stormy Atlantic)

Sir Michael Stoute   Highclere T'Bred Racing St James' Palace

PLACINGS: **31-**   RPR **88+**

Starts	1st	2nd	3rd	4th	Win & Pl
2	1	-	1	-	£6,522
10/14	Leic	7f Cls4 Mdn 2yo gd-sft			£5,175

Built on a highly promising debut (raced green when third in very strong company at Salisbury) when winning a fillies' maiden at Leicester in October by five lengths; looks a very smart prospect

at around a mile but unlikely to stay further on pedigree.

Tac De Boistron (Fr) *pictured left*

8 gr g Take Risks - Pondiki (Sicyos)

Marco Botti Australian Thoroughbred Bloodstock

PLACINGS: 41/5352160/3121/121- **RPR 119**

Starts		1st	2nd	3rd	4th	Win & Pl
35		9	4	3	6	£636,508
	10/14	Lonc	1m7¹/₂f Gp1 v soft			£166,658
	4/14	Asct	2m Cls1 Gp3 soft			£34,026
	10/13	Lonc	1m7¹/₂f Gp1 v soft			£116,138
	9/13	Ches	1m4¹/₂f Cls1 List soft			£21,904
	7/12	Lonc	1m6f Gp2 soft			£61,750
	11/11	StCl	1m7¹/₂f List heavy			£22,414
	7/11	Vich	1m7f 4yo Hcap v soft			£20,259
0	4/11	StCl	1m2¹/₂f 4yo Hcap heavy			£20,259
	6/10	Stra	1m2¹/₂f 3yo soft			£7,080

Has won Prix Royal-Oak at Longchamp in each of last two years, returning from a lengthy injury absence last season having been off since close second in Yorkshire Oaks; performance that day showed ability to handle good ground but has always seemed better on soft.

Take Cover

8 b g Singspiel - Enchanted (Magic Ring)

David C Griffiths Norcroft Park Stud

PLACINGS: 1/1602/27102/811846- **RPR 116**

Starts		1st	2nd	3rd	4th	Win & Pl
18		7	3	-	1	£124,852
	8/14	Gdwd	5f Cls1 Gp2 gd-fm			£56,710
	7/14	York	5f Cls1 List gd-fm			£22,684
92	10/13	York	5f Cls3 87-95 Hcap good			£12,291
79	9/12	Hayd	6f Cls3 74-87 Hcap heavy			£8,410
71	11/11	Sthl	6f Cls6 60-71 Hcap stand			£1,704
65	11/11	Sthl	6f Cls6 51-65 Hcap stand			£1,704
	10/11	Sthl	7f Cls5 Mdn stand			£2,386

Late-maturing sprinter who took form to another level last season with wins at Goodwood and York (both on good to firm ground); not beaten far in Nunthorpe Stakes and Prix de l'Abbaye and may do better again back on a quicker surface; can win big races over 5f.

Telescope (Ire)

5 b h Galileo - Velouette (Darshaan)

Sir Michael Stoute
Highclere Thoroughbred Racing -Wavertree

PLACINGS: 21/121/221234- **RPR 125**

Starts		1st	2nd	3rd	4th	Win & Pl
11		4	5	1	1	£682,383
	6/14	Asct	1m4f Cls1 Gp2 gd-fm			£120,962
	8/13	York	1m4f Cls1 Gp2 3yo gd-fm			£85,065
	7/13	Leic	1m2f Cls3 3yo gd-fm			£7,561
	9/12	NmkR	1m Cls4 Mdn 2yo stand			£4,528

One-time Derby favourite who took longer than expected to fulfil potential but came good at Royal Ascot last season when winning Hardwicke Stakes by seven lengths; ran another terrific race when second in King George to Taghrooda; should be a threat in top races over 1m4f.

Telmeyd

4 b g Dutch Art - Blithe (Pivotal)

William Haggas Sheikh Ahmed Al Maktoum

PLACINGS: 61141- **RPR 109**

Starts		1st	2nd	3rd	4th	Win & Pl
5		3			1	£36,455
97	10/14	Asct	6f Cls2 81-97 3yo Hcap good			£18,675
88	7/14	Ripn	6f Cls3 77-88 3yo Hcap good			£7,561
	5/14	Ches	6f Cls4 Mdn 3yo gd-sft			£7,763

Improving young sprinter who won three-year-old handicaps at Ripon and Ascot last season; still very much a work in progress (was slowly away at times and has had stalls work this winter) so should have more to offer, perhaps at Pattern level; could stay 7f in time.

Tendu

3 b f Oasis Dream - Arabesque (Zafonic)

John Gosden K Abdullah

PLACINGS: 715- **RPR 106**

Starts		1st	2nd	3rd	4th	Win & Pl
3		1	-	-	-	£8,492
	9/14	Kemp	6f Cls5 Mdn 2yo stand			£2,911

Supplemented for last season's Cheveley Park Stakes after runaway win in a Kempton maiden and did well for one so inexperienced when beaten little over three lengths in fifth; could start over a mile but pedigree strongly suggests she will end up as a sprinter.

Territories (Ire)

3 b c Invincible Spirit - Taranto (Machiavellian)

Andre Fabre (Fr) Godolphin Snc

PLACINGS: 3132- **RPR 112**

Starts		1st	2nd	3rd	4th	Win & Pl
4		1	1	2	-	£93,966
	7/14	Chan	6f 2yo soft			£14,167

Won only one of four starts last season but got much closer to Full Mast in the Prix Jean Luc Lagardere than he had in a Group 3 previously and might well have finished in front of him with a clear run; could be a smart miler.

The Corsican (Ire)

4 b c Galileo - Walklikeanegyptian (Danehill)

David Simcock Mrs Fitri Hay

PLACINGS: 31511- **RPR 105+**

Starts		1st	2nd	3rd	4th	Win & Pl
5		3		1	-	£33,939
93	9/14	Donc	1m2¹/₂f Cls2 89-103 Hcap gd-sft			£16,173
86	8/14	Gdwd	1m2f Cls2 83-100 3yo Hcap good			£12,450
	5/14	Kemp	1m4f Cls5 Mdn stand			£2,588

Sent straight over 1m4f last season but benefited from being dropped in trip when winning a pair of handicaps at Goodwood and Doncaster (very strong contest full of improvers); seen as a nice long-term type by his trainer and may well make his mark at Pattern level.

The Grey Gatsby (left) battles with Australia before winning the Irish Champion Stakes at Leopardstown

The Grey Gatsby (Ire)

4 gr c Mastercraftsman - Marie Vison (Entrepreneur)

Kevin Ryan   **F Gillespie**

PLACINGS: 1227/2011621-   RPR **126**

Starts	1st	2nd	3rd	4th	Win & Pl
11	4	4	-	-	£1,508,140
9/14	Leop	1m2f Gp1 gd-fm			£483,333
6/14	Chan	1m2½f Gp1 3yo good			£714,250
5/14	York	1m2½f Cls1 Gp2 3yo gd-sft			£85,065
7/13	York	6f Cls3 Auct Mdn 2yo gd-fm			£7,439

Dual Group 1 winner last season, beating Australia in an epic Irish Champion Stakes having earlier run away with Prix du Jockey-Club at Chantilly; also won Dante and finished second in Juddmonte International; will set standard in Group 1 races at around 1m2f.

The Wow Signal (Ire)

3 b c Starspangledbanner - Muravka (High Chaparral)

John Quinn   **Al Shaqab Racing**

PLACINGS: 1119-   RPR **116**

Starts	1st	2nd	3rd	4th	Win & Pl
4	3	-	-	-	£238,915
8/14	Deau	6f Gp1 2yo v soft			£166,658
6/14	Asct	6f Cls1 Gp2 2yo good			£68,052
5/14	Ayr	6f Cls4 Mdn 2yo gd-sft			£4,205

Leading juvenile early last season, though still has something to prove despite wins in Coventry Stakes (race didn't work out particularly well) and Prix Morny (faced only one serious rival); scoped dirty following tame defeat at Longchamp on only subsequent start.

Tiggy Wiggy (Ire) *below second left*

3 b f Kodiac - Kheleyf's Silver (Kheleyf)

Richard Hannon   Potensis Ltd C Giles Merriebelle Stables

PLACINGS: **11212111-**   RPR **117**

Starts		1st	2nd	3rd	4th	Win & Pl
8		6	2	-	-	£381,181
	9/14	NmkR	6f Cls1 Gp1 2yo gd-fm.................£117,673			
	8/14	York	6f Cls1 Gp2 2yo good.....................£85,065			
	7/14	Newb	5f Cls2 2yo good...........................£122,925			
	5/14	Sand	5f Cls1 List 2yo soft.......................£14,745			
	5/14	Sals	5f Cls3 2yo soft..............................£6,792			
	3/14	Kemp	5f Cls4 Mdn 2yo stand....................£3,881			

Blistering fast filly who got better and better as season went on; arguably produced best performance when running away with Super Sprint but settled well enough to see out extra furlong when landing Cheveley Park and Lowther Stakes; set to test stamina in 1,000 Guineas.

Together Forever (Ire)

3 b f Galileo - Green Room (Theatrical)

Aidan O'Brien (Ir)

Mrs John Magnier & Michael Tabor & Derrick Smith

PLACINGS: **423111-**   RPR **110**

Starts		1st	2nd	3rd	4th	Win & Pl
6		3	1	1	1	£170,856
	10/14	NmkR	1m Cls1 Gp1 2yo soft......................£133,269			
	10/14	Curr	1m List 2yo yield............................£22,750			
	9/14	Gowr	1m Mdn 2yo gd-fm...........................£8,338			

Improved rapidly towards the end of last season to win the Fillies' Mile, though may have got lucky in a weak renewal with main rivals struggling on soft ground; needs to improve again to take a hand in the Classics but may be versatile enough to operate over a variety of trips.

Toocoolforschool (Ire)

3 b g Showcasing - Spring Surprise (Hector Protector)

Karl Burke   Ontoawinner 6, M Hulin, E Burke

PLACINGS: **31221-**   RPR **114**

Starts	1st	2nd	3rd	4th	Win & Pl
5	2	2	1	-	£69,253
	9/14	Newb	6f Cls1 Gp2 2yo soft		£42,533
	8/14	Ripn	6f Cls5 Mdn 2yo good		£3,235

Won last season's Mill Reef Stakes by seven lengths; probably flattered by that run (only horse to cope with desperate ground) but at least proved his versatility with ground and had also produced good performances in defeat in the Acomb Stakes and a Listed race at Doncaster.

Toormore (Ire) *pictured below*

4 b c Arakan - Danetime Out (Danetime)

Richard Hannon   Middleham Park Racing Ix & James Pak

PLACINGS: **111/176233-**   RPR **122**

Starts	1st	2nd	3rd	4th	Win & Pl
9	4	1	2	-	£380,199
	4/14	NmkR	1m Cls1 Gp3 3yo good		£36,862
	9/13	Curr	7f Gp1 2yo good		£94,309
	7/13	Gdwd	7f Cls1 Gp2 2yo gd-sft		£42,533
	5/13	Leic	6f Cls4 Mdn 2yo good		£4,205

Champion juvenile in 2013 and won Craven Stakes on return last season; disappointing that he failed to win again (twice beaten at odds-on, including at 1-5 in Turkey) but bounced back to form when third in QEII on final start and could yet fulfil potential as a four-year-old.

Treve (Fr)

5 b m Motivator - Trevise (Anabaa)

Criquette Head-Maarek (Fr)　　　**Al Shaqab Racing**

PLACINGS: 1/1111/2341-　　　　　　**RPR 127**

Starts	1st	2nd	3rd	4th	Win & Pl
9	6	1	1	1	£5,391,948

10/14	Lonc	1m4f Gp1 good	£2,380,833
10/13	Lonc	1m4f Gp1 soft	£2,229,854
9/13	Lonc	1m4f Gp1 soft	£162,593
6/13	Chan	1m2½f Gp1 3yo good	£464,553
5/13	StCl	1m 3yo good	£13,821
9/12	Lonc	1m 2yo gd-sft	£10,000

Phenomenal dual winner of Prix de l'Arc de Triomphe who has come out of a brief retirement to be aimed at a third victory in Longchamp showpiece; had been beset by physical issues for much of last season but will set a stiff standard if staying fully fit.

Tropics (USA)

7 ch g Speightstown - Taj Aire (Taj Alriyadh)

Dean Ivory　　　　　　　　　　**Dean Ivory**

PLACINGS: 12116101/7509210425-　　**RPR 117**

Starts	1st	2nd	3rd	4th	Win & Pl
23	7	5	1	1	£341,271

	8/14	NmkJ	6f Cls1 List gd-fm	£22,684
	10/13	Asct	6f Cls1 Gp3 gd-sft	£39,697
	8/13	NmkJ	6f Cls1 List gd-sft	£22,684
100	7/13	York	6f Cls2 80-100 Hcap gd-fm	£31,125
94	6/13	Wind	6f Cls2 88-105 Hcap good	£18,675
84	5/13	Wind	6f Cls4 72-85 Hcap good	£4,852
	10/12	Kemp	7f Cls5 Mdn stand	£2,264

Shock 66-1 second in July Cup last season but had been progressive in 2013 and went on to prove that was no fluke by winning same Listed race at Newmarket for second successive year and finishing second in Champions Sprint at Ascot.

Tullius (Ire) *pictured far right*

7 ch g Le Vie Dei Colori - Whipped Queen (Kingmambo)

Andrew Balding Kennet Valley Thoroughbreds VI

PLACINGS: 02/11131/037/212444- RPR **121**

Starts		1st	2nd	3rd	4th	Win & Pl
24		8	6	2	3	£335,457

	4/14	Sand	1m Cls1 Gp2 soft	£53,875
	8/12	Sals	1m Cls1 Gp3 gd-sft	£31,191
	6/12	York	1m Cls1 List soft	£19,536
	5/12	Wind	1m¹/₂f Cls1 List soft	£18,714
92	5/12	NmkR	1m1f Cls2 84-104 Hcap soft	£27,390
77	5/11	Sand	1m Cls4 68-80 3yo Hcap good	£4,080
75	11/10	Ling	1m Cls4 75-82 2yo Hcap stand	£3,011
	10/10	Ling	7f Cls5 Mdn 2yo stand	£3,303

Proved himself a top-class miler last season, particularly on soft ground, winning Sandown Mile and finishing a close fourth in Queen Elizabeth II Stakes granted preferred conditions; also coped well enough with quicker surface when well-beaten second in Lockinge.

Vent De Force

4 b c Hurricane Run - Capriolla (In The Wings)

Hughie Morrison The Fairy Story Partnership

PLACINGS: 53/5116120- RPR **108**

Starts		1st	2nd	3rd	4th	Win & Pl
9		3	1	1	-	£98,666

85	8/14	York	1m6f Cls2 79-99 3yo Hcap good	£49,800
81	6/14	Hayd	1m6f Cls4 72-81 3yo Hcap soft	£5,175
72	5/14	Sand	1m6f Cls4 71-81 3yo Hcap gd-sft	£5,175

Rose through the ranks last season with a trio of handicap wins over 1m6f, most notably when outstaying rivals to win the Melrose at York; went close when stepped up to Group 2 level next time at Deauville (also came back with a bruised foot), though disappointed in Prix Royal-Oak.

Vert De Grece (Ire)

3 gr c Verglas - Tiny Petal (Grand Lodge)

Roger Varian Joseph G Murphy

PLACINGS: 2121- RPR **116+**

Starts		1st	2nd	3rd	4th	Win & Pl
4		2	2	-	-	£146,695

	10/14	StCl	1m Gp1 2yo soft	£119,042
	8/14	Leop	7f Mdn 2yo yield	£9,488

Moved to Roger Varian from John Joseph Murphy after running Gleneagles close in the National Stakes and soon went one better, winning an admittedly soft Group 1 at Saint-Cloud by four lengths; full sister won over just short of 1m2f and looks a strong stayer.

ONE TO FOLLOW

Flashy Memories Well-bred son of Dubawi and impressive winner of Redcar maiden late last season. In good hands and potential to do a lot better this year. *[Simon Turner, Racing Post Ratings]*

Wannabe Yours (Ire)

4 b c Dubawi - Wannabe Posh (Grand Lodge)

John Gosden   Normandie Stud Ltd

PLACINGS: 63/1110-   RPR **114+**

Starts	1st	2nd	3rd	4th	Win & Pl
6					£50,631
	8/14	Gdwd	1m Cls1 Gp3 3yo gd-fm		.....£34,026
84	6/14	Donc	1m Cls2 83-102 3yo Hcap soft		......£12,938
	5/14	Nott	1m¹/₂f Cls5 Mdn 3yo gd-fm		.....£3,235

Hugely progressive miler last season; won a handicap at Doncaster by nine lengths and successfully bridged gap to Pattern company when following up in a Group 3 at Goodwood; ran no race on final start at Newmarket but could yet strike at a higher level.

Western Hymn *pictured right*

4 b g High Chaparral - Blue Rhapsody (Cape Cross)

John Gosden   Rjh Geffen And Rachel Hood

PLACINGS: 1/116144-   RPR **114+**

Starts	1st	2nd	3rd	4th	Win & Pl
7	4			2	£223,911
	7/14	MsnL	1m2f Gp2 3yo v soft		.....£61,750
	4/14	Sand	1m2f Cls1 Gp3 3yo soft		.....£35,444
	4/14	Newb	1m2f Cls3 3yo gd-sft		.....£9,338
	12/13	Kemp	1m Cls5 Mdn 2yo stand		.....£2,588

Not far off last season's leading three-year-olds; won Group races at Sandown and Maisons-Laffitte and finished fourth in Champion Stakes (all on soft ground or worse) having been sixth in the Derby on quicker ground than ideal; should have more to offer at four.

Whiplash Willie

7 ch g Phoenix Reach - Santa Isobel (Nashwan)

Andrew Balding   J C & S R Hitchins

PLACINGS: 6413/27112/132244-   RPR **113**

Starts	1st	2nd	3rd	4th	Win & Pl
15	4	4	2	3	£129,592
93	5/14	Sals	1m6f Cls3 74-93 Hcap soft		.....£12,450
91	7/11	Gdwd	1m4f Cls2 77-100 3yo Hcap good		.....£24,900
79	6/11	Sals	1m4f Cls4 Mdn 3yo Hcap soft		.....£7,771
	10/10	Ling	1m Cls6 Auct Mdn 2yo stand		.....£2,047

Returned from missing two full seasons through injury by resuming previously progressive form last term, winning at Salisbury first time out and going on to run well in several top staying races; came closest when second in the Doncaster Cup and could win a similar prize.

ONE TO FOLLOW

Flaming Spear Justified favouritism and spreadeagled the opposition on his York debut in July, recording a time that underlined his potential. Some fancy targets were missed because of a setback, but he can make up for lost time.

[Dave Edwards, Topspeed]

Windshear

4 b c Hurricane Run - Portal (Hernando)

Richard Hannon   Michael Daniels

PLACINGS: 1/21222244-   RPR **113**

Starts	1st	2nd	3rd	4th	Win & Pl
9	2	5		2	£106,130
80	4/14	Sand	1m2f Cls3 77-86 3yo Hcap soft		.....£9,338
	9/13	Sand	1m Cls5 Mdn 2yo soft		.....£3,881

Desperately unlucky not to win more than once last season, finishing second in red-hot handicaps at Newbury and Royal Ascot and twice more at Group 3 level before creditable fourth in St Leger; probably over the top when fourth at 5-4 in a Listed race at Newmarket last time.

Winter Thunder

4 gr c New Approach - Summer Sonnet (Baillamont)

Saeed Bin Suroor   Godolphin

PLACINGS: 41151-   RPR **114**

Starts	1st	2nd	3rd	4th	Win & Pl
5	3			1	£50,543
105	10/14	NmkR	1m4f Cls2 74-105 App Hcap good		.....£32,345
89	7/14	NmkJ	1m2f Cls2 81-98 3yo Hcap gd-fm		.....£12,450
	6/14	NmkJ	1m2f Cls4 Mdn 3yo gd-fm		.....£5,499

Looked to have blown handicap mark when winning by 12 lengths at Newmarket in July but defied lofty rating of 105 to win apprentice handicap three months later (had been unsuited by soft ground in between); looks a surefire Group horse on that evidence and should progress.

Winters Moon (Ire)

3 ch f New Approach - Summertime Legacy (Darshaan)

Saeed Bin Suroor   Godolphin

PLACINGS: 1343-   RPR **109**

Starts	1st	2nd	3rd	4th	Win & Pl
4	1		2	1	£38,743
	7/14	NmkJ	7f Cls4 Mdn 2yo gd-sft		.....£6,469

Half-sister to a trio who gained black type over 1m2f and seemed to relish a test of stamina when staying on strongly into third in Fillies' Mile on soft ground; had previously failed to build on promising debut win but should progress over middle distances.

Words (Ire)

3 b f Dansili - Moonstone (Dalakhani)

Aidan O'Brien (Ir)   Derrick Smith & Mrs John Magnier & Michael Tabor

PLACINGS: 1-   RPR **89+**

Starts	1st	2nd	3rd	4th	Win & Pl
1	1				£9,487
	6/14	Curr	7f Mdn 2yo gd-fm		.....£9,488

Well-bred filly who won arguably the strongest maiden race all year at the Curragh last season, beating Raydara with a couple of other black-type fillies behind; out of an Irish Oaks winner (both of whose previous progeny won at Listed level) and should excel over middle distances.

Yuften

4 b c Invincible Spirit - Majestic Sakeena (King's Best)

William Haggas   **Saleh Al Homaizi & Imad Al Sagar**

PLACINGS: **23/152d4-**   RPR **116**

Starts	1st	2nd	3rd	4th	Win & Pl
6	1	1	1	2	£40,298
	5/14	NmkR	1m Cls4 Mdn 3yo gd-fm		£5,175

Coped well in face of some stiff tasks last season when pitched into Group 1 company straight after winning his maiden, finishing second in the Prix Jean Prat and fifth in St James's Palace; disappointing fourth at Salisbury on final start; described as a 'big baby' so should improve.

Zawraq (Ire)

3 b c Shamardal - Sundus (Sadler's Wells)

Dermot Weld (Ir)   **Hamdan Al Maktoum**

PLACINGS: **1-**   RPR **92+**

Starts	1st	2nd	3rd	4th	Win & Pl
1	1	-	-	-	£9,487
	10/14	Leop	7f Mdn 2yo yield		£9,488

Did very well to win only start at Leopardstown over 7f last season, battling back to claim what may well prove to be a notable scalp in Sir Isaac Newton; likely to start in a Guineas trial and should get a bit further (dam by Sadler's Wells won over 1m2f as did two half-brothers).

THIS SEASON'S KEY CONTENDERS LISTED BY TRAINER

Charlie Appleby
Charming Thought
Latharnach (USA)
Reckless Abandon

Michael Appleby
Danzeno

Andrew Balding
Elm Park
Here Comes When (Ire)
Tullius (Ire)
Whiplash Willie

Corine Barande-Barbe
Cirrus Des Aigles (Fr)

David Barron
Pearl Secret

Ralph Beckett
Air Pilot
Secret Gesture

Jim Bolger
Lucida (Ire)
Parish Boy
Pleascach (Ire)

Marco Botti
Euro Charline
Mount Athos (Ire)
Naadirr (Ire)
Tac De Boistron (Fr)

Clive Brittain
Rizeena (Ire)

Karl Burke
Toocoolforschool (Ire)

Henry Candy
Alonsoa (Ire)
Cape Peron
Limato (Ire)
Music Master

Mick Channon
Malabar

Peter Chapple-Hyam
Arod (Ire)

Roger Charlton
Al Kazeem
Captain Cat (Ire)

Paul Cole
Berkshire (Ire)

Tracey Collins
Captain Joy (Ire)

Robert Cowell
Intrinsic

Clive Cox
Kodi Bear (Ire)

Luca Cumani
Connecticut
Mount Logan (Ire)
Postponed (Ire)
Second Step (Ire)

Alain de Royer-Dupre
Dolniya (Fr)

Michael Dods
Mecca's Angel (Ire)

Michael Easterby
Aetna

David Elsworth
Arabian Queen (Ire)
Justice Day (Ire)
Justice Good (Ire)

Andre Fabre
Alea Iacta
Esoterique (Ire)
Fintry (Ire)
Flintshire
High Celebrity (Fr)
Miss France (Ire)
Territories (Ire)

James Fanshawe
High Jinx (Ire)
Hors De Combat
Ribbons

John Gosden
Christophermarlowe (USA)

Eagle Top
Fannaan (USA)
Faydhan (USA)
Flying Officer (USA)
Forever Now
Gm Hopkins
Golden Horn
Jellicle Ball (Ire)
Lady Correspondent (USA)
Marzocco (USA)
Muwaary
Remote
Richard Pankhurst
Romsdal
Star Of Seville
Tendu
Wannabe Yours (Ire)
Western Hymn

David Griffiths
Take Cover

William Haggas
Mutakayyef
Muthmir (Ire)
Telmeyd
Yuften

Mick Halford
Raydara (Ire)

Richard Hannon
Estidhkaar (Ire)
Ivawood (Ire)
Kool Kompany (Ire)
Marsh Hawk
Moheet (Ire)
Night Of Thunder (Ire)
Osaila (Ire)
Pether's Moon (Ire)
Shifting Power
Tiggy Wiggy (Ire)
Toormore (Ire)
Windshear

Jessica Harrington
Jack Naylor

Sabrina Harty
Ansgar (Ire)

Freddy Head
Solow

Criquette Head-Maarek
Epicuris
Full Mast (USA)
Treve (Fr)

Barry Hills
Fadhayyil (Ire)
Nafaqa (Ire)

Charlie Hills
Aces (Ire)
Cable Bay (Ire)
Cambridge
Commemorative
Cotai Glory
Dutch Connection
Just The Judge (Ire)
Kiyoshi
Muhaarar
Strath Burn

Tom Hogan
Gordon Lord Byron (Ire)

Dean Ivory
Tropics (USA)

Mark Johnston
Muraaqaba

David Lanigan
Biographer

Elie Lellouche
Ectot

Eddie Lynam
Agnes Stewart (Ire)
Anthem Alexander (Ire)
Sole Power

Ger Lyons
Ainippe (Ire)
Cappella Sansevero
Endless Drama (Ire)

George Margarson
Lucky Kristale

Evanna McCutcheon
Maarek

Hughie Morrison
Vent De Force

William Muir
Stepper Point

Willie Mullins
Pique Sous (Fr)

Joseph Murphy
Vert De Grece (Ire)

Peter Niven
Clever Cookie

Aidan O'Brien
Adelaide (Ire)
Aloft (Ire)
Cougar Mountain (Ire)
Dick Whittington (Ire)
Due Diligence (USA)
Easter (Ire)
Found (Ire)
Geoffrey Chaucer (USA)
Giovanni Canaletto (Ire)
Gleneagles (Ire)
Highland Reel (Ire)
Jamaica (Ire)

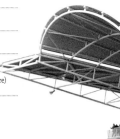

John F Kennedy (Ire)
Ol' Man River (Ire)
Order Of St George (Ire)
Sir Isaac Newton
Smuggler's Cove (Ire)
Together Forever (Ire)
Words (Ire)

David O'Meara
Custom Cut (Ire)
G Force (Ire)
Louis The Pious
Move In Time

Andy Oliver
Panama Hat

Hugo Palmer
Aktabantay
New Providence

Jonathan Pease
Karakontie (Jpn)

Jonathan Portman
Royal Razalma (Ire)

Sir Mark Prescott
Celestial Path (Ire)
Pallasator

John Quinn
The Wow Signal (Ire)

Jean-Claude Rouget
Avenir Certain (Fr)

Kevin Ryan
Astaire (Ire)
Flaming Spear (Ire)
Hot Streak (Ire)
The Grey Gatsby (Ire)

David Simcock
Breton Rock (Ire)
Madame Chiang
Sheikhzayedroad
The Corsican (Ire)

Bryan Smart
Moviesta (USA)

Olly Stevens
Extortionist (Ire)
Lightning Thunder

Sir Michael Stoute
Arab Spring (Ire)
Cannock Chase (USA)
Consort (Ire)
Convey
Gospel Choir
Hillstar
Integral
Provenance
Snow Sky
Stomachion (Ire)
Sympathy (USA)
Telescope (Ire)

Saeed Bin Suroor
Beautiful Romance

Sky Hunter
Winter Thunder
Winters Moon (Ire)

Marcus Tregoning
Bronze Angel (Ire)

Roger Varian
Aljamaaheer (Ire)
Battersea
Belardo (Ire)
Cursory Glance (USA)
Kingston Hill

Ed Vaughan
Adventure Seeker (Ire)

David Wachman
Queen Nefertiti (Ire)

Ed Walker
Lightning Moon (Ire)

Dermot Weld
Brooch (USA)

Fascinating Rock (Ire)
Forgotten Rules (Ire)
Free Eagle (Ire)
Mustajeeb
Zawraq (Ire)

Night Of
Thunder wins
last season's
2,000 Guineas

LEADING BRITISH FLAT TRAINERS: 2014

Trainer	Wins-runs	Wins (%)	2nd	3rd	4th	Win prize	Total prize	Profit/loss (£)
Richard Hannon	165–1129	15	162	161	129	£2,535,180	£4,462,370	-273.64
John Gosden	86–423	20	66	55	51	£2,704,927	£3,979,665	+22.33
Aidan O'Brien	11–81	14	8	9	5	£2,025,979	£2,882,212	-29.82
Richard Fahey	168–1283	13	177	153	137	£1,707,242	£2,645,329	-125.09
Mark Johnston	137–1001	14	124	138	108	£1,689,965	£2,580,079	-207.74
Roger Varian	61–366	17	61	59	35	£1,314,905	£2,155,996	-40.50
Sir Michael Stoute	62–363	17	61	35	44	£1,229,227	£2,123,316	-121.12
William Haggas	92–419	22	55	53	39	£1,255,332	£2,017,703	+40.55
Andrew Balding	72–433	17	50	53	58	£1,104,181	£1,677,681	-22.58
David O'Meara	94–673	14	68	92	63	£1,155,769	£1,619,183	-73.51
Saeed Bin Suroor	57–285	20	43	30	33	£731,458	£1,260,173	-61.53
Eddie Lynam	7–15	47	3	1	1	£1,083,161	£1,219,176	+12.25
Marco Botti	43–324	13	41	35	45	£613,018	£1,137,424	-66.10
Charlie Appleby	52–373	14	51	56	32	£626,174	£1,130,308	-127.81
Kevin Ryan	57–494	12	55	57	59	£541,224	£1,112,904	-130.77
Luca Cumani	48–264	18	44	38	23	£580,123	£1,052,555	-68.70
Lady Cecil	11–95	12	15	17	11	£937,437	£1,027,172	-46.68
David Simcock	40–290	14	35	40	30	£768,700	£1,023,955	-69.35
Mick Channon	67–612	11	94	89	72	£494,576	£904,473	-77.12
Roger Charlton	38–218	17	32	31	21	£371,127	£874,171	-13.40
Charlie Hills	48–410	12	45	47	36	£507,337	£823,368	-132.21
Tim Easterby	47–728	6	80	77	84	£319,181	£700,984	-316.98
Freddy Head	1–3	33	0	1	0	£632,345	£688,062	+3.00
Ralph Beckett	48–312	15	54	32	41	£395,956	£687,190	-62.90
Clive Cox	44–301	15	47	40	32	£303,659	£631,948	-75.19
Brian Ellison	47–469	10	47	45	51	£377,878	£599,623	-146.22
Karl Burke	48–334	14	42	59	37	£327,342	£591,304	-9.24
Dermot Weld	3–8	38	1	1	0	£306,234	£565,311	+4.50
Andre Fabre	3–11	27	3	2	1	£320,341	£518,098	+2.75
Henry Candy	31–214	14	17	26	24	£357,274	£508,740	-34.34
Tom Dascombe	39–320	12	30	43	41	£304,653	£505,218	-105.83
David Barron	40–306	13	34	20	34	£297,177	£461,880	-47.02
Michael Dods	37–280	13	43	32	35	£293,059	£440,448	-63.14
Ed Dunlop	17–235	7	28	24	29	£209,892	£429,156	-90.02
Robert Cowell	22–176	13	33	20	25	£238,434	£410,781	+6.48
Michael Appleby	36–259	14	25	24	30	£286,138	£399,768	+9.83
Peter Chapple-Hyam	16–147	11	18	17	17	£133,720	£399,491	-46.06
Marcus Tregoning	18–128	14	18	18	17	£333,025	£394,244	+1.01
Brian Meehan	31–250	12	32	26	30	£225,402	£380,800	-14.66
Clive Brittain	10–127	8	11	11	18	£261,180	£371,638	-30.00
Jim Goldie	45–450	10	49	40	65	£205,452	£364,160	-52.69
Hugo Palmer	18–115	16	20	13	8	£199,308	£360,678	-4.52
John Quinn	31–268	12	29	34	28	£227,964	£349,601	-67.11
William Muir	28–200	14	30	24	30	£122,664	£346,589	-14.06
Dean Ivory	10–101	10	12	6	10	£67,320	£313,136	-31.75
Hughie Morrison	21–171	12	17	15	26	£180,579	£309,776	-48.04
Ruth Carr	35–366	10	34	46	44	£176,397	£294,239	-77.08
James Fanshawe	16–177	9	19	22	27	£108,616	£288,811	-66.87
David Elsworth	17–121	14	12	9	19	£161,695	£271,519	-2.92
Keith Dalgleish	42–411	10	44	44	43	£164,115	£271,109	-158.46

Statistics for March 29 to November 8, 2014

LEADING BRITISH FLAT JOCKEYS: 2014

Jockey	Wins-runs	Wins (%)	2nd	3rd	4th	Win prize	Total prize	Profit/loss (£)
Richard Hughes	132–744	18	119	89	88	£1,901,956	£3,596,698	-177.86
Ryan Moore	128–649	20	99	73	75	£2,447,269	£4,004,637	-132.55
Graham Lee	126–816	15	96	79	102	£972,166	£1,385,234	-45.72
Joe Fanning	98–699	14	94	83	62	£1,257,544	£1,736,145	-40.95
Paul Mulrennan	93–621	15	65	69	71	£493,302	£737,835	-10.24
Andrea Atzeni	93–539	17	72	78	63	£2,036,997	£3,282,770	+45.73
Paul Hanagan	93–497	19	69	47	61	£2,063,680	£2,853,329	-39.05
William Buick	90–539	17	76	72	62	£1,536,785	£2,731,031	-56.89
Danny Tudhope	84–547	15	52	84	59	£862,155	£1,225,922	-110.87
Adam Kirby	78–514	15	62	59	52	£859,290	£1,261,011	-78.01
James Doyle	77–483	16	84	53	54	£2,077,853	£2,954,709	-35.26
Silvestre de Sousa	70–490	14	59	56	46	£787,294	£1,268,715	-17.99
Luke Morris	68–579	12	71	60	60	£435,985	£692,429	-166.18
George Baker	67–360	19	39	47	38	£514,745	£1,111,678	+34.08
Graham Gibbons	61–466	13	52	32	48	£399,632	£552,390	-74.59
Jim Crowley	61–447	14	48	44	39	£971,607	£1,431,356	+43.33
David Probert	59–492	12	35	54	62	£483,286	£790,625	-141.44
Oisin Murphy	56–452	12	67	49	56	£614,019	£914,491	-74.72
Tony Hamilton	52–445	12	65	56	47	£297,580	£495,975	-161.13
Kieren Fallon	52–404	13	30	50	40	£758,132	£1,182,171	-96.76
David Allan	51–474	11	56	59	50	£311,176	£542,598	-39.73
Phillip Makin	49–414	12	45	60	40	£244,811	£402,502	-131.31
P J McDonald	48–559	9	61	72	70	£234,061	£414,833	-203.47
Dane O'Neill	48–401	12	46	64	49	£295,101	£652,477	-97.55
Richard Kingscote	48–358	13	38	45	55	£459,475	£722,096	-55.06
Robert Winston	46–377	12	54	44	40	£225,825	£600,172	-86.57
Jamie Spencer	45–408	11	59	47	49	£438,877	£1,276,543	-178.24
Freddie Tylicki	44–306	14	45	40	29	£270,611	£485,370	-18.36
Jason Hart	43–421	10	42	34	44	£180,889	£276,030	-66.54
George Chaloner	42–318	13	44	28	27	£383,497	£530,845	-52.79
Martin Harley	42–284	15	42	29	43	£340,736	£601,117	-72.68
Franny Norton	41–395	10	53	65	50	£267,481	£568,502	-116.50
Martin Dwyer	41–300	14	33	30	38	£180,110	£468,976	+9.16
Tom Eaves	40–578	7	51	38	65	£180,351	£353,807	-300.88
Cam Hardie	40–384	10	55	44	47	£303,926	£487,271	-153.47
Connor Beasley	37–378	10	47	52	48	£219,324	£375,679	-154.93
Pat Dobbs	36–286	13	33	37	44	£270,341	£471,153	-48.31
Ben Curtis	35–318	11	39	37	31	£178,747	£322,590	-94.18
Fergus Sweeney	34–281	12	26	31	23	£240,330	£345,482	-84.06
Sean Levey	33–313	11	44	31	28	£195,562	£380,901	-116.72
Joey Haynes	32–272	12	34	29	31	£162,799	£280,070	-2.36
Jack Garritty	30–279	11	25	35	20	£209,539	£295,874	-43.94
David Nolan	30–227	13	36	33	22	£246,784	£421,143	+32.58
Ryan Tate	30–172	17	24	19	15	£158,877	£263,117	+21.60
Charles Bishop	29–179	16	22	17	19	£192,177	£243,290	+38.15
James Sullivan	28–422	7	38	49	49	£196,368	£328,646	-161.08
Willy Twiston-Davies	28–351	8	48	51	35	£134,354	£305,198	-128.94
Jimmy Fortune	28–307	9	33	33	41	£387,770	£677,046	-83.13
Tom Queally	27–374	7	35	30	50	£334,973	£537,104	-122.56
Andrew Mullen	27–285	9	25	24	28	£199,346	£286,407	-47.88

Statistics for March 29 to November 8, 2014

RACING POST RATINGS: LAST SEASON'S LEADING TWO-YEAR-OLDS

KEY: Horse name, best RPR figure, finishing position when earning figure, (details of race where figure was earned)

Acaster Malbis (FR) 95 2 (1m, Newb, GS, Sep 19)
Accepted (IRE) 103 3 (5f, Donc, Gd, Sep 12)
Accipiter 94 5 (6f, Kemw, SD, Sep 6)
Aces (IRE) 109 3 (7f, Donc, Gd, Sep 13)
Adaay (IRE) 102 8 (6f, Asco, Gd, Jun 17)
Agnes Stewart (IRE) 109 2 (1m, Newm, Sft, Oct 17)
Ahlan Emarati (IRE) 107 3 (6f, York, Gd, Aug 23)
Ainippe (IRE) 102 1 (5f, Curr, Gd, Aug 23)
Aktabantay 104 1 (7f 16y, Sand, GS, Aug 30)
Al Fareej (IRE) 96 2 (5f 34y, Newb, Sft, Aug 15)
Aloft (IRE) 112 2 (1m, Donc, Sft, Oct 25)
Alonsoa (IRE) 97 4 (7f, Newj, Sft, Aug 9)
Angelic Lord (IRE) 105 5 (6f, Newj, GF, Jul 10)
Anthem Alexander (IRE) 115 2 (6f, Newm, GF, Sep 27)
Approbare (IRE) 96 5 (6f, Curr, Yld, Aug 31)
Arabian Queen (IRE) 101 5 (7f, Newj, Sft, Aug 9)
Astrelle (IRE) 98 2 (7f, Newm, Gd, Oct 4)
Astrophysics 105 2 (5f, Donc, Gd, Sep 12)
Azraff (IRE) 94 1 (1m 3y, Newc, Gd, Aug 25)
Baitha Alga (IRE) 107 1 (5f, Asco, GF, Jun 19)
Basateen (IRE) 103 3 (7f, York, GF, Aug 20)
Battle Of Marathon (USA) 103 3 (1m, Curr, GF, Sep 28)
Beach Belle 103 4 (6f, Curr, Sft, Aug 10)
Beacon 106 1 (5f, Donc, Gd, Sep 12)
Belardo (IRE) 119 1 (7f, Newm, Sft, Oct 17)
Bertie Le Belge (IRE) 97 4 (1m, Leop, GF, Sep 13)
Best Of Times 97 1 (6f 212y, Sali, Gd, Oct 1)
Bond's Girl 95 2 (6f, York, GS, Oct 11)
Bonnie Grey 96 2 (7f, Good, Gd, Aug 23)
Bossy Guest (IRE) 98 2 (6f, Ripo, Gd, Aug 25)
Bronze Maquette (IRE) 102 1 (5f 34y, Newb, Sft, Aug 15)
Burnt Sugar (IRE) 110 1 (6f, Kemw, SD, Sep 6)
Calypso Beat (USA) 101 2 (7f, Newj, Sft, Aug 9)
Cappella Sansevero 112 4 (6f, Newm, GF, Sep 13)
Captain My Captain (IRE) 97 1 (6f, Naas, Yld, Oct 19)
Carry On Deryck 95 6 (7f, Donc, Gd, Sep 12)
Celestial Path (IRE) 111 3 (1m, Donc, Sft, Oct 25)
Chadic 95 6 (7f, Good, GF, Jul 30)
Charming Thought 117 1 (6f, Newm, Sft, Oct 17)
Christophermarlowe (USA) 97 1 (1m 114y, Epso, Gd, Sep 28)
Clonard Street 105 2 (1m, Curr, GF, Sep 28)
Cock Of The North 102 4 (7f 16y, Sand, GS, Aug 30)
Code Red 102 1 (6f, Donc, Sft, Oct 25)
Commemorative 104 1 (1m, Newm, Gd, Oct 11)
Convergence (IRE) 103 4 (1m, Curr, GF, Sep 28)
Cotai Glory 110 (5f, Donc, Gd, Sep 12)
Cursory Glance (USA) 112 1 (7f, Curr, GF, Sep 14)
Dark Reckoning 99 1 (6f, Ayr, Gd, Sep 20)
Diaz (IRE) 95 3 (7f, Newb, GS, Aug 16)
Dick Whittington (IRE) 114 1 (6f, Curr, Sft, Aug 10)
Disegno (IRE) 102 2 (7f, Asco, Gd, Jul 26)
Dr No 102 7 (6f, Asco, Gd, Jun 17)
Dutch Connection 108 3 (7f, Curr, GF, Sep 14)
Elite Gardens (USA) 104 1 (6f 212y, Sali, Gd, Sep 12)
Elm Park 118 1 (1m, Donc, Sft, Oct 25)
Elysian Flyer (IRE) 97 1 (6f, Sali, Gd, Oct 1)
Endless Drama (IRE) 96 1 (6f, Naas, Yld, Oct 19)
Estidhkaar (IRE) 116 1 (7f, Donc, Gd, Sep 13)
Fadhayyil (IRE) 108 2 (7f, Newm, Gd, Sep 26)
Faithful Creek (IRE) 100 3 (1m, Leop, GF, Sep 13)
Fanciful Angel (IRE) 100 4 (6f, Kemw, SD, Sep 6)
Fannaan (USA) 100 1 (7f, Newm, Sft, Oct 22)
Fast Act (IRE) 105 2 (5f, Good, GF, Jul 29)
Faydhan (USA) 99 1 (6f, Hayd, GS, Jul 3)
Fendale 96 5 (5f, Ayr, Gd, Sep 19)
Fit For The Job 95 1 (7f 100y, Tipp, GF, Aug 28)
Flaming Spear (IRE) 95 1 (6f, York, GF, Jul 12)
Forte 98 6 (1m, Newm, Sft, Oct 17)
Found (IRE) 110 3 (7f, Curr, GF, Sep 14)

Four Seasons (IRE) 98 1 (7f, Kemw, SD, Nov 5)
Fox Trotter (IRE) 100 2 (7f, Newb, Sft, Oct 25)
Future Empire 104 2 (7f 16y, Sand, GS, Aug 30)
Geordie George (IRE) 95 3 (6f, York, GF, Aug 20)
George Dryden (IRE) 97 6 (5f, Donc, Gd, Sep 12)
Glenalmond (IRE) 107 4 (6f, York, Gd, Aug 23)
Gleneagles (IRE) 116 1 (7f, Curr, GF, Sep 14)
Good Place (USA) 96 1 (1m, Asco, Gd, Sep 6)
Hall Of Fame (IRE) 103 3 (7f, Curr, GF, Aug 24)
Hawkesbury 104 2 (7f, Newb, GS, Aug 16)
Heartbreak Hero 104 2 (6f 110y, Donc, Gd, Sep 11)
High Celebrity (FR) 111 3 (6f, Newm, GF, Sep 27)
Highland Reel (IRE) 110 1 (7f, Good, GF, Jul 30)
Home Of The Brave (IRE) 101 3 (6f, Kemw, SD, Sep 6)
Hootenanny (USA) 109 1 (5f, Asco, Gd, Jun 17)
I Am Beautiful (IRE) 99 7 (7f, Curr, GF, Aug 24)
I Will Excel (IRE) 96 7 (6f, Curr, GF, Jun 28)
Intense Style (IRE) 101 1 (6f, Dunw, SD, Sep 26)
Irish Rookie (IRE) 95 1 (1m, Newm, GS, Nov 1)
Itorio (IRE) 100 4 (6f 63y, Curr, GF, Jul 19)
Ivawood (IRE) 117 2 (6f, Newm, Sft, Oct 17)
Izzthatright (IRE) 99 1 (6f, Ripo, Gd, Sep 12)
Jack Naylor 107 1 (1m, Curr, Gd, Aug 31)
Jacobean (IRE) 100 4 (1m, Donc, Sft, Oct 25)
Jamaica (IRE) 101 4 (7f, York, Gd, Aug 20)
Jeanne Girl (IRE) 101 4 (7f, Curr, GF, Aug 24)
John F Kennedy (IRE) 113 1 (1m, Leop, GF, Sep 13)
Johnny Barnes (IRE) 99 1 (7f 9y, Leic, Hvy, Oct 14)
Jungle Cat (IRE) 109 2 (6f, York, Gd, Aug 23)
Justice Good (IRE) 105 4 (6f, Asco, Gd, Jun 17)
Kibaar 98 2 (6f, York, GF, Aug 20)
King Of Normandy (FR) 96 3 (7f, Newb, Sft, Oct 25)
Kodi Bear (IRE) 114 2 (7f, Newm, Sft, Oct 17)
Kool Kompany (IRE) 112 2 (6f, Curr, Sft, Aug 10)
Latharnach (USA) 97 1 (7f 16y, Sand, Gd, Sep 17)
Legatissimo (IRE) 100 2 (1m, Curr, Gd, Aug 31)
Lexington Times (IRE) 103 3 (7f 16y, Sand, GS, Aug 30)
Likely (GER) 97 1 (5f, Carl, Gd, May 26)
Limato (IRE) 116 1 (6f, Redc, Gd, Oct 4)
Littlemissblakeney 95 5 (5f, Asco, GF, Jun 18)
Local Time 98 1 (7f, Newm, Gd, Oct 4)
Lola Beaux 97 2 (7f, Curr, GF, Sep 28)
Louie De Palma 101 2 (6f, Good, GF, Jul 31)
Lucida (IRE) 111 1 (7f, Newm, Gd, Sep 26)
Maftool (USA) 111 1 (7f, Newm, Gd, Sep 25)
Make It Up 97 1 (7f, Good, Gd, Sep 2)
Malabar 108 4 (7f, Curr, GF, Sep 14)
Markaz (IRE) 104 2 (7f, Newm, Gd, Sep 25)
Marsh Hawk 105 4 (1m, Newm, Sft, Oct 17)
Mattmu 107 1 (6f, York, GS, Oct 11)
Medrano 98 2 (1m, Hayd, Gd, Sep 6)
Mind Of Madness (IRE) 102 2 (5f, Asco, GF, Jun 19)
Misterioso (IRE) 95 4 (1m, Newm, GF, Sep 27)
Montalcino (IRE) 95 2 (1m, Asco, GF, Sep 6)
Moonraker 101 2 (5f, York, Gd, Aug 23)
Mubtaghaa (IRE) 101 1 (6f, York, Gd, Aug 21)
Muhaarar 113 3 (6f, Newm, Sft, Oct 17)
Mukhmal (IRE) 99 4 (5f, Good, GF, Jul 29)
Muraaqaba 105 1 (7f, Newj, Sft, Aug 9)
Nafaqa (IRE) 109 2 (1m, Newm, GF, Sep 27)
New Providence 103 3 (7f, Newm, Gd, Sep 26)
Newsletter (IRE) 102 3 (5f, Asco, GF, Jun 18)
Ol' Man River (IRE) 114 1 (1m, Curr, GF, Sep 28)
Order Of St George (IRE) 102 2 (1m 1f, Leop, Yld, Oct 26)
Osaila (IRE) 108 5 (7f, Curr, GF, Sep 14)
Pallister 95 5 (7f 16y, Sand, GS, Aug 30)
Parish Boy 103 1 (1m 1f, Leop, Yld, Oct 26)
Parsley (IRE) 99 2 (6f, Ayr, GF, Sep 20)
Pastoral Girl 95 2 (6f, Asco, Gd, Jul 26)
Patience Alexander (IRE) 100 3 (6f, Asco, GF, Jun 20)
Peacock 103 3 (7f, Donc, Gd, Sep 12)
Portamento (IRE) 104 1 (6f, Hayd, Sft, Oct 17)

Prince Gagarin (IRE) 99 1 (1m 4y, Pont, Sft, Oct 20)
Prize Exhibit 97 3 (7f, Newm, Gd, Oct 4)
Profitable (IRE) 99 5 (5f, Newm, Sft, Oct 17)
Qualify (IRE) 105 1 (7f, Curr, GF, Sep 28)
Quinta Verde (IRE) 98 3 (6f, Curr, GF, Jun 29)
Rapid Applause 107 2 (6f, Curr, Yld, Aug 31)
Raydara (IRE) 110 1 (7f, Curr, GF, Aug 24)
Realtra (IRE) 95 4 (6f, York, Gd, Aug 21)
Restorer 102 2 (1m, Newm, Gd, Oct 11)
Richard Pankhurst 114 1 (7f, Asco, GF, Jun 21)
Room Key 102 5 (7f, Donc, Gd, Sep 13)
Royal Navy Ship (USA) 103 2 (7f, Leop, Sft, Oct 25)
Royal Razalma (IRE) 104 1 (5f, Newm, Sft, Oct 17)
Russian Punch 98 1 (7f, Newb, Sft, Oct 25)
Salateen 99 3 (1m, Newm, GF, Sep 27)
Secret Brief (IRE) 101 6 (7f, Newm, Sft, Oct 17)
Shagah (IRE) 103 3 (1m, Donc, Gd, Sep 12)
Shepherd's Purse 105 4 (6f, Curr, Yld, Aug 31)
Showing Character 97 1 (5f 16y, Ches, GF, Jul 11)
Simply A Star (IRE) 95 3 (5f, Curr, Gd, Aug 23)
Sixty (IRE) 96 6 (6f, Good, GF, Jul 31)
Smaih (GER) 102 1 (7f, Newb, Sft, Oct 25)
Smuggler's Cove (IRE) 109 1 (7f, Dunw, SD, Oct 10)
Snoano 98 1 (1m, Newb, GS, Sep 19)
Spanish Pipedream (USA) 96 4 (5f, Asco, GF, Jun 18)
Squats (IRE) 102 4 (5f, Newm, Sft, Oct 17)
Steip Amach (IRE) 102 1 (7f, Leop, Sft, Oct 25)
Stellar Glow (IRE) 97 3 (7f, Curr, GF, Sep 28)
Strath Burn 102 2 (5f, Newm, Sft, Oct 17)
Stroll Patrol 100 5 (7f, Newm, Gd, Sep 26)

Strong Chemistry 97 4 (1m, Newm, Gd, Oct 11)
Sulaalaat 95 2 (6f 212y, Sali, Gd, Sep 12)
Sunset Glow (USA) 101 2 (6f, Asco, GF, Jun 20)
Supreme Occasion (IRE) 100 4 (1m, Donc, Gd, Sep 12)
Surewecan 97 2 (5f 218y, Leic, GF, Sep 22)
Tendu 106 5 (6f, Newm, GF, Sep 27)
Terror (IRE) 107 4 (6f, Newm, GF, Sep 27)
Teruntum Star (FR) 96 1 (6f, Hayd, Gd, Sep 6)
The Great War (USA) 104 1 (6f, Curr, GF, Sep 28)
The Warrior (IRE) 107 6 (6f, Newm, Sft, Oct 17)
The Wow Signal (IRE) 111 1 (6f, Asco, Gd, Jun 17)
Tiggy Wiggy (IRE) 117 1 (6f, Newm, GF, Sep 27)
Tigrilla (IRE) 102 4 (7f, Newm, Gd, Sep 26)
Together Forever (IRE) 110 1 (1m, Newm, Sft, Oct 17)
Tombelaine (USA) 105 2 (1m, Leop, GF, Sep 13)
Toocoolforschool (IRE) 114 1 (6f 8y, Newb, Sft, Sep 20)
Toogoodtobetrue (IRE) 104 3 (7f, Curr, GF, Aug 24)
Toscanelli (IRE) 97 5 (7f, Curr, GF, Sep 14)
Toscanini (IRE) 111 2 (7f, Curr, GF, Sep 14)
Tupi (IRE) 102 2 (7f, Good, GF, Jul 30)
Union Rose 97 3 (5f, Asco, GF, Sep 6)
Vert De Grece (IRE) 112 2 (7f, Curr, GF, Aug 24)
Volatile (SWE) 101 3 (5f, Newm, Sft, Oct 17)
War Envoy (USA) 110 2 (7f, Donc, Gd, Sep 13)
Wet Sail (USA) 102 3 (6f, Redc, Gd, Oct 4)
White Lake 101 4 (7f, Donc, Gd, Sep 12)
Winters Moon (IRE) 109 3 (1m, Newm, Sft, Oct 17)
Zafilani (IRE) 98 3 (1m 1f, Leop, Yld, Oct 26)
Zuhoor Baynoona (IRE) 95 1 (5f, Muss, Gd, Oct 11)

RACING POST RATINGS: LAST SEASON'S TOP PERFORMERS 3YO+

Absolutely So (IRE) 113 1 (7f, York, Gd, Aug 22)
Abstraction (IRE) 106 2 (5f, Tipp, GF, Aug 8)
Addictive Dream (IRE) 109 3 (5f, Epso, Gd, Jun 7)
Adelaide (IRE) 112 2 (1m 4f, Asco, GF, Jun 20)
Adventure Seeker (IRE) 105 2 (1m 4f, Newm, Gd, Oct 11)
Aeolus 109 1 (6f, Hayd, GS, May 31)
Aetna 106 1 (6f, York, Sft, May 14)
Ahtoug 112 5 (5f, Asco, Gd, Jun 17)
Ahzeemah (IRE) 117 2 (2m, Good, GF, Jul 31)
Air Pilot 115 1 (1m 2f, Newm, Gd, Nov 1)
Ajjaadd (USA) 106 2 (5f, Donc, Sft, Oct 25)
Ajmany (IRE) 106 2 (1m 2f, Newj, GF, Jul 26)
Al Kazeem 122 2 (1m 2f, Asco, Hvy, Oct 18)
Al Saham 106 1 (1m 3f 135y, Wind, Gd, Jun 28)
Al Thakhira 107 3 (7f, Donc, Gd, Sep 11)
Albasharah (USA) 113 1 (1m 2f, Newm, Gd, Oct 11)
Alben Star (IRE) 113 2 (6f, Newj, GF, Aug 23)
Alejandro (IRE) 105 1 (7f, York, GF, Jul 26)
Alex My Boy (IRE) 110 2 (1m 6f, Good, Gd, Aug 23)
Alfred Hutchinson 105 3 (1m 1y, Linw, SD, Apr 18)
Algar Lad 104 1 (5f, Asco, GF, Sep 6)
Alive Alive Oh 105 3 (1m 1f, Curr, Gd, Aug 31)
Aljamaaheer (IRE) 117 3 (6f, Asco, GF, Jun 21)
Alkasser (IRE) 107 1 (7f, Curr, GF, May 5)
All Set To Go (IRE) 105 3 (1m 2f, Nava, Sft, Apr 12)
Almargo (IRE) 106 2 (7f, Leop, GF, Sep 13)
Altano (GER) 105 7 (2m 4f, Asco, GF, Jun 19)
Amarillo (IRE) 107 5 (7f, Good, GF, Jul 29)
American Devil (FR) 106 5 (6f, Asco, GF, Jun 21)
American Hope (USA) 109 2 (1m, Asco, Gd, Jul 26)
Amralah (IRE) 115 1 (1m 2f 95y, Hayd, Gd, Aug 9)
An Saighdiur (IRE) 111 1 (6f, Cork, Hvy, Apr 6)
Angel Gabrial (IRE) 111 5 (2m 88y, York, Gd, Aug 22)
Anjaal 111 3 (7f, Good, GF, Jul 29)
Annecdote 107 3 (7f, Ling, Gd, May 10)
Annunciation 107 2 (6f, Hayd, Sft, May 10)
Anodin (IRE) 119 3 (1m, Asco, Gd, Jun 17)
Another Wise Kid (IRE) 105 2 (6f 5y, Hami, Gd, Sep 21)
Ansgar (IRE) 117 1 (7f, Donc, Gd, Sep 13)
Answered 105 1 (1m 2f, Leop, Sft, Oct 25)

Anticipation (IRE) 109 1 (1m, Newj, GS, Jul 10)
Arab Spring (IRE) 115 1 (1m 4f, Asco, GF, Jun 21)
Arabian Comet (IRE) 105 2 (1m 4f, York, Gd, Aug 21)
Arctic Fire (GER) 104 2 (1m 6f, Kill, Sft, May 13)
Area Fifty One 108 1 (1m 4f, Donc, Sft, Mar 30)
Arod (IRE) 113 1 (1m 1f 218y, Leic, GF, Jul 17)
Artigiano (USA) 109 2 (1m 75y, Nott, Sft, Jun 4)
Ashpan Sam 111 1 (6f, Epso, Gd, Jun 7)
Astaire (IRE) 113 2 (6f, York, Sft, May 14)
Aussie Reigns (IRE) 106 2 (1m 6f 21y, Sali, Gd, Sep 4)
Australia 129 1 (1m 2f 88y, York, GF, Aug 20)
Awake My Soul (IRE) 105 1 (1m 2f, Ayr, Sft, Aug 11)
Ayaar (IRE) 104 5 (1m, Asco, GF, Jun 18)
Ayrad (IRE) 110 3 (1m 4f, Newm, Gd, Sep 26)
B Fifty Two (IRE) 109 1 (5f 110y, Ches, GS, Aug 30)
Baccarat (IRE) 116 1 (6f, Asco, GF, Jun 21)
Balducci 105 3 (1m, York, Gd, Aug 21)
Baltic Knight (IRE) 114 1 (1m 75y, Nott, GS, Nov 5)
Balty Boys (IRE) 108 2 (1m, Hayd, Gd, Sep 6)
Barkston Ash 104 1 (6f, Thir, Gd, May 17)
Barracuda Boy (IRE) 106 1 (5f 216y, Wolw, SD, Apr 5)
Battalion (IRE) 112 1 (1m 4f 10y, Ripo, GS, Apr 26)
Bayrir (FR) 112 3 (1m 2f 60y, Donc, GS, Sep 10)
Be My Gal 104 1 (1m, Good, GS, May 3)
Belgian Bill 109 5 (1m, Good, GF, Aug 1)
Belle D'or (USA) 108 2 (7f, Newm, Gd, Sep 26)
Berkshire (IRE) 117 1 (1m 1f, Newm, Sft, Oct 17)
Bertiewhittle 105 6 (7f, Hayd, Gd, Apr 26)
Big Break 106 1 (7f 100y, Tipp, Gd, Oct 5)
Big Orange 112 1 (1m 6f, Asco, Gd, Oct 3)
Billingsgate (IRE) 104 1 (1m, Kemw, SD, Oct 30)
Biographer 114 2 (1m 2f, Asco, Hvy, Oct 18)
Blaine 108 1 (5f 89y, York, GF, Aug 20)
Blue Surf 104 3 (1m 4f 10y, Epso, Gd, Jun 7)
Body And Soul (IRE) 108 2 (5f, York, GS, May 31)
Bold Sniper 110 2 (1m 2f, Asco, GF, Jun 20)
Bold Thady Quill (IRE) 107 2 (1m, Curr, GF, Jun 27)
Bookrunner (USA) 108 (1m, Newm, GF, May 3)
Boom And Bust (IRE) 104 6 (7f 2y, Ches, GF, Jul 12)
Bow Creek (IRE) 118 1 (1m, Leop, GF, Sep 13)

Bracelet (IRE) 112 1 (1m 4f, Curr, GF, Jul 19)
Brae Hill (IRE) 104 1 (1m, Donc, Sft, Mar 29)
Bragging (USA) 113 1 (7f, York, Gd, Aug 21)
Brass Ring 111 4 (2m 2f, Newm, Gd, Oct 11)
Brazos (IRE) 109 3 (7f, Newb, GS, Aug 16)
Brendan Brackan (IRE) 114 2 (1m, Leop, Sft, May 11)
Breton Rock (IRE) 116 1 (7f, Newb, GS, Aug 16)
Bronze Angel (IRE) 116 1 (1m, Asco, Hvy, Oct 18)
Brooch (USA) 105 1 (1m 1f 100y, Gowr, GF, Sep 21)
Brown Panther 119 1 (1m 6f, Curr, GF, Sep 14)
Brown Sugar (IRE) 104 3 (7f, Newb, GS, Sep 19)
Bunker (IRE) 105 5 (1m 2f 88y, York, GS, May 15)
Burano (IRE) 104 8 (1m, Newb, Gd, Apr 12)
Cable Bay (IRE) 110 2 (7f, Newm, Sft, Oct 17)
Cafe Society (FR) 107 7 (1m 5f 61y, Newb, GS, Aug 16)
Caledonia Lady 105 1 (6f 15y, Nott, GS, May 10)
Camborne 109 7 (1m 6f, York, Gd, May 16)
Cannock Chase (USA) 111 1 (1m 2f, Asco, GF, Jun 19)
Capo Rosso (IRE) 105 1 (7f 32y, Wolw, SD, Oct 25)
Captain Cat (IRE) 117 1 (1m, Hayd, Gd, Sep 6)
Captain Joy (IRE) 104 1 (7f, Dunw, SD, Oct 24)
Captain Ramius (IRE) 108 5 (6f, Ripo, GS, Apr 26)
Carla Bianca (IRE) 108 1 (1m 1f, Curr, Gd, Aug 31)
Carlo Bugatti (IRE) 105 7 (1m 4f, Asco, GF, Jun 19)
Caspar Netscher 104 7 (6f, Hayd, Gd, Sep 6)
Caspian Prince (IRE) 107 2 (5f, Curr, Gd, Jul 20)
Cat O'mountain (USA) 111 1 (1m 2f 150y, Dunw, SD, Oct 3)
Cavalryman 118 1 (2m, Good, GF, Jul 31)
Century (IRE) 104 2 (2m, Asco, GF, Jun 20)
Certerach (IRE) 111 2 (1m 6f, Curr, GF, Jun 29)
Championship (IRE) 104 1 (1m, Donc, Gd, Sep 13)
Chance To Dance (IRE) 108 1 (1m 2f, Leop, GF, Jul 17)
Charm Spirit (IRE) 124 1 (1m, Asco, Hvy, Oct 18)
Chicquita (IRE) 113 3 (1m 4f, Asco, Hvy, Oct 18)
Chil The Kite 117 2 (1m, Asco, GF, Jun 18)
Chopin (GER) 113 4 (1m, Newb, GF, May 17)
Circumvent 104 4 (1m, Kemw, SD, Apr 19)
Cirrus Des Aigles (FR) 125 1 (1m 4f 10y, Epso, Gd, Jun 7)
Clayton 110 2 (1m 2f 18y, Epso, GS, Apr 23)
Clever Cookie 110 1 (1m 6f, York, GS, May 31)
Clon Brulee (IRE) 112 3 (1m 2f 7y, Sand, GS, Aug 30)
Cloudscape (IRE) 109 4 (1m 4f, Good, GF, Jul 30)
Complicate (AUS) 108 1 (6f, Warw, Sft, Aug 25)
Connecticut 110 3 (1m 6f, York, Gd, Aug 23)
Continuum 104 4 (1m 4f, Asco, GS, May 10)
Contributer (IRE) 115 1 (1m 2f, Asco, GF, Jun 20)
Cordite (IRE) 107 3 (1m 60y, Leic, GS, Oct 7)
Cougar Mountain (IRE) 112 5 (6f, Newj, GS, Jul 12)
Coulsty (IRE) 108 2 (7f 122y, Ches, GS, Aug 16)
Criteria (IRE) 105 3 (1m 4f, Asco, GF, Jun 19)
Cubanita 111 3 (1m 3f 5y, Newb, Sft, Sep 20)
Custom Cut (IRE) 120 1 (1m, Newm, Gd, Sep 26)
Dabadiyan (IRE) 105 4 (1m 6f, Curr, GF, Jun 29)
Danadana (IRE) 107 2 (1m 1f 192y, Good, Gd, Sep 24)
Dank 104 5 (1m 2f, Asco, GF, Jun 18)
Danzeno 117 2 (6f, Asco, Sft, Oct 4)
Dare To Achieve 104 1 (1m 4f 17y, Hami, GS, May 16)
Dark Emerald (IRE) 106 1 (1m, Newm, GS, Sep 20)
Darwin (USA) 119 3 (1m, Good, GF, Jul 30)
Dashing Star 106 4 (1m 3f 200y, Hayd, GS, Jul 5)
Day Of Conquest 105 2 (7f, Good, GF, Jul 31)
De Rigueur 110 2 (2m 2f, Newm, Gd, Oct 11)
Demora 109 4 (5f, Asco, GF, Jul 12)
Dick Doughtywylie 107 2 (1m 2f, Linw, SD, Apr 18)
Dinkum Diamond (IRE) 112 3 (5f, Muss, Sft, Jun 14)
Domination 105 3 (2m 78y, Sand, GF, Jul 5)
Don't Call Me (IRE) 105 2 (1m, Ayr, GF, Sep 20)
Dont Bother Me (IRE) 106 2 (7f, Asco, Gd, Jul 26)
Double Bluff (IRE) 110 1 (1m 4f, Good, GF, Aug 2)
Due Diligence (USA) 116 2 (6f, Curr, Gd, Jun 21)
Duke Of Clarence (IRE) 106 2 (1m 4f, Newj, Gd, May 31)
Duke Of Firenze 105 1 (5f, Catt, Sft, Oct 18)
Dungannon 106 1 (5f, Donc, Sft, Oct 25)
Dutch Rose (IRE) 105 1 (7f, York, GS, May 31)
Eagle Top 119 4 (1m 4f, Asco, Gd, Jul 26)
Eastern Belle 106 4 (1m 1f 192y, Good, GF, Aug 2)

Eastern Impact (IRE) 109 1 (6f, Newj, GS, Aug 16)
Eastern Rules (IRE) 109 2 (7f, Leop, GF, Jun 19)
Ebanoran (IRE) 110 1 (1m 2f, Leop, Sft, May 11)
Edelmira (IRE) 106 1 (1m 4f, Cork, Sft, Aug 5)
Edge Of Sanity (IRE) 105 1 (2m 88y, York, GF, Aug 20)
Educate 113 3 (1m 2f 88y, York, GS, Oct 11)
El Salvador (IRE) 109 2 (1m 4f 110y, Lime, Sft, Apr 26)
Elidor 106 4 (1m 6f 132y, Donc, GS, Sep 12)
Elite Army 109 1 (1m 4f, Asco, GF, Jun 19)
Elkaayed (USA) 106 4 (1m 5f 61y, Newb, GF, May 17)
Elleval (IRE) 108 6 (1m 208y, York, Gd, Aug 23)
Emell 109 2 (1m, Good, Gd, Aug 23)
Emirates Flyer 104 2 (1m 141y, Wolw, SD, Oct 9)
Empire Storm (GER) 113 3 (1m, Asco, Hvy, Oct 18)
Empoli (GER) 112 4 (1m 4f 10y, Epso, Gd, Jun 7)
Encke (USA) 110 3 (1m 6f, Curr, GF, Sep 14)
Energia Davos (BRZ) 108 1 (1m 2f 95y, Hayd, Gd, Aug 9)
Energizer (GER) 104 6 (1m 2f, Asco, GF, Jun 20)
Ennistown 108 1 (1m 2f 6y, Pont, GF, Sep 25)
Epsom Hill (SWE) 104 2 (1m 6f, Hayd, Gd, Sep 6)
Ernest Hemingway (IRE) 114 1 (1m 6f, Curr, GF, Jun 29)
Ertijaal (IRE) 108 3 (6f 18y, Ches, GS, Aug 3)
Es Que Love (IRE) 116 4 (7f, Donc, Gd, Sep 13)
Esoterique (IRE) 114 1 (1m 1f, Newm, GF, May 4)
Estimate (IRE) 115 2 (2m 4f, Asco, GF, Jun 19)
Etaab (USA) 107 1 (1m, Newm, Gd, Sep 26)
Eton Forever (IRE) 113 6 (6f, Asco, Hvy, Oct 18)
Eton Rifles (IRE) 111 2 (5f, Hayd, GS, May 31)
Euphrasia (IRE) 106 3 (1m 2f 110y, Curr, Sft, May 25)
Euro Charline 111 3 (1m, Asco, GF, Jun 20)
Evita Peron 105 5 (7f, Donc, Gd, Sep 11)
Expert (IRE) 104 2 (6f, Newm, Gd, Apr 16)
Extortionist (IRE) 115 3 (5f, York, Gd, Aug 22)
Extra Noble 105 3 (1m 2f 6y, Newb, GF, May 17)
Extremity (IRE) 106 1 (1m, Thir, GS, Sep 6)
Eye Of The Storm (IRE) 107 1 (1m 4f, Leop, Yld, Aug 7)
Famous Kid (USA) 104 1 (1m 4f, Newm, GF, Sep 27)
Farraaj (IRE) 120 1 (1m 2f 88y, York, GF, Jul 12)
Fascinating Rock (IRE) 110 2 (1m 2f, Leop, Sft, May 11)
Fattsota 107 2 (1m 2f 88y, York, GS, Oct 11)
Fencing (USA) 113 2 (1m, York, Gd, Jun 14)
Field Of Dream 112 1 (1m, Asco, Gd, Jun 18)
Fiesolana (IRE) 115 2 (1m, Curr, Hvy, May 24)
Final Score (IRE) 106 5 (1m 4f, Asco, GF, Jun 19)
Fintry (IRE) 116 3 (1m, Newm, Gd, Oct 4)
Fire Fighting (IRE) 111 2 (1m 4f, Newm, Gd, Oct 4)
Fire Ship 111 2 (1m, Newm, Gd, Nov 1)
First Flight (IRE) 104 2 (1m 2f 6y, Newb, Sft, Sep 20)
First Mohican 110 3 (1m 5f 61y, Newb, GF, May 17)
First Prophet 105 1 (1m, York, Gd, Jun 14)
Fiesolana (IRE) 115 2 (1m, Curr, Hvy, May 24)
Flintshire 121 2 (1m 4f 10y, Epso, Gd, Jun 7)
Flying Officer (USA) 111 2 (2m, Newm, Gd, Sep 25)
Flying The Flag (IRE) 108 5 (1m 208y, York, Gd, Aug 23)
Flyman 104 1 (6f, Donc, Sft, Mar 30)
Focus On Venice (IRE) 105 2 (7f, Curr, GF, May 5)
Forever Now 111 6 (1m 6f 132y, Donc, Gd, Sep 13)
Forgotten Rules (IRE) 117 1 (2m, Asco, Hvy, Oct 18)
Forgotten Voice (IRE) 111 6 (2m 88y, York, Gd, Aug 22)
Fort Knox 111 2 (7f, Newb, GF, May 17)
Fountain Of Youth (IRE) 108 1 (5f, Curr, GF, Jun 28)
Foxtrot Romeo (IRE) 108 1 (5f 216y, Wolw, SD, Nov 7)
Francis Of Assisi (IRE) 107 2 (7f, Leop, Yld, Oct 26)
Free Eagle (IRE) 120 3 (1m 2f, Asco, Hvy, Oct 18)
Free Wheeling (AUS) 104 9 (7f, Asco, GF, Sep 6)
Freedom's Light 107 1 (1m 4f 8y, Pont, Gd, Jun 22)
French Navy 118 1 (1m, Newm, Gd, Nov 1)
G Force 121 1 (6f, Hayd, Gd, Sep 6)
Gabrial (IRE) 105 1 (1m 60y, Leic, Sft, Oct 27)
Gabrial's Kaka (IRE) 109 2 (1m, Hayd, Gd, Apr 26)
Gabriel's Lad (IRE) 114 1 (7f, Asco, GS, May 10)
Garswood 114 2 (7f, Newj, Sft, Jun 28)
Gatewood 109 1 (1m 4f, Asco, GS, May 10)
Gathering Power (IRE) 109 7 (6f, Asco, Hvy, Oct 18)
Geoffrey Chaucer (USA) 112 3 (1m 2f, Leop, Sft, May 11)
Georgian Bay (IRE) 105 1 (7f, Kemw, SD, Apr 19)
Gifted Girl (IRE) 106 3 (1m 1f, Newm, GF, May 4)
Giovanni Boldini (USA) 109 3 (7f, Asco, Gd, Jun 18)

Girolamo (GER) 109 4 (2m 78y, Sand, Sft, May 29)
Glen Moss (IRE) 107 3 (7f, York, Gd, Aug 22)
Glen's Diamond 108 8 (1m 6f, York, Gd, May 16)
Glorious Empire (IRE) 106 1 (7f, Newj, Sft, Aug 14)
Glorious Protector (IRE) 109 4 (1m 3f 5y, Newb, Sft, Sep 20)
Glory Awaits (IRE) 112 7 (1m, Asco, Gd, Jun 17)
Gm Hopkins 108 1 (1m 1f, Newm, Gd, Sep 26)
Go Far 106 1 (5f 216y, Wolw, SD, Sep 6)
Go For Goal (IRE) 109 1 (1m, Leop, Hvy, Mar 30)
Golden Town (IRE) 107 1 (1m, Newj, Sft, Jul 12)
Goldream 109 2 (5f, Hayd, Gd, Sep 27)
Gordon Lord Byron (IRE) 121 1 (6f, Asco, Hvy, Oct 18)
Gospel Choir 116 1 (1m 6f, York, Gd, May 16)
Grandeur (IRE) 111 1 (1m 1f 192y, Good, Gd, Sep 24)
Graphic (IRE) 114 2 (1m, Asco, GS, Apr 30)
Great Hall 104 2 (1m 6f, Hayd, Gd, Sep 27)
Great White Eagle (USA) 105 4 (7f, Curr, GF, May 5)
Green Door (IRE) 109 2 (5f 16y, Ches, GF, Jul 11)
Gregorian (IRE) 117 3 (6f, Newj, GS, Jul 12)
Grendisar (IRE) 107 2 (1m 4f, Linw, SD, Apr 18)
Grey Mirage 104 4 (1m 1y, Linw, SD, Apr 18)
Groundbreaking 106 1 (1m 2f, Newm, GF, May 16)
Guerre (USA) 108 1 (5f, Naas, Gd, Apr 28)
Guest Of Honour (IRE) 117 1 (1m, Asco, GF, Jul 12)
Hadaatha (IRE) 104 1 (1m 2f 21y, Yarm, Gd, Sep 17)
Hall Of Mirrors (IRE) 112 1 (1m 2f, Curr, GF, Aug 24)
Hallelujah 105 1 (6f, Kemw, SD, Oct 8)
Hamelin (IRE) 104 2 (1m 4f, Asco, GS, May 10)
Hamza (IRE) 114 1 (6f, Newm, Gd, Apr 17)
Harris Tweed 109 2 (1m 3f 183y, Leic, Sft, Oct 27)
Hartnell 111 1 (1m 5f, Newj, GF, Jul 10)
Hasopop (IRE) 106 5 (7f 1y, Linw, SD, Oct 30)
Havana Beat (IRE) 106 1 (2m 78y, Sand, GF, Jul 5)
Havana Cooler (IRE) 106 2 (1m 6f, Good, GF, Jul 29)
Hawkeyethenoo (IRE) 106 6 (7f, Asco, GF, Sep 6)
Heaven's Guest (IRE) 115 3 (7f, Newj, GS, Jul 12)
Heavy Metal 106 2 (1m, Good, GF, Aug 1)
Heeraat (IRE) 114 2 (6f 8y, Newb, Gd, Jul 19)
Helene Happy Star (IRE) 108 5 (1m 2f, Asco, GF, Jun 19)
Here Comes When (IRE) 118 1 (7f, Newm, Sft, Oct 17)
High Jinx (IRE) 112 2 (2m 78y, Sand, Sft, May 29)
High On Life 108 1 (5f, Hayd, Gd, Sep 27)
Highland Acclaim (IRE) 107 2 (6f, York, GS, Oct 11)
Highland Colori (IRE) 104 5 (7f, York, Gd, Aug 22)
Highland Knight (IRE) 111 4 (1m 114y, Epso, Gd, Jun 6)
Hillstar 117 1 (1m 3f 5y, Newb, Sft, Sep 20)
Homage (IRE) 104 1 (1m 67y, Wind, Gd, Jun 29)
Hoodna (IRE) 107 3 (7f, Newj, GS, Jul 12)
Hoof It 108 3 (6f, Kemw, SD, Mar 29)
Hors De Combat 113 2 (1m, Good, GF, Aug 1)
Horsted Keynes (FR) 108 2 (7f, Asco, GF, Jun 20)
Hot Streak (IRE) 116 1 (5f, Hayd, Sft, May 24)
I'm Yours 104 1 (1m 1f 100y, Gowr, Sft, Apr 27)
Ihtimal (IRE) 110 5 (1m 4f 10y, Epso, Gd, Jun 6)
Impulsive Moment (IRE) 105 3 (1m 3f 16y, Hami, GF, Jul 18)
Inchila 112 4 (1m 4f 10y, Epso, Gd, Jun 6)
Indignant 106 3 (7f, Good, GF, Aug 1)
Inis Meain (USA) 112 1 (1m 2f, Curr, Yld, Apr 13)
Integral 119 1 (1m, Newm, Gd, Oct 4)
Intibaah 114 5 (6f, Asco, Hvy, Oct 18)
Intransigent 115 1 (7f, Asco, Sft, Oct 4)
Intrinsic 106 1 (6f, Good, GF, Aug 2)
Inyordreams 105 1 (6f, Newm, Gd, Oct 4)
It's Somewhat (USA) 114 3 (1m 2f 7y, Sand, GF, Jul 5)
J Wonder (USA) 110 1 (7f, Good, GF, Aug 1)
Jack Dexter 116 3 (6f, Asco, Hvy, Oct 18)
Jack's Revenge (IRE) 104 2 (7f, Newm, GF, Sep 27)
Jallota 107 2 (7f, Newb, GS, Sep 19)
Jamesie (IRE) 109 1 (6f, Curr, Gd, Aug 23)
Jimmy Styles 107 2 (5f 34y, Newb, GS, Apr 11)
Jordan Princess 104 2 (1m 4f, Newm, Gd, Sep 26)
Joyeuse 109 2 (6f, York, GF, Jul 11)
Just The Judge (IRE) 108 3 (1m 2f, Curr, GF, Jun 29)
Justice Day (IRE) 111 1 (6f, Hayd, GS, Jul 5)
Justineo 110 1 (6f, Donc, GF, Aug 2)
Kalann (IRE) 109 3 (2m 2f, Donc, GS, Sep 12)

Kanes Pass (IRE) 105 1 (7f, Leop, Yld, Oct 26)
Kenhope (FR) 105 4 (1m, Leop, GF, Sep 13)
Kernoff (IRE) 105 1 (6f, Dunw, SD, Oct 31)
Khione 104 9 (1m 6f, York, Gd, May 16)
Kickboxer (IRE) 106 2 (5f, Asco, GS, Oct 4)
Kingfisher (IRE) 113 2 (1m 4f, Curr, GF, Jun 28)
Kingman 128 1 (1m, Asco, Gd, Jun 17)
Kings Fete 108 3 (1m 6f, Good, Gd, Aug 23)
Kingsbarns (IRE) 111 2 (1m 2f, Curr, GF, Aug 24)
Kingsgate Native (IRE) 115 2 (5f, Newm, GF, May 3)
Kingston Hill 123 2 (1m 4f 10y, Epso, Gd, Jun 7)
Kiyoshi 111 1 (7f, Donc, Gd, Sep 11)
Krypton Factor 109 2 (6f, Kemw, SD, Oct 8)
L'amour De Ma Vie (USA) 116 2 (1m, Asco, GF, Jun 18)
Ladies Are Forever 111 2 (6f, York, GF, Sep 7)
Lady Lara (IRE) 108 3 (1m 208y, York, Gd, Aug 23)
Lahinch Classics (IRE) 104 2 (1m 1f, Curr, GF, Jul 20)
Lancelot Du Lac (ITY) 104 5 (6f, Kemw, SD, Mar 29)
Leading Light (IRE) 121 1 (1m 6f, Nava, Gd, May 18)
Leitir Mor (IRE) 109 5 (1m, Leop, GF, Sep 13)
Lesstalk In Paris (IRE) 111 2 (1m, Asco, GF, Jun 20)
Lightning Moon (IRE) 114 1 (6f, Asco, Sft, Oct 4)
Lightning Thunder 110 2 (1m, Curr, Sft, May 25)
Line Of Reason (IRE) 105 3 (5f, Beve, GF, Aug 30)
Litigant 104 1 (1m 7f 169y, Linw, SD, Apr 18)
Lockwood 110 4 (1m, York, Gd, Jun 14)
Long John (AUS) 112 3 (1m, Asco, GF, Jul 12)
Lord Van Percy 107 2 (1m 6f, York, Gd, Aug 23)
Louis The Pious 114 1 (6f, Ayr, GF, Sep 20)
Lucky Beggar (IRE) 110 1 (5f 34y, Newb, GS, Apr 11)
Lustrous 106 2 (1m 4f, Asco, GF, Jun 19)
Maarek 118 1 (6f, York, Sft, May 14)
Madame Chiang 115 1 (1m 4f, Asco, Hvy, Oct 18)
Magic City (IRE) 106 3 (1m, Asco, Gd, Aug 9)
Magician (IRE) 124 2 (1m 2f, Asco, GF, Jun 18)
Magnolia Beach (IRE) 106 4 (1m 2f 150y, Dunw, SD, Oct 3)
Magnus Maximus 104 1 (6f, Newm, Gd, Apr 16)
Maid In Rio (IRE) 106 1 (2m, Asco, Gd, Jul 25)
Manalapan (IRE) 107 2 (1m 6f, Leop, Gd, Jul 17)
Manderley (IRE) 107 4 (1m, Newm, GF, May 4)
Mango Diva 105 1 (1m 1f, Curr, GF, Jul 20)
Marsh Daisy 105 1 (1m 1f 192y, Good, Sft, May 22)
Marvellous (IRE) 117 1 (1m, Curr, Sft, May 25)
Marzocco (USA) 112 5 (1m 6f 132y, Donc, Gd, Sep 13)
Masamah 108 2 (5f, Muss, Sft, Jun 14)
Mass Rally (IRE) 108 9 (5f 89y, York, GF, Aug 20)
Maverick Wave (USA) 106 3 (1m 1f 103y, Wolw, SD, Nov 6)
Mecca's Angel (IRE) 115 1 (5f 34y, Newb, Sft, Sep 20)
Medicean Man 113 4 (5f, Asco, Gd, Jun 17)
Mekong River (IRE) 110 1 (1m 2f, Curr, GF, Jun 29)
Menorah (IRE) 107 9 (2m 78y, Sand, Sft, May 29)
Michaelmas (USA) 104 1 (1m, Naas, GF, Jul 23)
Mick's Yer Man 106 1 (6f, Asco, Sft, Apr 30)
Mighty Yar (IRE) 105 2 (1m 4f, York, Gd, Jul 11)
Miner's Lamp (IRE) 109 1 (1m 4f, Newm, GF, May 17)
Miracle Of Medinah 105 2 (7f 2y, Ches, GF, Jul 12)
Mirza 110 2 (5f, Beve, GF, Aug 30)
Miss France (IRE) 117 2 (1m, Newm, Gd, Oct 4)
Missunited (IRE) 115 3 (2m 4f, Asco, GF, Jun 19)
Mizzou (IRE) 109 3 (1m 6f, Asco, Gd, Oct 3)
Monsieur Joe (IRE) 111 1 (5f, York, GS, May 15)
Montiridge (IRE) 110 2 (1m 14y, Sand, Sft, Apr 25)
Morache Music 111 1 (7f, Donc, Gd, Aug 16)
Mount Athos (IRE) 113 1 (1m 5f 61y, Newb, GF, May 17)
Mount Logan (IRE) 108 1 (1m 4f, Donc, Gd, Sep 13)
Move In Time 111 2 (5f 89y, York, GF, Aug 20)
Moviesta (USA) 115 3 (5f, Good, GF, Aug 1)
Mubaraza (IRE) 106 2 (2m, Ripo, GS, Apr 30)
Mukhadram 122 3 (1m 4f, Asco, Gd, Jul 26)
Mull Of Killough (IRE) 117 1 (1m 1f, Newm, Gd, Apr 17)
Munaaser 105 2 (1m 1f, Newm, Gd, Sep 26)
Mushir 104 1 (7f, Thir, GF, Aug 1)
Music Master 115 1 (6f 8y, Newb, Gd, Jul 19)
Music Theory (IRE) 110 2 (7f 1y, Linw, SD, Oct 30)
Musical Comedy 106 1 (6f 8y, Newb, Gd, May 16)
Mustajeeb 121 1 (7f, Asco, Gd, Jun 18)

Mutakayyef 116 2 (1m 1f, Newm, Sft, Oct 17)
Muteela 109 1 (7f, Redc, Gd, Oct 4)
Muthmir (IRE) 115 1 (5f 140y, Donc, Gd, Sep 13)
Mutual Regard (IRE) 116 1 (1m 6f, York, Gd, Aug 23)
Muwaary 115 2 (7f, Asco, Gd, Jun 18)
My Ambivalent (IRE) 114 3 (1m 4f 10y, Epso, Gd, Jun 7)
My Good Brother (IRE) 105 1 (6f, Dunw, SD, Oct 3)
My Titania (IRE) 108 4 (1m, Asco, GF, Jun 20)
Naadirr (IRE) 112 1 (6f, York, GF, Sep 7)
Nabucco 112 3 (1m 1f 192y, Good, Sft, May 24)
Narniyn (IRE) 113 2 (1m 1f 192y, Good, GF, Aug 2)
Nautilus 108 1 (1m 6f, Hayd, Gd, Sep 6)
Navajo Chief 106 1 (1m, York, GS, May 15)
Nearly Caught (IRE) 106 6 (2m 2f, Newm, Gd, Oct 11)
Night Of Thunder (IRE) 124 1 (1m, Newm, GF, May 3)
Ninjago 111 2 (6f, Good, GF, Aug 2)
Noble Mission 123 1 (1m 2f, Asco, Hvy, Oct 18)
Noble Protector 108 1 (1m 4f, Newj, GF, Jul 19)
Noble Storm (USA) 109 1 (5f, Thir, Gd, May 17)
Nocturnal Affair (SAF) 105 3 (5f, Naas, Gd, Apr 28)
Noozhoh Canarias (SPA) 114 6 (1m, Newm, GF, May 3)
Obliterator (IRE) 108 1 (1m 2f 150y, Dunw, SD, Oct 17)
Observational 105 1 (1m 3f, Good, Sft, May 23)
Ocean Tempest 121 1 (7f 122y, Ches, GS, Aug 30)
Odeliz (IRE) 108 3 (1m 2f 88y, York, GS, May 15)
Odeon 106 4 (1m 2f 88y, York, GS, May 15)
Olympic Glory (IRE) 125 1 (1m, Newb, GF, May 17)
Online Alexander (IRE) 107 1 (5f, York, Gd, Aug 23)
Orchestra (IRE) 112 1 (1m 4f 66y, Ches, Sft, May 8)
Oriental Fox (GER) 108 6 (2m 19y, Newc, GF, Jun 28)
Our Channel (USA) 104 8 (1m, Good, GF, Aug 1)
Outback Traveller (IRE) 110 1 (7f, Asco, Gd, Oct 3)
Outstrip 119 3 (1m, Asco, Gd, Jun 17)
Pacific Heights (IRE) 106 1 (7f 2y, Ches, GS, May 31)
Paene Magnus (IRE) 106 2 (1m, Curr, GF, Jun 28)
Pale Mimosa (IRE) 112 1 (2m 88y, York, Gd, Aug 22)
Pallasator 115 1 (1m 4f, Asco, GF, Jul 27)
Panama Hat 116 2 (1m 4f, Curr, GF, Sep 14)
Parbold (IRE) 109 5 (7f, Newm, Gd, Apr 16)
Parish Hall (IRE) 113 2 (1m 4f, Asco, Sft, Oct 4)
Passing Star 105 5 (7f, Good, GF, Jul 31)
Patentar (FR) 111 1 (7f, Ling, GF, Sep 13)
Peace Burg (FR) 113 3 (1m, Newj, Sft, Jul 11)
Pearl Of Africa (IRE) 108 1 (1m, Leop, Gd, Jun 12)
Pearl Secret 117 2 (5f, Hayd, Sft, May 24)
Pelerin (IRE) 107 1 (1m, Dunw, SD, Oct 31)
Penitent 114 1 (7f, Hayd, GS, May 31)
Pether's Moon (IRE) 117 1 (1m 4f, Asco, Sft, Oct 4)
Pinzolo 109 2 (1m 3f 135y, Wind, Gd, Aug 23)
Piri Wango (IRE) 109 4 (7f, Leop, GF, Sep 13)
Pollyana (IRE) 110 4 (1m 4f, Asco, Hvy, Oct 18)
Polybius 106 1 (6f, Kemw, SD, Sep 22)
Pomology (USA) 113 1 (1m 3f 200y, Hayd, GS, Jul 5)
Postponed (IRE) 121 1 (1m 4f, York, GF, Aug 20)
Pretzel (IRE) 108 2 (1m, Newj, GS, Jul 10)
Prince Bishop (IRE) 121 1 (1m 4f, Kemw, SD, Sep 6)
Prince Of All 113 7 (1m, Asco, Gd, Jun 17)
Prince Of Johanne (IRE) 106 3 (1m, York, GS, May 15)
Prince's Trust 111 1 (7f 1y, Linw, SD, Oct 30)
Princess Loulou (IRE) 106 3 (1m, Curr, Hvy, May 24)
Producer 116 5 (1m, Asco, Gd, Jun 17)
Professor 114 1 (7f, Hayd, GS, Jul 19)
Purr Along 111 1 (1m, Curr, Hvy, May 24)
Quaduna 108 4 (1m 1f, Newm, GF, May 4)
Queen Catrine (IRE) 108 2 (1m, Asco, GF, Jun 18)
Queen Of Ice 108 1 (1m 4f, Newm, Gd, Sep 26)
Queensberry Rules (IRE) 105 1 (1m 2f 88y, York, Gd, Aug 23)
Quest For Peace (IRE) 107 5 (1m 3f 5y, Newb, Sft, Sep 20)
Quiz Mistress 106 5 (1m 3f 200y, Hayd, GS, Jul 5)
Racy 105 1 (5f, Asco, GF, Jul 27)
Ralston Road (IRE) 110 1 (1m 6f, York, GS, May 31)
Rangali 110 7 (7f, York, Gd, Aug 22)
Rawaki (IRE) 112 2 (1m 4f 17y, Hami, GS, May 16)
Reckless Abandon 113 3 (6f, Newj, GF, Aug 23)
Red Avenger (USA) 105 1 (1m, Good, GF, Aug 1)
Red Cadeaux 111 4 (1m 5f 61y, Newb, GS, Aug 16)

Red Galileo 110 2 (1m 4f, Newm, Gd, Sep 26)
Red Rocks Point (IRE) 108 2 (1m 1f 100y, Gowr, GF, Jul 1)
Rene Mathis (GER) 105 2 (7f, Good, Gd, Aug 23)
Renew (IRE) 107 4 (1m 4f, Newm, GF, May 3)
Repeater 106 2 (2m 78y, Sand, GF, Jul 5)
Rerouted (USA) 113 3 (7f, Hayd, GS, Jul 19)
Retirement Plan 107 2 (1m 6f 132y, Donc, GS, Sep 12)
Rewaaya (IRE) 107 1 (1m 3f 183y, Leic, Sft, Oct 27)
Rex Imperator 107 2 (6f, Wind, Gd, Jun 2)
Rivellino 108 3 (6f, Asco, GF, Jun 21)
Rizeena (IRE) 113 1 (1m, Asco, GF, Jun 20)
Robin Hoods Bay 105 3 (1m 2f, Linw, SD, Apr 18)
Robot Boy (IRE) 110 1 (5f, Newc, GF, Jun 27)
Rocky Ground (IRE) 114 1 (6f, Wind, Gd, Jun 2)
Romsdal 118 3 (1m 4f 10y, Epso, Gd, Jun 7)
Royal Diamond (IRE) 115 2 (1m 6f, Nava, Gd, May 18)
Russian Soul (IRE) 112 2 (6f, Fair, GF, Jul 13)
Ruwaiyan (USA) 108 4 (6f, Good, GF, Aug 2)
Saayerr 107 4 (7f, Newm, Gd, Apr 16)
Safety Check (IRE) 108 1 (7f, Asco, GF, Sep 6)
Salutation (IRE) 108 2 (1m 4f, York, Gd, Aug 22)
Sandiva (IRE) 107 5 (1m, Asco, GF, Jun 20)
Santefisio 105 6 (7f, Asco, Gd, Jun 20)
Scotland (GER) 109 3 (1m 4f, Asco, GF, Jun 20)
Scream Blue Murder (IRE) 106 1 (6f, Curr, Sft, Aug 10)
Seal Of Approval 112 4 (1m 6f, York, Gd, May 16)
Secret Gesture 111 2 (1m 2f 88y, York, GF, Jul 26)
Secret Number 111 2 (1m 4f, Kemw, SD, Sep 6)
Seeking Magic 107 2 (5f, Epso, Gd, Jun 7)
Seismos (IRE) 114 1 (1m 5f 61y, Newb, GS, Aug 16)
Sennockian Star 110 1 (1m 1f 192y, Good, Gd, Jul 29)
Shamshon (IRE) 109 1 (5f, York, Gd, May 15)
Sharestan (IRE) 113 1 (1m 2f 7y, Sand, Sft, May 29)
Sheikhzayedroad 115 1 (1m 2f 88y, York, GF, Jul 26)
Shifting Power 117 4 (1m, Newm, GF, May 3)
Shining Emerald 107 2 (1m, Leop, Hvy, Mar 30)
Short Squeeze (IRE) 112 1 (1m, York, Gd, Aug 21)
Shwaiman (IRE) 108 3 (1m 6f, York, GS, May 31)
Side Glance 107 9 (1m, Asco, Gd, Jun 17)
Silk Sari 112 2 (1m 4f, Asco, Hvy, Oct 18)
Simenon (IRE) 113 5 (2m 4f, Asco, GF, Jun 19)
Sir Maximilian (IRE) 109 1 (5f, Dunw, SD, Oct 24)
Sirius Prospect (USA) 110 2 (7f, York, GS, May 31)
Sizzler 105 3 (2m 4f, Asco, Gd, Jun 17)
Sky Hunter 117 1 (1m 4f 5y, Newb, Sft, Oct 25)
Sky Lantern (IRE) 110 5 (1m, Asco, GF, Jun 18)
Slade Power (IRE) 123 1 (6f, Asco, GF, Jun 21)
Smoothtalkinrascal (IRE) 106 1 (5f, Muss, GF, Apr 18)
Snow Sky 117 2 (1m 4f, York, Gd, Aug 20)
Soft Falling Rain (SAF) 115 6 (1m, Asco, Gd, Jun 17)
Sole Power 120 1 (5f, Asco, Gd, Jun 17)
Songcraft (IRE) 106 4 (1m 6f, Good, Gd, Aug 23)
Spa's Dancer (IRE) 107 2 (1m 2f, Redc, GS, May 26)
Speed Hawk (USA) 105 1 (5f 43y, Yarm, Gd, Sep 17)
Spinatrix 114 1 (6f, York, GS, Oct 11)
Sruthan (IRE) 114 1 (7f, Curr, Yld, Apr 13)
Steeler (IRE) 113 4 (1m, Good, GF, Aug 1)
Stepper Point 117 1 (5f, Curr, GF, Sep 14)
Steps (IRE) 115 4 (5f, Epso, Gd, Jun 7)
Streetcar To Stars 107 4 (1m 6f, Curr, GF, Aug 24)
Stuccodor (IRE) 105 3 (1m 100y, Cork, Sft, Oct 18)
Sudden Wonder (IRE) 111 2 (1m 2f, Newm, Gd, Nov 1)
Suegioo (FR) 107 3 (1m 6f 132y, Donc, GS, Sep 12)
Sultanina 116 1 (1m 1f 192y, Good, GF, Aug 2)
Sun On The Run (IRE) 109 1 (1m 100y, Cork, Sft, Oct 18)
Suzi's Connoisseur 107 1 (7f 9y, Leic, Hvy, Oct 14)
Swan Song 105 5 (5f, Epso, Gd, Jun 7)
Sweet Lightning 105 5 (1m, Newb, Gd, Apr 12)
Tac De Boistron (FR) 119 2 (1m 6f, York, Gd, May 16)
Taghrooda 125 1 (1m 4f, Asco, Gd, Jul 26)
Tahira (GER) 105 2 (1m 2f 75y, Ches, Gd, Jun 14)
Take Cover 116 1 (5f, Good, GF, Aug 1)
Talent 105 3 (1m 3f 200y, Hayd, GS, Jul 5)
Tales Of Grimm (USA) 106 4 (1m, York, GS, May 15)
Talmada (USA) 106 2 (1m 2f, Newm, Gd, Oct 11)
Tapestry (IRE) 121 1 (1m 4f, York, Gd, Aug 21)

Tarana (IRE) 106 2 (1m 4f, List, Gd, Sep 17)
Tarfasha (IRE) 112 1 (1m 2f, Curr, GF, Sep 14)
Tariq Too 106 3 (7f, Thir, GS, Apr 12)
Tasaday (USA) 111 2 (1m 3f 5y, Newb, Sft, Sep 20)
Tawhid 110 4 (7f, Newm, Sft, Oct 17)
Telescope (IRE) 125 1 (1m 4f, Asco, GF, Jun 21)
Telmeyd 109 1 (6f, Asco, Gd, Oct 3)
Tenor (IRE) 115 5 (1m 1f, Newm, GF, Sep 27)
Tested 109 1 (7f 100y, Tipp, GF, Aug 28)
Tha'ir (IRE) 105 5 (1m 4f, Donc, Gd, Sep 13)
That Is The Spirit 105 1 (7f, Epso, Gd, Jun 6)
That's Plenty (IRE) 105 1 (1m, Curr, Hvy, May 24)
The Corsican (IRE) 105 1 (1m 2f 60y, Donc, GS, Sep 11)
The Fugue 125 1 (1m 2f, Asco, GF, Jun 18)
The Grey Gatsby (IRE) 126 1 (1m 2f, Leop, GF, Sep 13)
The Lark 106 5 (1m 2f 88y, York, GS, May 15)
The Rectifier (USA) 111 1 (1m, Sali, Gd, Jun 29)
Thistle Bird 115 1 (1m 2f, Curr, GF, Jun 29)
Tiger Cliff (IRE) 114 3 (1m 6f, York, Gd, May 16)
Times Up 112 3 (2m 88y, York, Gd, Aug 22)
Tinghir (IRE) 106 1 (1m 1f 103y, Wolw, SD, Oct 4)
Tobann (IRE) 105 3 (1m, Leop, GF, Sep 13)
Token Of Love 108 1 (1m, Hayd, Gd, Aug 9)
Toormore (IRE) 122 3 (1m, Asco, Hvy, Oct 18)
Top Notch Tonto (IRE) 117 2 (1m, York, Gd, Aug 21)
Torchlighter (IRE) 105 1 (1m 2f, Newj, Gd, Jul 10)
Toronado (IRE) 124 1 (1m, Asco, Gd, Jun 17)
Trade Storm 113 2 (7f, Hayd, GS, Jul 19)
Trading Leather (IRE) 116 3 (1m 2f, Leop, GF, Sep 13)
Tres Coronas (IRE) 108 2 (1m 2f 88y, York, Sft, May 14)
Treve (FR) 119 3 (1m 2f, Asco, GF, Jun 18)
Trinityelitedotcom (IRE) 109 2 (6f 1y, Linw, SD, Apr 18)

Tropics (USA) 117 2 (6f, Asco, Hvy, Oct 18)
True Story (IRE) 114 2 (1m 2f 7y, Wind, Gd, Aug 23)
Trumpet Major (IRE) 111 4 (1m 1f, Newm, GF, May 3)
Tullius (IRE) 121 4 (1m, Asco, Hvy, Oct 18)
Two For Two (IRE) 106 3 (1m, Ayr, GF, Sep 20)
Undrafted (USA) 116 4 (6f, Newj, GS, Jul 12)
Valonia 107 4 (7f, Donc, Gd, Sep 11)
Vancouverite 111 2 (1m 2f 6y, Newb, Gd, Jul 19)
Venus De Milo (IRE) 110 2 (1m 2f, Curr, GF, Jun 29)
Verrazano (USA) 122 2 (1m, Asco, Gd, Jun 17)
Viztoria (IRE) 108 1 (6f, Curr, Yld, Oct 12)
Volume 111 3 (1m 4f, Curr, GF, Jul 19)
Wadi Al Hattawi (IRE) 105 7 (1m 4f, Asco, GF, Jun 21)
Waila 106 2 (1m 4f 8y, Pont, Gd, Jun 22)
Wannabe Better (IRE) 107 1 (7f, Leop, GF, Jun 19)
Wannabe Yours (IRE) 114 1 (1m, Good, GF, Aug 1)
War Command (USA) 118 4 (1m, Asco, Gd, Jun 17)
Watchable 107 1 (6f, Curr, GF, Sep 14)
We'll Go Walking (IRE) 105 8 (1m 4f, Asco, Hvy, Oct 18)
Western Hymn 113 4 (1m 2f, Asco, Hvy, Oct 18)
Wexford Town (IRE) 105 5 (1m 6f, Leop, GF, Jul 17)
Whiplash Willie 113 2 (1m 5f 89y, Ches, GS, Aug 30)
Willing Foe (USA) 113 2 (1m 5f 61y, Newb, GS, Aug 16)
Wind Fire (USA) 105 1 (5f 6y, Sand, Gd, Jun 14)
Windfast (IRE) 108 4 (7f, Asco, Gd, Jun 18)
Windhoek 114 3 (1m 2f 88y, York, GF, Jul 26)
Windshear 113 4 (1m 6f 132y, Donc, Gd, Sep 13)
Winter Thunder 114 1 (1m 4f, Newm, Gd, Oct 4)
Yuften 116 5 (1m, Asco, Gd, Jun 17)
Zambucca (SAF) 105 5 (1m 2f 88y, York, GF, Jul 26)
Zarwaan 105 5 (1m, Asco, GF, Jun 19)
Zurigha (IRE) 109 3 (1m, Asco, Gd, Jul 25)

*Telescope (left) powers home
in the Hardwicke Stakes at
Royal Ascot under Ryan Moore*

TOPSPEED: LAST SEASON'S LEADING TWO-YEAR-OLDS

KEY: Horse name, best Topspeed figure, finishing position when earning figure, (details of race where figure was earned)

Acaster Malbis (FR) 84 2 (1m, Newb, GS, Sep 19)
Accepted (IRE) 86 5 (6f, York, Gd, Aug 23)
Adulation (IRE) 83 1 (5f, Catt, GF, Jul 2)
Agnes Stewart (IRE) 82 1 (1m, Donc, Gd, Sep 12)
Ahlan Emarati (IRE) 97 3 (6f, York, Gd, Aug 23)
Ainippe (IRE) 85 1 (5f, Naas, GF, Jul 23)
Aktabantay 89 2 (7f, Newj, GS, Jul 12)
Al Fareej (IRE) 85 2 (5f 34y, Newb, Sft, Aug 15)
Angelic Lord (IRE) 85 5 (6f, Newj, GF, Jul 10)
Anthem Alexander (IRE) 107 3 (6f, York, Gd, Aug 21)
Arabian Queen (IRE) 89 6 (5f, Asco, GF, Jun 18)
Astrelle (IRE) 80 1 (7f, Newj, GS, Aug 16)
Astrophysics 81 2 (5f, Donc, Gd, Sep 12)
Azmaam (IRE) 85 4 (7f, Newm, GF, Oct 4)
Baitha Alga (IRE) 98 1 (5f, Asco, GF, Jun 19)
Ballymore Castle (IRE) 83 5 (7f, Newm, GF, Oct 4)
Bamboccianti 81 1 (5f 89y, York, GF, Sep 7)
Bartel (IRE) 82 1 (7f 3y, Yarm, Gd, Sep 17)
Basateen (IRE) 99 1 (7f, Donc, Gd, Jul 24)
Beacon 88 3 (5f, Good, GF, Jul 29)
Belardo (IRE) 88 1 (7f, Newb, GS, Aug 16)
Best Of Times 85 1 (1m, Good, Gd, Aug 22)
Blackbriar 80 1 (6f, Cork, Gd, Aug 5)
Blue Aegean 81 1 (5f 13y, Nott, Sft, Jun 4)
Bocca Baciata (IRE) 81 1 (1m, Nava, Yld, Oct 8)
Bond's Girl 82 1 (6f 110y, Donc, Gd, Sep 11)
Bossy Guest (IRE) 86 3 (7f, Newm, GF, Oct 4)
Brando 80 2 (5f 89y, York, GS, Oct 10)
Bronze Maquette (IRE) 92 1 (5f 34y, Newb, Sft, Aug 15)
Burnt Sugar (IRE) 86 1 (5f 6y, Linw, SD, Aug 2)
Calypso Beat (USA) 81 1 (6f, Newj, GF, Jun 28)
Canny Kool 81 1 (5f, Beve, GF, Sep 17)
Cappella Sansevero 94 4 (6f, Newm, Sft, Oct 17)
Carry On Deryck 84 6 (7f, Donc, Gd, Sep 17)
Celestial Path (IRE) 81 1 (1m, Hayd, Gd, Sep 6)
Charming Thought 102 1 (6f, Newm, Sft, Oct 17)
Christophermarlowe (USA) 95 1 (1m 114y, Epso, Gd, Sep 28)
Clonard Street 80 1 (1m 100y, Galw, Sft, Aug 2)
Clouds Rest 81 1 (5f 34y, Newb, Gd, May 16)
Cock Of The North 84 4 (7f 16y, Sand, GS, Aug 30)
Code Red 90 1 (6f 15y, Nott, Gd, Oct 8)
Commemoration 95 1 (1m, Newm, Gd, Oct 11)
Cotai Glory 91 1 (5f, Good, GF, Jul 29)
Crafty Choice 86 1 (1m 1f, Nott, Sft, Oct 8)
Cursory Glance (USA) 106 2 (6f, York, Gd, Aug 21)
Dance Of Fire 80 1 (1m, Donc, Gd, Sep 13)
Dark Reckoning 83 1 (6f, Ayr, GF, Sep 20)
Diaz (IRE) 84 2 (7f, Hayd, GS, Jul 3)
Dick Whittington (IRE) 94 1 (6f 63y, Curr, GF, Jul 19)
Disegno (IRE) 84 2 (7f, Asco, Gd, Jul 26)
Dominada (IRE) 80 6 (7f, York, GF, Aug 20)
Dr No 81 1 (6f 15y, Nott, Gd, May 20)
Dutch Connection 101 1 (7f, York, GF, Aug 20)
East Coast Lady (IRE) 85 2 (6f 110y, Donc, Gd, Sep 11)
Elm Park 97 1 (1m, Newm, GF, Sep 27)
Encore D'or 81 1 (5f 216y, Wolw, SD, Oct 11)
Escalating 80 1 (5f, Kemw, SD, Apr 19)
Estidhkaar (IRE) 103 1 (7f, Newj, GS, Jul 12)
Evening Rain (USA) 83 1 (6f 1y, Linw, SD, Oct 15)
Explosive Lady (IRE) 81 2 (6f 63y, Curr, GF, Sep 14)
Fadhayyil (IRE) 100 2 (7f, Newm, Gd, Sep 26)
Faithful Creek (IRE) 81 3 (1m, Leop, Gd, Sep 13)
Fast Act (IRE) 89 2 (5f, Good, GF, Jul 29)
Faydhan (USA) 88 1 (6f, Hayd, GS, Jul 3)
Feeling Easy (IRE) 80 4 (6f 110y, Donc, Gd, Sep 11)
Field Game 85 1 (5f, Catt, GS, Oct 28)
Fieldsman (USA) 81 1 (7f, Epso, Gd, Sep 28)
Fit For The Job (IRE) 80 1 (7f, Galw, Sft, Aug 1)
Flaming Spear (IRE) 87 1 (6f, York, GF, Jul 12)

Flash Fire (IRE) 84 1 (6f 15y, Nott, GF, Aug 15)
Found (IRE) 85 3 (7f, Curr, GF, Sep 14)
Four Seasons (IRE) 83 1 (7f, Kemw, SD, Nov 5)
Fox Trotter (IRE) 84 4 (6f, Good, GF, Jul 31)
Fruity (IRE) 80 4 (6f 63y, Curr, GF, Sep 14)
Future Empire 87 3 (1m, Newm, Gd, Oct 11)
Geordie George (IRE) 80 3 (6f, York, GF, Aug 20)
Glenalmond (IRE) 95 4 (6f, York, Gd, Aug 23)
Gleneagles (IRE) 83 1 (7f, Curr, GF, Sep 14)
Good Contact (USA) 92 2 (1m 114y, Epso, Gd, Sep 28)
Handsome Dude 85 1 (5f 89y, York, GS, Oct 10)
Harold Peto (IRE) 80 1 (1m, Nava, Sft, Oct 22)
Harry's Dancer (IRE) 84 2 (5f, Thir, GF, Aug 1)
Hawkesbury 86 1 (7f, Donc, GF, Jun 27)
Haxby (IRE) 87 5 (5f, Asco, Gd, Jun 17)
Heartbreak Hero 89 2 (6f 110y, Donc, Gd, Sep 11)
High Celebrity (FR) 89 3 (6f, Newm, GF, Sep 27)
Home Cummins (IRE) 88 1 (6f 110y, Donc, Gd, Sep 11)
Home Of The Brave (IRE) 87 1 (6f, Newj, GF, Jul 25)
Hootenanny (USA) 106 1 (5f, Asco, Gd, Jun 17)
I Am Beautiful (IRE) 82 1 (6f, Curr, GF, Jun 29)
Itorio (IRE) 84 4 (6f 63y, Curr, GF, Jul 19)
Ivawood (IRE) 107 1 (6f, Good, GF, Jul 31)
Izzthatright (IRE) 83 1 (5f 212y, Catt, Gd, Aug 15)
Jack Naylor 81 1 (1m, Curr, Gd, Aug 31)
Jacobean (IRE) 85 2 (7f, Curr, Yld, Oct 12)
Jamaica (IRE) 94 4 (7f, York, GF, Aug 20)
Jeanne Girl (IRE) 81 2 (6f, Curr, GF, Jun 29)
John F Kennedy (IRE) 98 1 (1m, Leop, GF, Sep 13)
Juncart 81 1 (5f, Hayd, Sft, Oct 17)
Jungle Cat (IRE) 99 2 (6f, York, Gd, Aug 23)
Justice Good (IRE) 82 1 (5f 10y, Wind, Gd, Jun 2)
Kasb (IRE) 81 1 (7f, Newj, GF, Aug 23)
Kibaar 84 2 (6f, York, GF, Aug 20)
Kodi Bear (IRE) 89 1 (7f, Asco, Gd, Jul 26)
Kool Kompany (IRE) 91 2 (6f, Curr, Sft, Aug 10)
Lady Of Dubai 81 1 (1m, Newm, Gd, Sep 20)
Lexington Times (IRE) 85 3 (7f 16y, Sand, GS, Aug 30)
Lieutenant Kaffee (USA) 83 1 (7f, Hayd, GS, Jul 3)
Likely (GER) 86 1 (5f, Carl, Gd, May 26)
Limato (IRE) 90 1 (6f 8y, Newb, GF, Jul 18)
Littlemissblakeney 90 5 (5f, Asco, GF, Jun 18)
Lola Beaux 92 2 (7f, Curr, GF, Sep 28)
Lord Ben Stack (IRE) 82 1 (1m, Hayd, GS, Sep 4)
Louie De Palma 86 2 (6f, Good, GF, Jul 31)
Lucida (IRE) 103 1 (7f, Newm, Gd, Sep 26)
Maftool (USA) 103 1 (7f, Newm, Gd, Sep 25)
Make It Up 82 1 (7f, Good, Gd, Sep 2)
Malabar 83 4 (7f, Curr, GF, Sep 14)
Markaz (IRE) 95 2 (7f, Newm, Gd, Sep 25)
Marsh Hawk 90 1 (7f, Newj, Sft, Aug 9)
Marshall Jennings (IRE) 87 2 (1m, Donc, Gd, Sep 13)
Mattmu 89 1 (6f, York, GS, Oct 11)
Merdon Castle (IRE) 83 2 (5f 10y, Wind, GF, May 19)
Miami Carousel (IRE) 82 1 (6f, York, Sft, Oct 10)
Midterm Break (IRE) 90 1 (6f 63y, Curr, GF, Sep 14)
Mind Of Madness (IRE) 92 2 (5f, Asco, GF, Jun 19)
Moonraker 83 2 (5f, York, Gd, Aug 23)
Mubtaghaa (IRE) 91 3 (5f, Asco, Gd, Jun 17)
Muhaarar 100 1 (6f, York, Gd, Aug 23)
Mukhmal (IRE) 82 4 (5f, Good, GF, Jul 29)
Muraaqaba 83 1 (7f, Newj, Sft, Aug 9)
Nafaqa (IRE) 96 1 (7f, Donc, Gd, Sep 12)
Natural Pearl (IRE) 82 1 (1m 5y, Bath, Fm, Sep 14)
Nebulla 81 1 (1m 75y, Nott, GS, Nov 5)
New Providence 94 3 (7f, Newm, Gd, Sep 26)
Newsletter (IRE) 98 3 (5f, Asco, GF, Jun 18)
Order Of St George (IRE) 86 2 (1m 1f, Leop, Yld, Oct 26)
Osaila (IRE) 82 5 (7f, Curr, GF, Sep 14)
Outlaw Country (IRE) 87 2 (7f, Newm, GF, Oct 4)
Pamona (IRE) 86 1 (7f, Newm, Sft, Oct 22)
Parish Boy 88 1 (1m 1f, Leop, Yld, Oct 26)

Parsley (IRE) 82 2 (6f, Ayr, GF, Sep 20)
Peacock 93 3 (7f, Donc, Gd, Sep 12)
Percy Alleline 84 2 (7f, Good, Sft, Oct 12)
Primrose Valley 83 1 (5f, Newc, GF, Aug 22)
Prince Bonnaire 84 2 (6f, Ripo, Gd, Aug 16)
Profitable (IRE) 89 2 (5f, Hayd, Gd, Sep 26)
Publilia 84 1 (6f 5y, Hami, GF, Jul 18)
Pulcinella 84 2 (7f, Newm, Sft, Oct 17)
Qualify (IRE) 101 1 (7f, Curr, GF, Sep 28)
Queen Nefertiti (IRE) 81 1 (7f, Leop, Gd, Jun 12)
Rapid Applause 89 3 (6f 63y, Curr, GF, Jul 19)
Raydara (IRE) 83 1 (7f, Curr, GF, Aug 24)
Realtra (IRE) 84 4 (6f, York, Gd, Aug 21)
Restorer 92 2 (1m, Newm, Gd, Oct 11)
Richard Pankhurst 92 1 (7f, Asco, GF, Jun 21)
Risen Sun 85 5 (7f, Donc, Gd, Sep 12)
Rosie's Premiere (IRE) 89 1 (5f, Hayd, Gd, Sep 26)
Rotherwick 86 1 (1m 1f, Newm, GS, Nov 1)
Royal Navy Ship (USA) 90 1 (7f, Curr, Yld, Oct 12)
Royal Razalma (IRE) 84 1 (5f, Newm, Sft, Oct 17)
Rule The Waves (USA) 84 1 (1m 100y, Kill, Gd, Aug 22)
Russian Punch 87 1 (7f, Newb, Sft, Oct 25)
Salateen 88 1 (7f, Donc, Gd, Sep 10)
Sarista (IRE) 83 4 (5f, Asco, Gd, Jun 17)
Secret Brief (IRE) 89 1 (7f, Newm, GF, Oct 4)
Shagah (IRE) 86 2 (7f, Newb, Sft, Oct 25)
She's A Worldie (IRE) 81 3 (5f, Thir, GS, Aug 2)
Smuggler's Cove (IRE) 85 1 (7f, Dunw, SD, Oct 10)
Snoano 88 1 (1m, Newb, GS, Sep 19)
Son Of Africa 87 1 (6f, Good, GF, Aug 1)

Spanish Pipedream (USA) 91 4 (5f, Asco, GF, Jun 18)
Squats (IRE) 88 1 (5f, Asco, GF, Sep 6)
Stellar Glow (IRE) 91 3 (7f, Curr, GF, Sep 28)
Storm Rock 81 1 (1m, York, GS, Oct 10)
Strath Burn 90 1 (5f 34y, Newb, Gd, Jul 3)
Stroll Patrol 90 5 (7f, Newm, Gd, Sep 26)
Strong Chemistry 86 1 (7f, Kemw, SD, Sep 22)
Sulaalaat 83 1 (6f 15y, Nott, GF, Jul 31)
Sunset Sail 86 3 (6f, Good, GF, Aug 1)
Tamadhor (IRE) 83 1 (7f, Leop, GF, Sep 13)
Tendu 82 5 (6f, Newm, GF, Sep 27)
Terror (IRE) 90 1 (6f, Warw, GS, Aug 25)
The Great War (USA) 92 1 (6f, Curr, GF, Sep 28)
The Warrior (IRE) 88 6 (6f, Newm, Sft, Oct 17)
The Wow Signal (IRE) 85 1 (6f, Asco, Gd, Jun 17)
Tiggy Wiggy (IRE) 112 1 (6f, York, Gd, Aug 21)
Tigrilla (IRE) 92 4 (7f, Newm, Gd, Sep 26)
Tombelaine (USA) 88 2 (1m, Leop, GF, Sep 13)
Toocoolforschool (IRE) 100 1 (6f 8y, Newb, Sft, Sep 20)
Toscanini (IRE) 92 2 (6f 63y, Curr, GF, Jul 19)
Union Rose 92 2 (5f, Asco, Gd, Jun 17)
Very Special (IRE) 81 1 (6f 3y, Yarm, Gd, Sep 18)
Vimy Ridge 81 1 (6f, Thir, GF, Jul 25)
War Envoy (USA) 81 3 (6f, Naas, Yld, Jun 2)
What Say You (IRE) 86 1 (7f, Newj, Gd, Aug 22)
White Lake 91 4 (7f, Donc, Gd, Sep 12)
Yeenaan (FR) 82 1 (1m 67y, Wind, Hvy, Oct 20)
Zephuros (IRE) 83 1 (7f, Newj, GF, Jun 28)
Zuhoor Baynoona (IRE) 92 1 (5f, Muss, Gd, Oct 11)

TOPSPEED: LAST SEASON'S TOP PERFORMERS 3YO+

Abseil (USA) 89 1 (1m 3y, Yarm, Gd, Apr 21)
Absolutely So (IRE) 107 1 (7f, York, Gd, Aug 22)
Abstraction (IRE) 95 2 (5f, Tipp, GF, Aug 8)
Addictive Dream (IRE) 104 3 (5f, Epso, Gd, Jun 7)
Adelaide (IRE) 107 2 (1m 4f, Asco, GF, Jun 20)
Adventure Seeker (IRE) 94 2 (1m 6f, York, Gd, Aug 23)
Aertex (IRE) 87 1 (7f, Newb, GF, May 17)
Aetna 90 1 (6f, York, Sft, May 14)
Agent Murphy 89 1 (1m 1f, Sand, Gd, Jun 14)
Air Pilot 87 1 (1m 2f, Newm, Gd, Nov 1)
Ajjaadd (USA) 99 2 (5f, Donc, Sft, Oct 25)
Ajmany (IRE) 93 1 (1m 1f 198y, Sali, Gd, Oct 1)
Al Kazeem 119 2 (1m 2f, Asco, Hvy, Oct 18)
Al Saham 97 1 (1m 4f, Asco, GS, May 10)
Al Thakhira 87 3 (7f, Donc, Gd, Sep 11)
Albasharah (USA) 106 1 (1m 2f, Newm, Gd, Oct 11)
Alben Star (IRE) 103 4 (6f, Newm, GF, May 4)
Alejandro (IRE) 88 3 (7f, Hayd, GS, Jul 5)
Alex My Boy (IRE) 87 8 (1m 6f 132y, Donc, Gd, Sep 13)
Alfred Hutchinson 95 3 (1m 1y, Linw, SD, Apr 18)
Algar Lad 92 1 (5f, Asco, GF, Sep 6)
Alive Alive Oh 95 2 (1m 1f 100y, Gowr, Yld, Aug 13)
Aljamaaheer (IRE) 102 3 (6f, Newm, Gd, Apr 17)
Almargo (IRE) 96 2 (7f, Leop, GF, Sep 13)
Alwilda 93 3 (1m 5f, Linw, SD, Oct 30)
American Hope (USA) 98 2 (1m, Asco, Gd, Jul 26)
Amralah (IRE) 92 1 (1m 2f 95y, Hayd, Gd, Aug 9)
Ancient Sands (IRE) 94 6 (1m 4f, Naas, Yld, Oct 19)
Angel Gabrial (IRE) 92 1 (2m, Ripo, GS, Apr 26)
Annunciation 93 2 (6f, Pont, Gd, Apr 14)
Anodin 87 3 (1m, Asco, Gd, Jun 17)
Another Wise Kid (IRE) 97 2 (6f, Ripo, Gd, Aug 4)
Ansaab 88 1 (1m 4y, Pont, Gd, Apr 14)
Ansgar (IRE) 92 1 (7f, Donc, Gd, Sep 13)
Arab Dawn 91 2 (1m 4f, Linw, SD, Oct 15)
Arab Spring 110 1 (1m 4f, Asco, GF, Jun 21)
Arabian Comet (IRE) 91 2 (1m 6f, Good, GF, Jul 31)
Arnold Lane 87 3 (6f, Wind, GS, Jun 28)
Arod (IRE) 101 4 (1m 4f 10y, Epso, Gd, Jun 7)
Artigiano (USA) 93 2 (1m 75y, Nott, Sft, Jun 4)

Ashpan Sam 96 1 (6f, Epso, Gd, Jun 7)
Askaud (IRE) 95 6 (1m, York, GS, May 15)
Astaire (IRE) 99 2 (6f, York, Sft, May 14)
Astronereus (IRE) 89 2 (1m 4f, Asco, Gd, Aug 9)
Auction (IRE) 90 4 (1m, Asco, GF, Sep 6)
Aussie Reigns (IRE) 94 8 (1m 4f, Asco, GF, Jun 21)
Australia 119 1 (1m 4f 10y, Epso, Gd, Jun 7)
Avenue Gabriel 89 1 (1m, Naas, Yld, Oct 19)
Awake My Soul (IRE) 97 1 (1m 2f, Ayr, Sft, Aug 11)
Ayrad (IRE) 97 8 (1m 2f, Asco, Hvy, Oct 18)
B Fifty Two (IRE) 100 1 (5f 110y, Ches, GS, Aug 30)
Baccarat (IRE) 111 1 (6f, Asco, GF, Jun 21)
Balducci 97 3 (1m, York, Gd, Aug 21)
Baltic Knight (IRE) 94 2 (1m 67y, Wind, GS, Jun 28)
Balty Boys (IRE) 91 7 (1m 2f 7y, Sand, GS, Aug 30)
Bancnuanaheireann (IRE) 94 2 (1m, Newm, GS, Nov 1)
Baraweez (IRE) 95 1 (7f, Leop, GF, Sep 13)
Barkston Ash 93 3 (6f, Hayd, GS, May 24)
Barnet Fair 90 1 (6f, Good, GF, Aug 2)
Barracuda Boy (IRE) 93 1 (6f, Hayd, Gd, Sep 27)
Bartack (IRE) 91 1 (1m, Ripo, Gd, Aug 16)
Battalion (IRE) 87 3 (1m 4f 5y, Newb, Sft, Oct 25)
Bayrir (FR) 92 3 (1m 2f 150y, Dunw, SD, Oct 3)
Bazaar (IRE) 97 2 (1m 4f, Naas, Yld, Oct 19)
Beacon Lady 87 1 (1m 2f 18y, Epso, Sft, Aug 25)
Bear Behind (IRE) 92 1 (6f, Hayd, GS, May 24)
Beau Nash (IRE) 89 3 (7f, Good, Sft, May 24)
Belle D'or (USA) 87 2 (1m, Newm, Gd, Sep 26)
Bertiewhittle 91 6 (7f, Hayd, Gd, Apr 26)
Beyond Brilliance (IRE) 92 3 (1m 1f 100y, Gowr, Yld, Aug 13)
Big Break 88 4 (7f, Leop, GF, Jun 19)
Big Orange 88 4 (2m, Asco, GF, Jun 20)
Bilimbi (IRE) 89 1 (1m, Muss, GF, Apr 18)
Biographer 87 2 (2m, Asco, Hvy, Oct 18)
Black Shadow 87 2 (1m 2f 18y, Epso, Gd, Jun 7)
Blaine 91 3 (6f, Ayr, GF, Sep 20)
Blithe Spirit 92 1 (5f 16y, Ches, Sft, May 9)
Blue Hussar (IRE) 96 1 (1m 4f, Naas, Yld, Oct 19)
Blue Surf 94 3 (1m 4f 10y, Epso, Gd, Jun 7)
Bold Lass (IRE) 90 1 (1m, Asco, GF, Sep 6)

Bold Sniper 95 2 (1m 2f, Asco, GF, Jun 20)
Bold Thady Quill (IRE) 96 3 (7f, Leop, GF, Sep 13)
Bondesire 91 2 (6f, York, Gd, Jun 13)
Bookrunner (USA) 87 (1m, Newm, GF, May 3)
Boom And Bust (IRE) 88 (1m, York, Gd, Aug 21)
Boomerang Bob (IRE) 93 5 (6f, Asco, GF, Jun 21)
Boomshackerlacker (IRE) 87 8 (1m 2f, Asco, GF, Jun 20)
Borderlescott 90 5 (5f, York, GF, Jul 11)
Born In Bombay 91 1 (1m, Asco, GF, Jun 19)
Bow Creek (IRE) 106 2 (1m, Asco, GF, Jun 19)
Brae Hill (IRE) 96 1 (1m, Donc, Sft, Mar 29)
Bragging (USA) 88 2 (7f, Donc, Gd, Sep 11)
Brass Ring 96 4 (2m 2f, Newm, Gd, Oct 11)
Brazos (IRE) 92 3 (7f, Newb, GS, Apr 11)
Brendan Brackan (IRE) 99 3 (7f, Leop, GF, Jun 19)
Breton Rock (IRE) 96 1 (7f, Newb, GS, Aug 16)
Bronze Angel (IRE) 109 1 (1m, Asco, Hvy, Oct 18)
Brown Panther 101 1 (1m 6f, Curr, GF, Sep 14)
Buckstay (IRE) 90 2 (1m, Good, GF, Jul 29)
Bunker (IRE) 93 5 (1m 4f, Asco, GF, Jun 20)
Buonarroti (IRE) 92 (1m 4f, Naas, Yld, Oct 19)
Cafe Society (FR) 93 7 (1m 5f 61y, Newb, GS, Aug 16)
Caledonia Lady 94 3 (5f 11y, Bath, Fm, Apr 19)
Califante 89 4 (1m 100y, Kill, Gd, Jul 14)
Cannock Chase (USA) 95 1 (1m 2f, Asco, GF, Jun 19)
Capo Rosso (IRE) 98 1 (7f 32y, Wolw, SD, Oct 25)
Captain Cat (IRE) 103 1 (1m 1y, Linw, SD, Apr 18)
Captain Cullen (IRE) 91 1 (6f, Curr, Yld, Aug 31)
Captain Joy (IRE) 88 1 (7f, Dunw, SD, Oct 24)
Captain Ramius (IRE) 90 2 (6f, Donc, Sft, Mar 29)
Carla Bianca (IRE) 102 1 (1m 1f 100y, Gowr, Yld, Aug 13)
Caspian Prince (IRE) 101 2 (5f, Curr, Gd, Jul 20)
Cat O'mountain (USA) 98 1 (1m 2f 150y, Dunw, SD, Oct 3)
Cavalryman 92 4 (2m 88y, York, Gd, Aug 22)
Century (IRE) 92 2 (2m, Asco, GF, Jun 20)
Chance To Dance (IRE) 100 1 (1m 2f, Leop, GF, Jul 17)
Charm Spirit (IRE) 97 5 (1m, Newm, GF, May 3)
Chatez (IRE) 89 2 (1m, Hayd, Sft, May 10)
Chicago (IRE) 92 (1m 4f, Naas, Yld, Oct 19)
Chicquita (IRE) 92 3 (1m 4f, Asco, Hvy, Oct 18)
Chil The Kite 96 2 (1m, Asco, GF, Jun 18)
Cirrus Des Aigles (FR) 107 5 (1m 2f, Asco, Hvy, Oct 18)
Clayton 97 2 (1m 2f 18y, Epso, GS, Apr 23)
Clear Spring (IRE) 89 8 (6f, Ripo, Gd, Aug 16)
Clever Cookie 94 1 (1m 2f 88y, York, Sft, May 14)
Clockmaker (IRE) 89 1 (7f, Good, Gd, Jun 8)
Clon Brulee (IRE) 104 3 (1m 2f 7y, Sand, GS, Aug 30)
Cloudscape (IRE) 101 4 (1m 4f, Good, GF, Jul 30)
Colonel Mak 93 1 (6f, Ripo, Hvy, Jun 4)
Communicator 91 3 (1m 6f, Hayd, Gd, Sep 6)
Complicit (IRE) 93 3 (1m 2f 7y, Wind, Gd, Aug 23)
Compton Park 93 1 (6f, Thir, Gd, Aug 29)
Confessional 91 3 (6f, Ripo, Gd, Aug 16)
Connecticut 103 3 (1m 6f, York, Gd, Aug 23)
Continuum 89 9 (1m 4f, Asco, GF, Jun 21)
Contributer (IRE) 100 1 (1m 2f, Asco, GF, Jun 20)
Cosmic Cannonball (IRE) 92 4 (1m 1f 100y, Gowr, Yld, Aug 13)
Cosmic Chatter 88 3 (6f, Ripo, Hvy, Jun 4)
Cougar Mountain (IRE) 99 9 (5f, York, Gd, Aug 22)
Coulsty (IRE) 91 2 (6f 18y, Ches, GS, Aug 3)
Criteria (IRE) 89 3 (1m 6f 132y, Donc, GS, Sep 11)
Custom Cut (IRE) 96 1 (1m 4y, Pont, GF, Jul 27)
Dalkova 92 2 (1m 100y, Kill, Gd, Jul 14)
Danadana (IRE) 88 2 (1m 1f 192y, Good, Gd, Sep 24)
Dank 88 5 (1m 2f, Asco, GF, Jun 18)
Danzeno 102 2 (6f, Asco, Sft, Oct 4)
Dare To Achieve 95 1 (1m 4f 17y, Hami, GS, May 16)
Dark Emerald (IRE) 88 2 (7f, Hayd, GS, Jul 5)
Darwin (USA) 88 2 (7f, Curr, GF, Jul 19)
Dashing Star 96 5 (1m 4f, Asco, GF, Jun 21)
De Rigueur 96 2 (2m 2f, Newm, Gd, Oct 11)
Deeds Not Words (IRE) 93 1 (6f, Newj, Sft, Jul 11)
Demora 102 4 (5f, Asco, Gd, Jul 12)
Devilment 89 3 (1m 3f, Kemw, SD. Sep 24)
Dinkum Diamond (IRE) 94 3 (5f, Muss, Sft, Jun 14)
Discussiontofollow (IRE) 96 1 (5f, Asco, GF, Jul 12)

Dont Bother Me (IRE) 91 3 (6f, Newj, Gd, May 31)
Double Bluff (IRE) 102 1 (1m 4f, Good, GF, Aug 2)
Double Discount (IRE) 89 1 (1m 3f, Kemw, SD, Oct 8)
Dream Walker (FR) 90 1 (1m, Newm, GS, Nov 1)
Drifting Mist 88 3 (1m 4f, List, Gd, Sep 17)
Dubai Dynamo 88 1 (7f 122y, Ches, Gd, Jun 14)
Due Diligence (USA) 94 2 (6f, Asco, Gd, Jun 21)
Duke Of Firenze 97 1 (5f, Catt, Sft, Oct 18)
Dungannon 100 1 (5f, Donc, Sft, Oct 25)
Dusky Queen (IRE) 91 2 (7f, Newb, Sft, Oct 25)
Eagle Top 114 1 (1m 4f, Asco, GF, Jun 20)
Earth Drummer (IRE) 89 3 (7f 32y, Wolw, SD, Oct 25)
Eastern Impact (IRE) 94 1 (6f, Newm, GF, May 17)
Eastern Rules (IRE) 97 2 (7f, Leop, GF, Jun 19)
Ebanoran (IRE) 90 9 (1m 4f 10y, Epso, Gd, Jun 7)
Edge Of Sanity (IRE) 89 2 (2m, Curr, GF, Jun 28)
Educate 90 9 (1m 1f, Newm, GF, Sep 27)
Egyptian Warrior (IRE) 88 4 (1m 4f, Curr, GF, Jun 29)
Elhaame (IRE) 91 3 (1m 2f 95y, Hayd, Gd, Aug 9)
Elidor 97 4 (1m 4f, Asco, GF, Jun 21)
Elusivity (IRE) 88 2 (5f, York, GS, May 15)
Empire Storm (GER) 105 3 (1m, Asco, Hvy, Oct 18)
Energia Davos (BRZ) 102 1 (1m 2f 95y, Hayd, Gd, Aug 9)
Energia Fribby (BRZ) 89 1 (1m 4f 66y, Ches, Gd, Sep 13)
Energizer (GER) 89 6 (1m 2f, Asco, GF, Jun 20)
Epsom Hill (SWE) 96 2 (1m 6f, Hayd, Gd, Sep 6)
Ertijaal (IRE) 90 3 (6f 18y, Ches, GS, Aug 3)
Es Que Love (IRE) 103 2 (6f, Newm, Gd, Apr 17)
Estimate (IRE) 91 2 (2m 88y, York, Gd, Aug 22)
Etaab (USA) 88 1 (1m, Newm, Gd, Sep 26)
Eton Forever (IRE) 96 6 (6f, Asco, Hvy, Oct 18)
Eton Rifles (IRE) 88 2 (5f, Hayd, GS, May 31)
Euro Charline 96 1 (1m, Asco, Gd, Jul 25)
Examiner (IRE) 88 2 (1m 208y, York, GS, Oct 11)
Expert (IRE) 91 6 (6f, Newm, GF, May 17)
Extortionist (IRE) 106 3 (5f, York, Gd, Aug 22)
Extra Noble 89 2 (1m, Muss, Sft, Apr 18)
Eye Of The Storm (IRE) 89 1 (1m 4f, Leop, Yld, Aug 7)
Farquhar (IRE) 89 1 (1m 4f, Newm, Gd, Oct 11)
Farraaj (IRE) 110 1 (1m 2f 18y, Epso, Gd, Jun 6)
Fascinating Rock (IRE) 93 8 (1m 4f 10y, Epso, Gd, Jun 7)
Fattsota 93 4 (1m 2f 95y, Hayd, Gd, Aug 9)
Feedyah (USA) 89 6 (1m, Asco, GF, Jun 18)
Field Of Dream 92 1 (1m, Asco, GF, Jun 18)
Fiesolana (IRE) 90 4 (1m, Asco, GF, Jun 18)
Fire Fighting (IRE) 91 1 (1m 4f, Newm, Gd, Oct 11)
Fire Ship 94 2 (1m, Newm, Gd, Nov 1)
Flight Risk (IRE) 91 4 (6f, Curr, Sft, Aug 10)
Flintshire 92 2 (1m 4f 10y, Epso, Gd, Jun 7)
Forever Now 98 6 (1m 6f 132y, Donc, Gd, Sep 13)
Forgotten Rules (IRE) 89 1 (2m, Asco, Hvy, Oct 18)
Forgotten Voice (IRE) 93 4 (1m 4f, Asco, GF, Jun 21)
Fort Bastion (IRE) 98 2 (1m, York, GS, May 15)
Fountain Of Youth (IRE) 93 1 (5f, Curr, GF, Jun 28)
Foxtrot Romeo (IRE) 95 2 (5f 216y, Wolw, SD, Sep 6)
Free Eagle (IRE) 115 3 (1m 2f, Asco, Hvy, Oct 18)
Freedom's Light 98 1 (1m 4f 8y, Pont, Gd, Jun 22)
French Navy 101 1 (1m, Newm, Gd, Nov 1)
From Frost 88 1 (1m 4f, Souw, SD, Jun 30)
Fury 91 1 (1m 14y, Chep, Hvy, Aug 25)
G Force (IRE) 102 6 (5f, York, Gd, Aug 22)
Gabrial (IRE) 90 4 (1m 4f 66y, Ches, Gd, Sep 13)
Gabrial's Kaka (IRE) 99 5 (1m, York, Gd, Aug 21)
Gabrial's King (IRE) 90 2 (1m 5f 194y, Wolw, SD, Nov 7)
Gabriel's Lad (IRE) 98 4 (7f, York, Gd, Aug 22)
Gamesome (FR) 89 2 (6f, Wind, GS, Jun 28)
Garswood 96 2 (7f, Newj, Sft, Jun 28)
Gatewood 89 1 (1m 4f, Asco, GS, May 10)
Gathering Power (IRE) 92 7 (6f, Asco, Hvy, Oct 18)
George Guru 91 5 (1m 1y, Linw, SD, Apr 18)
Georgian Bay (IRE) 88 1 (7f, Kemw, SD, Apr 19)
Gifted Girl (IRE) 91 2 (1m 1f 198y, Sali, GF, Aug 13)
Giovanni Boldini (USA) 92 3 (7f, Asco, Gd, Jun 18)
Gladiatrix 89 1 (5f 10y, Wind, GS, Jul 7)
Glen Moss (IRE) 99 3 (7f, York, Gd, Aug 22)
Glenard 90 5 (1m 6f, Hayd, Gd, Sep 6)

FOR YOUR FREE 30-DAY TRIAL GO TO **racingpost.com/ipad**

Glorious Empire (IRE) 96 1 (7f, Newj, Sft, Aug 14)
Glorious Protector (IRE) 92 1 (1m 3f 135y, Wind, Gd, Aug 23)
Glory Awaits (IRE) 102 2 (7f, York, Gd, Aug 22)
Go Far 99 1 (5f 216y, Wolw, SD, Sep 6)
God Willing 88 4 (1m 208y, York, GS, Oct 11)
Golden Steps (FR) 89 1 (6f, Donc, Gd, Jun 15)
Golden Town (IRE) 98 1 (1m, Newj, Sft, Jul 12)
Goldream 100 2 (5f, Hayd, Gd, Sep 27)
Gordon Lord Byron (IRE) 107 1 (6f, Asco, Hvy, Oct 18)
Graceful Grit (IRE) 90 4 (1m, Asco, GF, Jun 18)
Grandeur (IRE) 92 1 (1m 1f 192y, Good, Gd, Sep 24)
Graphic (IRE) 90 2 (1m 114y, Epso, Gd, Jun 6)
Great Minds (IRE) 92 1 (6f, Curr, Hvy, May 25)
Green Door (IRE) 94 2 (5f 16y, Ches, GF, Jul 11)
Green Howard 91 1 (1m, Muss, Gd, Sep 5)
Gregorian (IRE) 99 3 (6f, Newj, GS, Jul 12)
Grendisar (IRE) 99 2 (1m 4f, Linw, SD, Apr 18)
Grey Mirage 93 4 (1m 1y, Linw, SD, Apr 18)
Groovejet 93 2 (1m 6f 132y, Donc, GS, Sep 11)
Groundbreaking 88 (1m 4f, Asco, GF, Jun 21)
Guest Of Honour (IRE) 94 1 (1m, Asco, GF, Jul 12)
Hall Of Mirrors (IRE) 92 5 (1m 2f, Asco, GF, Jun 20)
Hamelin (IRE) 96 2 (1m 4f, Asco, GS, May 10)
Hamza (IRE) 105 1 (6f, Newm, Gd, Apr 17)
Hartnell 95 7 (1m 6f 132y, Donc, Gd, Sep 13)
Hassle (IRE) 90 6 (1m 6f, Hayd, Gd, Sep 6)
Havana Cooler (IRE) 96 3 (1m 4f, Asco, GF, Jun 21)
Hay Chewed (IRE) 88 2 (5f 6y, Sand, Gd, Jun 14)
Heaven's Guest (IRE) 104 1 (7f, Newj, GS, Jul 12)
Heavy Metal 90 5 (1m, Asco, Hvy, Oct 18)
Helene Happy Star (IRE) 89 5 (1m 2f, Asco, GF, Jun 19)
Here Comes When (IRE) 95 1 (7f 122y, Ches, Sft, May 9)
Hi There (IRE) 89 4 (1m 2f 18y, Epso, GS, Apr 23)
Hidden Gold (IRE) 95 1 (1m 5f, Linw, SD, Oct 30)
High On Life 100 1 (5f, Hayd, Gd, Sep 27)
Highland Acclaim (IRE) 98 2 (6f, York, GS, Oct 11)
Highland Colori (IRE) 95 5 (7f, York, Gd, Aug 22)
Highland Knight (IRE) 99 2 (1m 1y, Linw, SD, Apr 18)
Hillbilly Boy (IRE) 95 1 (7f, Newj, GS, May 30)
Hillstar 100 2 (1m 4f, Asco, GF, Jun 21)
Hoodna (IRE) 99 3 (7f, Newj, GS, Jul 12)
Hoof It 97 3 (6f, Kemw, SD, Mar 29)
Hors De Combat 106 2 (1m, Good, GF, Aug 1)
Hot Streak (IRE) 103 5 (5f, York, Gd, Aug 22)
Huntsmans Close 91 1 (6f, Ayr, GF, Sep 20)
Ifwecan 88 1 (1m, Muss, Gd, Jun 7)
Ihtimal (IRE) 91 3 (1m, Newm, GF, May 4)
Inchila 90 4 (1m 4f 10y, Epso, Gd, Jun 6)
Indignant 93 3 (6f, York, GF, Jul 11)
Ingleby Angel (IRE) 90 2 (1m, Ayr, Gd, Jul 21)
Integral 102 1 (1m, Asco, GF, Jun 18)
Intibaah 98 5 (6f, Asco, Hvy, Oct 18)
Intransigent 98 1 (6f 18y, Ches, GS, Aug 3)
Invincible Strike (IRE) 88 4 (5f 216y, Wolw, SD, Sep 6)
Inxile (IRE) 89 1 (5f, Good, GF, Jul 29)
It's Somewhat (USA) 103 3 (1m 4f, Good, GF, Jul 30)
Jack Dexter 101 3 (6f, Asco, Hvy, Oct 18)
Jamesie (IRE) 96 2 (6f, Curr, Sft, Aug 10)
Joey's Destiny (IRE) 91 1 (6f 15y, Nott, Gd, Jun 12)
John Constable (IRE) 91 2 (1m 2f, Curr, Sft, May 24)
Jordan Princess 95 2 (1m 4f, Newm, Gd, Sep 26)
Joyeuse 99 2 (6f, York, GF, Jul 11)
Justice Day (IRE) 101 1 (5f, Asco, GS, Oct 4)
Justineo 89 6 (5f, Newm, GF, May 3)
Kernoff (IRE) 93 1 (5f, Curr, GF, Jun 27)
Khubala (IRE) 88 2 (5f, Asco, Sft, Oct 4)
Kickboxer (IRE) 96 2 (5f, Asco, GS, Oct 4)
Kimberella 93 1 (6f 18y, Ches, GF, Jul 12)
Kingman 107 2 (1m, Newm, GF, May 3)
Kings Fete 95 2 (1m 4f, Good, GF, Aug 2)
Kingsgate Native (IRE) 97 2 (5f 6y, Sand, GF, Jul 5)
Kingston Hill 116 2 (1m 4f 10y, Epso, Gd, Jun 7)
Kiyoshi 92 1 (7f, Donc, Gd, Sep 11)
Kosika (USA) 90 1 (1m, Newb, Gd, Jul 19)
L'amour De Ma Vie (USA) 99 2 (1m, Asco, GF, Jun 18)
La Banderilla (FR) 91 4 (1m 2f, Newm, Gd, Oct 11)

Ladies Are Forever 101 1 (6f, York, GF, Jul 11)
Lady Lara (IRE) 93 5 (1m, Asco, GF, Jun 18)
Lady Pimpernel 96 1 (1m 1f 198y, Sali, GF, Aug 13)
Lahaag 89 9 (1m 4f, Asco, GF, Jun 21)
Lahinch Classics (IRE) 88 2 (1m 2f 6y, Newb, Gd, May 16)
Lancelot Du Lac (ITY) 93 5 (5f, Donc, Sft, Oct 25)
Leading Light (IRE) 92 1 (1m 6f, Curr, GF, Aug 24)
Leitir Mor (IRE) 92 5 (7f, Leop, GF, Jun 19)
Levitate 90 4 (1m, Asco, Hvy, Oct 18)
Lexi's Hero (IRE) 90 1 (6f 18y, Ches, GS, Aug 16)
Lightning Moon (IRE) 99 1 (6f, Asco, Sft, Oct 4)
Lightning Thunder 93 2 (1m, Newm, GF, May 4)
Lily Rules (IRE) 90 2 (1m 2f 88y, York, Sft, May 14)
Line Of Reason (IRE) 97 1 (5f, York, GF, Jul 11)
Linguine (FR) 88 3 (1m 4f 17y, Hami, GS, Aug 22)
Livia's Dream (IRE) 92 4 (1m 5f, Linw, SD, Oct 30)
Llanarmon Lad (IRE) 96 2 (1m 2f 95y, Hayd, Gd, Aug 9)
Lord Van Percy 90 2 (1m 6f, York, Gd, Aug 23)
Louis The Pious 102 1 (6f, Ayr, GF, Sep 20)
Lucky Beggar (IRE) 89 1 (5f 34y, Newb, GS, Apr 11)
Lucky Bridle (IRE) 90 8 (1m 4f, Naas, Yld, Oct 19)
Lustrous 88 1 (1m, York, Gd, May 16)
Lyn Valley 93 1 (1m 1f 192y, Good, GF, Jul 31)
Maarek 105 1 (6f, York, Sft, May 14)
Madame Chiang 96 1 (1m 4f, Asco, Hvy, Oct 18)
Madeed 90 3 (1m 2f 95y, Hayd, Gd, Sep 5)
Magician 102 8 (1m 2f, Asco, GF, Jun 18)
Magnolia Beach (IRE) 93 2 (1m 2f, Leop, GF, Jul 17)
Magnus Maximus 90 1 (6f, Newm, Gd, Apr 16)
Manderley (IRE) 89 4 (1m, Newm, GF, May 4)
Marmalady (IRE) 89 1 (5f 161y, Bath, Fm, Sep 13)
Marsh Daisy 91 1 (1m 1f 192y, Good, Sft, May 22)
Marzocco (USA) 99 5 (1m 6f 132y, Donc, Gd, Sep 13)
Masamah (IRE) 94 5 (5f, Asco, GF, Jul 12)
Mass Rally 91 4 (6f, York, Sft, May 14)
Masterpaver 90 1 (1m 5f 194y, Wolw, SD, Nov 7)
Maverick Wave (USA) 95 2 (1m, Asco, Hvy, Oct 18)
Mecca's Angel (IRE) 108 1 (5f 34y, Newb, Sft, Sep 20)
Midnite Angel (IRE) 88 1 (1m, Newj, Sft, Jun 28)
Mighty Yar (IRE) 88 1 (1m 4f, Newm, GF, May 4)
Milly's Gift 95 2 (5f, Asco, GF, Jul 12)
Minalisa 89 2 (6f, Ayr, GF, Sep 20)
Miner's Lamp (IRE) 91 6 (1m 4f, Asco, GF, Jun 20)
Miss France 94 1 (1m, Newm, GF, May 4)
Miss Marjurie (IRE) 94 2 (1m 5f, Linw, SD, Oct 30)
Missunited (IRE) 96 1 (1m 6f, Good, GF, Jul 31)
Mizzou (IRE) 88 1 (1m 4f, Donc, GF, Aug 2)
Monsieur Joe (IRE) 104 1 (5f, York, GS, May 15)
Montaly 88 1 (1m 3f 200y, Hayd, Gd, Aug 9)
Morache Music 88 2 (6f, Hayd, GS, Jul 5)
More Questions (IRE) 88 2 (5f 182y, Nava, GF, Jun 14)
Mount Athos (IRE) 90 1 (1m 5f 61y, Newb, GF, May 17)
Mount Logan (IRE) 92 1 (1m 4f, Donc, Gd, Sep 13)
Move In Time 90 2 (5f 89y, York, GF, Aug 20)
Moviesta (USA) 106 4 (5f, York, Gd, Aug 22)
Mubaraza (IRE) 97 2 (2m, Ripo, GS, Apr 26)
Mukhadram 121 3 (1m 4f, Newm, Gd, Oct 26)
Mull Of Killough (IRE) 92 2 (1m, Asco, GF, Jul 12)
Music Master 100 1 (6f, Warw, Gd, Apr 24)
Mustajeeb 105 1 (7f, Asco, Gd, Jun 18)
Mutakayyef 92 2 (1m 2f, Asco, GF, Jun 19)
Muteela 95 1 (1m, Asco, GF, Jun 18)
Muthmir (IRE) 99 1 (6f, York, GF, Jul 26)
Mutual Regard (IRE) 100 1 (1m 6f, York, Gd, Aug 23)
Muwaary 99 2 (7f, Asco, Gd, Jun 18)
My Good Brother (IRE) 94 3 (5f, Curr, Gd, Jul 20)
Naadirr (IRE) 92 1 (6f, York, GF, Sep 7)
Nabucco 88 1 (1m 4f, Newm, Gd, Sep 26)
Nautilus 102 1 (1m 6f, Hayd, Gd, Sep 6)
Navajo Chief 102 1 (1m, York, GS, May 15)
Nearly Caught (IRE) 93 2 (2m 45y, Hayd, Gd, May 24)
New Story 88 1 (1m 2f 95y, Hayd, Gd, Jul 18)
Nicholascopernicus (IRE) 89 1 (1m 2f 7y, Wind, Sft, Aug 11)
Night Of Thunder (IRE) 109 1 (1m, Newm, GF, May 3)
Ninjago 103 3 (6f, Newm, GF, May 4)
Noble Citizen (USA) 90 6 (1m 1y, Linw, SD, Apr 18)

Noble Mission 120 1 (1m 2f, Asco, Hvy, Oct 18)
Noble Protector 97 1 (1m 4f, Newj, GF, Jul 19)
Noble Silk 91 4 (1m 5f 194y, Wolw, SD, Nov 7)
Noble Storm (USA) 92 1 (5f, Thir, Gd, May 17)
Noozhoh Canarias (SPA) 95 6 (1m, Newm, GF, May 3)
Normal Equilibrium 88 1 (5f, Ling, Gd, May 9)
Observational 92 6 (1m 4f, Good, GF, Jul 30)
Ocean Tempest 91 1 (7f 122y, Ches, GS, Aug 30)
Odeon 94 4 (1m 2f 88y, York, GS, May 15)
Olympic Glory (IRE) 99 1 (1m, Newb, GF, May 17)
Online Alexander (IRE) 89 1 (5f, York, Gd, Aug 23)
Open Eagle (IRE) 89 1 (1m 2f, Redc, Sft, Nov 4)
Orchestra (IRE) 101 1 (1m 4f 66y, Ches, Sft, May 8)
Our Gabrial (IRE) 89 1 (1m 4f, Asco, Gd, Aug 9)
Out Do 96 1 (6f, Ripo, Gd, Aug 16)
Outback Traveller (IRE) 100 1 (7f, Asco, Gd, Oct 3)
Palace (IRE) 89 1 (1m 100y, Kill, Gd, Jul 14)
Pale Mimosa (IRE) 92 1 (2m 88y, York, Gd, Aug 22)
Pallasator 102 1 (1m 4f, Asco, GF, Jul 27)
Panama Hat 100 1 (1m 2f 150y, Dunw, SD, Aug 17)
Parish Hall (IRE) 90 6 (1m 2f, Asco, GF, Jun 18)
Pearl Blue (IRE) 94 1 (5f, Newj, GS, Jul 10)
Pearl Secret 102 2 (5f, Hayd, Sft, May 24)
Pelerin (IRE) 88 1 (1m, Dunw, SD, Oct 31)
Penhill 88 1 (1m 4f 10y, Ripo, Sft, Jul 19)
Penny Drops 89 2 (7f, Good, Sft, May 24)
Perfect Blessings (IRE) 92 1 (6f, Donc, Sft, Apr 26)
Pether's Moon (IRE) 99 7 (1m 2f, Asco, Hvy, Oct 18)
Pinzolo 94 3 (1m 4f 66y, Ches, Gd, Sep 13)
Pipers Note 92 5 (6f, Ripo, Gd, Aug 16)
Piri Wango (IRE) 100 4 (7f, Leop, GF, Sep 13)
Pollyana (IRE) 91 4 (1m 4f, Asco, Hvy, Oct 18)
Polybius 89 1 (6f, Kemw, SD, Sep 22)
Pomology (USA) 93 1 (1m 3f 200y, Hayd, GS, Jul 5)
Postponed (IRE) 110 1 (1m 4f, York, GF, Aug 20)
Presburg (IRE) 90 1 (1m 2f 7y, Sand, GF, Jul 4)
Prince Bishop (IRE) 100 1 (1m 4f, Kemw, SD, Sep 6)
Prince Of All 96 2 (1m 2f 150y, Dunw, SD, Oct 3)
Prince Of Johanne (IRE) 100 3 (1m, York, GS, May 15)
Princess Loulou (IRE) 88 2 (1m, Good, GS, May 3)
Princess Pearlita (IRE) 88 2 (1m 4f, Naas, Yld, Oct 19)
Producer 89 4 (1m 2f 88y, York, GF, Jul 26)
Professor 108 2 (6f, Asco, GF, Jun 21)
Provenance 89 5 (1m 2f, Newm, Gd, Oct 11)
Pupil (IRE) 88 2 (1m 114y, Epso, Gd, Sep 28)
Purr Along 90 3 (1m, Asco, GF, Jun 18)
Quartz (IRE) 90 1 (1m 1f 100y, Gowr, Gd, Sep 21)
Queen Catrine (IRE) 101 2 (1m, Asco, GF, Jun 18)
Queen Of Ice 100 1 (1m 4f, Newm, Gd, Sep 26)
Quick Jack (IRE) 88 3 (2m 2f, Newm, Gd, Oct 11)
Racy 99 1 (5f, Asco, GF, Jul 27)
Rangali 101 7 (5f, York, Gd, Aug 22)
Rawaki (IRE) 103 2 (1m 4f 17y, Hami, GS, May 16)
Rebellious Guest 93 3 (1m 3f, Kemw, SD, Mar 29)
Reckless Abandon 102 2 (5f, Donc, Gd, Sep 10)
Red Avenger (USA) 94 6 (1m, York, Gd, Aug 21)
Red Cadeaux 99 4 (1m 5f 61y, Newb, GS, Aug 16)
Red Galileo 98 5 (1m 4f 10y, Epso, Gd, Jun 7)
Red Pike (IRE) 93 1 (6f, Newm, GS, Oct 31)
Red Refraction (IRE) 89 2 (6f, Ripo, Gd, Aug 16)
Red Stargazer (IRE) 94 1 (1m, Hayd, Sft, May 10)
Rekdhat (IRE) 90 1 (1m, Muss, GF, Sep 28)
Remember 91 2 (6f, Newj, Sft, Jul 11)
Rene Mathis (GER) 91 3 (6f, York, GF, Jul 26)
Reroute (IRE) 89 2 (5f 11y, Bath, Fm, Apr 19)
Rewaaya (IRE) 92 1 (1m 4f, Newm, GS, Sep 20)
Rivellino 101 3 (6f, Asco, GF, Jun 21)
Rizeena (IRE) 88 1 (1m, Asco, Gd, Jun 20)
Roachdale House (IRE) 89 1 (7f 2y, Ches, GS, Jun 28)
Robot Boy (IRE) 102 3 (5f, Asco, GF, Jul 12)
Rocky Bleier 88 1 (1m 4f, Naas, Yld, Oct 19)
Rocky Ground (IRE) 97 6 (6f, Asco, GF, Jun 21)
Romsdal 109 3 (1m 4f 10y, Epso, Gd, Jun 7)
Roseburg (IRE) 96 1 (1m 2f 95y, Hayd, GS, Jul 5)
Royal Rascal 92 2 (7f, Newc, GF, Jun 28)
Ruler Of The World (IRE) 93 9 (1m 2f, Asco, Hvy, Oct 18)

Russian Realm 88 7 (1m, York, Gd, Aug 21)
Russian Soul (IRE) 99 3 (5f, Tipp, GF, Aug 8)
Ruwaiyan (USA) 90 2 (7f, Good, Gd, Jun 8)
Rydan (IRE) 93 1 (1m 3f, Kemw, SD, Sep 24)
Rye House (IRE) 94 5 (1m 2f 88y, York, Sft, May 14)
Saab Almanal 90 6 (1m 2f 88y, York, GS, May 15)
Salutation (IRE) 97 2 (1m 4f, Asco, GF, Jun 21)
Scotland (GER) 102 3 (1m 4f, Asco, GF, Jun 20)
Scream Blue Murder (IRE) 96 1 (6f, Curr, Sft, Aug 10)
Seal Of Approval 97 3 (1m 5f 61y, Newb, GS, Aug 16)
Second Step (IRE) 88 3 (1m 4f, Good, GF, Aug 2)
Secret Gesture 96 2 (1m 2f 88y, York, GF, Jul 26)
Secret Number 89 2 (1m 4f, Kemw, SD, Sep 6)
Secret Witness 89 5 (5f, York, GS, May 15)
Secretinthepark 91 6 (6f, Newm, GF, May 4)
Seeking Magic 102 2 (5f, Epso, Gd, Jun 7)
Seismos (IRE) 103 1 (1m 5f 61y, Newb, GS, Aug 16)
Semeen 90 1 (1m 6f 17y, Yarm, Gd, Sep 18)
Sennockian Star 95 2 (1m 2f 75y, Ches, Sft, May 8)
Shamshon (IRE) 89 1 (5f, York, Gd, May 15)
Sharestan (IRE) 92 5 (1m 4f, Asco, GF, Jun 21)
Shea Shea (SAF) 89 (5f, York, Gd, Aug 22)
Sheikhzayedroad 106 6 (1m 2f, Asco, Hvy, Oct 18)
Shifting Power 99 4 (1m, Newm, GF, May 3)
Short Squeeze (IRE) 105 1 (1m, York, Gd, Aug 21)
Silent Bullet (IRE) 91 2 (7f 16y, Sand, Gd, Jun 14)
Silk Sari 105 1 (1m 6f 132y, Donc, GS, Sep 11)
Silvanus (IRE) 90 1 (5f, Catt, GF, Jul 23)
Silwana 90 3 (1m 6f, Leop, GF, Sep 13)
Sir Guy Porteous (IRE) 90 2 (1m 114y, Epso, GF, Jul 10)
Sir Maximilian (IRE) 100 1 (5f, Curr, Gd, Jul 20)
Sirius Prospect (USA) 90 8 (6f, Asco, GF, Jun 21)
Sirvino 88 2 (1m 6f, Muss, GF, Apr 18)
Sky Hunter 106 1 (1m 4f 5y, Newb, Sft, Oct 25)
Sky Lantern 90 5 (1m, Asco, GF, Jun 18)
Slade Power (IRE) 106 1 (6f, Newj, GS, Jul 12)
Slipper Orchid (IRE) 90 1 (1m, Dunw, SD, Oct 10)
Smoothtalkinrascal (IRE) 97 (5f, Epso, Gd, Jun 7)
Snow Sky 105 2 (1m 4f, York, GF, Aug 20)
Sole Power 111 1 (5f, York, Gd, Aug 22)
Soviet Rock (IRE) 91 2 (1m 1f 198y, Sali, Gd, Oct 1)
Spa's Dancer (IRE) 97 4 (1m 2f 7y, Sand, GS, Aug 30)
Special Meaning 89 1 (1m 4f, Good, GS, May 3)
Speed Hawk 89 3 (5f 216y, Wolw, SD, Sep 6)
Spinatrix 107 1 (6f, York, GS, Oct 11)
Squire Osbaldeston (IRE) 88 4 (1m 2f 75y, Ches, Sft, May 8)
Srucahan (IRE) 90 1 (6f, Curr, Sft, Apr 13)
Sruthan (IRE) 92 1 (7f, Curr, Yld, Apr 13)
Stand My Ground (IRE) 93 2 (1m, Donc, Sft, Mar 29)
Stay De Night (IRE) 89 6 (7f, Leop, GF, Sep 13)
Steeler (IRE) 90 4 (1m, Good, GF, Aug 1)
Stepper Point 109 2 (5f, York, Gd, Aug 22)
Steps 111 4 (5f, Epso, Gd, Jun 7)
Storm King 89 1 (7f 100y, Beve, GF, Aug 30)
Stormardal (IRE) 88 5 (1m 2f 18y, Epso, Gd, Sep 28)
Strictly Silver (IRE) 91 1 (1m 2f, Ayr, GF, Jun 21)
Sultannia 88 2 (1m 3f 200y, Hayd, GS, Jul 5)
Sun On The Run (IRE) 93 1 (7f, Cork, Hvy, Apr 6)
Supplicant 90 9 (6f, Ripo, Gd, Aug 16)
Swan Song 100 5 (5f, Epso, Gd, Jun 7)
Swivel 91 1 (1m 4f 17y, Hami, GS, Aug 22)
Tac De Boistron (FR) 88 1 (2m, Asco, Sft, Apr 30)
Taghrooda 121 1 (1m 4f, Asco, Gd, Jul 26)
Tahira (GER) 90 7 (1m 2f 88y, York, Sft, May 14)
Take Cover 106 1 (5f, Good, Gd, Jul 31)
Talent 91 4 (1m 6f, Good, GF, Jul 31)
Tales Of Grimm (USA) 100 4 (1m, York, GS, May 15)
Talmada (USA) 98 2 (1m 2f, Newm, Gd, Oct 11)
Tangerine Trees 89 (5f, Epso, Gd, Jun 7)
Tapestry (IRE) 94 1 (1m 4f, York, Gd, Aug 21)
Tarana (IRE) 99 2 (1m 4f, List, Gd, Sep 17)
Tarfasha (IRE) 92 2 (1m 4f 10y, Epso, Gd, Jun 6)
Tarziyna (IRE) 90 5 (1m 1f 100y, Gowr, Yld, Aug 13)
Tatlisu (IRE) 91 3 (6f, Ripo, Gd, Aug 16)
Telescope (IRE) 122 2 (1m 4f, Asco, Gd, Jul 26)
Telmeyd 96 1 (6f, Asco, Gd, Oct 3)

Treve makes history at Longchamp by recording back-to-back wins in the Arc

Tenor (IRE) 97 5 (1m 1f, Newm, GF, Sep 27)
Tha'ir (IRE) 89 3 (1m 2f 7y, Sand, GF, Jul 4)
That Is The Spirit 97 1 (7f, York, GS, May 14)
That's Plenty (IRE) 89 3 (1m 2f 75y, Ches, Sft, May 8)
The Fugue 109 1 (1m 2f, Asco, GF, Jun 18)
The Grey Gatsby (IRE) 101 1 (1m 2f 88y, York, GS, May 15)
The Rectifier (USA) 96 3 (1m, Hayd, Gd, Apr 26)
This Is The Day 88 1 (1m 2f 95y, Hayd, Gd, Sep 27)
Timeless Call 92 1 (5f, Cork, GF, Jun 15)
Times Up 92 3 (2m 88y, York, Gd, Aug 22)
Tobann (IRE) 89 2 (7f, Curr, GF, Jun 28)
Toe The Line (IRE) 88 1 (1m 6f, Leop, GF, Sep 13)
Tooreen Legend (IRE) 88 2 (1m 4f, Curr, GF, Jun 29)
Toormore (IRE) 100 1 (1m, Newm, Gd, Apr 17)
Top Diktat 88 1 (1m 2f 7y, Wind, Sft, Apr 28)
Top Notch Tonto (IRE) 110 2 (1m, York, Gd, Aug 21)
Torchlighter (IRE) 92 1 (1m 2f, Newj, Gd, Jul 10)
Toronado (IRE) 93 1 (1m, Asco, Gd, Jun 17)
Totalize 91 1 (1m 6f, York, Gd, Jun 13)
Trading Leather (IRE) 105 5 (1m 4f, Asco, Gd, Jul 26)
Tres Coronas (IRE) 104 2 (1m 2f 88y, York, Sft, May 14)
Treve (FR) 103 3 (1m 2f, Asco, GF, Jun 18)
Trinityelitedotcom (IRE) 97 1 (6f, Kemw, SD, Mar 29)
Tropics (USA) 102 2 (6f, Asco, Hvy, Oct 18)
True Story 107 2 (1m 2f 7y, Wind, Gd, Aug 23)
Tullius (IRE) 92 2 (1m, Newb, GF, May 17)
Two For Two (IRE) 89 1 (1m, Ayr, GF, Jun 21)
Undrafted (USA) 98 4 (6f, Newj, GS, Jul 12)
Vanity Rules 95 3 (1m 4f, Newm, Gd, Sep 26)
Vastonea (IRE) 89 4 (1m 2f 150y, Dunw, SD, Aug 17)
Vent De Force 92 1 (1m 6f, York, Gd, Aug 23)
Venus De Milo (IRE) 94 1 (1m 4f, Cork, GF, Jun 15)

Verrazano (USA) 91 2 (1m, Asco, Gd, Jun 17)
Viewpoint (IRE) 95 1 (1m 4f, Linw, SD, Apr 18)
Vintage Nouveau (IRE) 93 1 (1m 4f, List, Gd, Sep 17)
Vital Evidence (USA) 89 2 (1m 2f 7y, Sand, GF, Jul 4)
Viva Verglas (IRE) 88 2 (5f 16y, Ches, Sft, May 9)
Volume 91 3 (1m 4f 10y, Epso, Gd, Jun 6)
Wadi Al Hattawi (IRE) 93 1 (1m 4f, York, GS, May 31)
Wahgah (USA) 89 3 (1m 2f, Newm, Gd, Oct 11)
Waila 97 2 (1m 4f 8y, Pont, Gd, Jun 22)
Wannabe Better (IRE) 96 1 (7f, Leop, GF, Jun 19)
Wannabe Yours (IRE) 107 1 (1m, Good, GF, Aug 1)
War Command (USA) 91 7 (1m 2f 7y, Sand, GF, Jul 5)
Watchable 88 4 (6f, Ripo, Hvy, Jun 4)
Wee Jean 91 1 (7f, Good, Sft, May 24)
Western Hymn 108 4 (1m 2f, Asco, Hvy, Oct 18)
What About Carlo (FR) 92 1 (1m 2f 18y, Epso, Gd, Jun 7)
Whiplash Willie 88 2 (2m 2f, Donc, GS, Sep 12)
Whispering Warrior (IRE) 88 3 (1m 1f 198y, Sali, Gd, Oct 1)
Willbeme 89 1 (6f, York, Gd, Jun 13)
Willing Foe (USA) 102 2 (1m 5f 61y, Newb, GS, Aug 16)
Wind Fire (USA) 92 1 (5f 6y, Sand, Gd, Jun 14)
Windfast (IRE) 90 4 (1m, Good, GF, Aug 1)
Windhoek 98 3 (1m 2f 88y, York, GF, Jul 26)
Windshear 104 2 (1m 4f, Good, GF, Jul 30)
Winter Thunder 88 1 (1m 2f, Newj, GF, Jul 19)
Won Diamond 89 5 (1m 4f, Naas, Yld, Oct 19)
Wrangler 88 1 (1m 4f, Sali, Sft, May 4)
Yeeoow (IRE) 93 2 (6f, Newm, GF, May 4)
Zalty (FR) 89 4 (6f, York, GF, Jul 26)
Zambucca (SAF) 88 5 (1m 2f 88y, York, GF, Jul 26)
Zarwaan 97 5 (1m, Asco, GF, Jun 19)
Zurigha (IRE) 94 3 (1m, Asco, Gd, Jul 25)

INDEX OF HORSES

Abbey Angel 21-22
Ablan 96
Able Friend 100
Absolutely So 6-7
Aces 108
Acolyte 98
Adelaide 108
Adventure Seeker 108
Aerovelocity 100, 104
Aetna 108
African Story 28
Agent Murphy 98
Agnes Stewart 76, 77, 108-109, 129, 136
Ainippe 109
Air Pilot 109
Akeed Champion 18
Aktabantay 109, 122
Al Kazeem 86, 109-110
Al Naamah 106
Al Saham 49
Al Thakhira 14
Alben Star 20
Alea Iacta 106, 110
Alex My Boy 47
Alfajer 12-13
Aljamaaheer 70, 110
All About Time 136
Almela 96
Aloft 110
Alonsoa 110
Alpha Bravo 106
Angel Gabrial 20, 24
Ansgar 110
Anthem Alexander 95, 106, 110
Arab Spring 110-112
Arabian Queen 112
Arcano Gold 22
Arod 112
Astaire 62, 112
Astrelle 13, 15
Avenir Certain 106, 112-113
Baccarat 24
Baitha Alga 41
Bajan 70
Balducci 56
Ballymore Castle 18-20
Baltic Comtesse 106
Bartel 92
Basateen 41
Battersea 70, 113
Beautiful Romance 28, 113
Belardo 68, 69, 72, 113, 131
Berkshire 113-114, 137
Best Of Times 27, 85
Biographer 79, 114
Blaine 62, 67

Blue Wave 50
Bocca Baciata 98
Bogart 64
Bond's Girl 24
Bookrunner 107
Bow Creek 47
Brazen Beau 100
Breton Rock 114
Bronze Angel 114
Brooch 114
Cable Bay 14, 114
California Chrome 100, 101
Calypso Beat 62
Cambridge 114
Cannock Chase 114-115, 137
Cape Peron 115
Cappella Sansevero 115
Captain Cat 115
Captain Colby 64
Captain Joy 115
Celestial Path 115
Charlie Croker 64
Charm Spirit 138
Charming Thought 26, 64, 115-117
Chesil Beach 7
Christophermarlowe 34, 80, 117
Cirrus Des Aigles 117
Clariden 105
Clever Cookie 118
Commemorative 118
Connecticut 118
Consort 118
Convey 98, 119
Cosmic Statesman 140
Cotai Glory 119, 132
Cougar Mountain 119
Coulsty 42
Cursory Glance 68, 69, 72, 119
Custom Cut 54, 59, 60, 120
Dance Of Fire 5
Danzeno 92, 94, 120, 132
De Rigueur 17
Deep Field 101
Dick Whittington 120, 142
Dissident 102
Dolniya 107, 120
Dominant 94
Dubday 102-103
Due Diligence 120
Duke Of Clarence 20-21
Dutch Connection 32, 79, 120, 123
Eagle Top 34-36, 120-121
Earth Drummer 55-56
Easter 121
Eastern Impact 20

Ectot 121
Eesha 107
Elite Gardens 28, 94
Elm Park 4, 9, 63, 92, 98, 110, 121, 137
Endless Drama 121
Entitling 137
Epicuris 105, 121
Epiphaneia 104
Ervedya 78, 107
Es Que Love 94
Esoterique 121-122
Estidhkaar 40, 109, 122
Eton Forever 70
Euro Charline 11, 122
Excilly 96
Extortionist 122
Fadhayyil 122-123
Fanciful Angel 14
Fannaan 32, 92-93, 123
Farham 98
Farraaj 70
Fascinating Rock 123
Fast Act 63
Faufiler 107
Faydhan 32, 33, 79, 123
Festive Fare 27
Fintry 106, 123
Fire Fighting 48-49
Flaming Spear 62, 96, 124, 156
Flashy Memories 22, 154
Flight Officer 110
Flintshire 105-106, 124
Flying Officer 124
Fontanelice 105
Forever Now 36, 124
Forgotten Rules 77, 79, 114, 124, 125
Found 76, 78, 81, 84, 107, 125, 129
Free Eagle 77, 125
Frontier Fighter 57
Full Mast 105, 106, 125, 147
Future Empire 27
G Force 54, 59, 80, 126
Gabrial 18
Gabrial's Kaka 18, 19
Gentildonna 104
Geoffrey Chaucer 126
Giovanni Canaletto 75, 78, 126
Gleneagles 75-76, 105, 106, 120, 125, 126, 154
Glory Awaits 62
Gm Hopkins 126
Golden Horn 32, 126
Golden Spun 129
Gold-Fun 102, 103-104

Gordon Lord Byron 77, 80, 127
Gospel Choir 127
Greatest Hits 93
Hail The Hero 57
Hamza 67
Hartnell 47
Havana Beat 6
Hawkesbury 92-93
Heaven's Guest 22, 24
Heavy Metal 47
Here Comes When
 6, 93, 114, 127
High Celebrity 95, 106, 112,
 127-128
High Jinx 128
Highland Acclaim 57
Highland Reel 75, 93, 128
Hillstar 128
Home Cummins 21
Hootenanny 104, 107
Hors De Combat 128
Hot Streak 61, 62, 67, 128
Integral 122, 128-129, 141
Intrinsic 129
Ivawood 40, 64, 117, 129
Jack Hobbs 34
Jack Naylor 129
Jamaica 129
Jellicle Ball 34, 129
John F Kennedy 74, 93, 129
Johnny Barnes 34
Just The Judge 129-130
Justice Day 130
Justice Good 130
Justineo 70, 71
Karakontie 107, 121, 130
Kingston Hill 68, 72, 130, 142
Kiyoshi 130-131
Kodi Bear 68, 131
Kool Company 41, 131
Lacing 18, 21
Lady Correspondent 34, 131
Lady Dutch 12
Lap Of Luxury 34, 96
Latharnach 28, 131
Legend's Gate 29
Lesha 64
Lexington Abbey 64
Liberty Sky 21
Light Breaks 120
Lightning Moon 92, 132
Lightning Thunder 132
Likely 96
Limato 132
Local Time 13, 27
Louis The Pious 54, 59, 132-133
Lucida 76, 77, 122, 133, 137, 141

Luck Of The Kitten 104
Lucky Kristale 133
Lyn Valley 50
Maarek 133
Madame Chiang 133
Made In Rio 48
Maftool 27
Main Sequence 106
Make Believe 106
Malabar 78
Malabar 133
Manatee 106
Marsh Hawk 40, 133, 137
Marzocco 133-134
Master Apprentice 5
Mattmu 96
Maverick Wave 50
Mcguigan 96-97
Mecca's Angel 134
Mexican Gold 106
Migwar 107
Miss France 122, 134
Mister Universe 47-48
Mistrusting 28
Moheet 41, 97, 135
Montaly 7
Moohaarib 12
Mount Athos 136
Mount Logan 136
Move In Time 55, 59, 136
Moviesta 136
Muatadel 50
Muhaarar 136
Muraaqaba 47, 136
Music Master 136-137
Mustajeeb 137
Mutakayyef 137
Muthmir 64, 93, 99, 137
Muwaary 36, 137
My Fairy 97
Mymatechris 7
Naadirr 11-12, 137
Nabatean 7
Nafaqa 137
New Agenda 97
New Providence 137
New Story 99
Night Generation 88
Night Of Thunder 42, 43, 44, 138
Ninjago 42-43
Noble Mission 86
Nucifera 105, 107
Ol' Man River 75, 84, 93, 138
One And Only 104
Onesie 14
Online Alexander 63, 67
Order Of St George 138, 140

Oriental Fox 49-50
Osaila 40-41, 138
Out Do 55
Outlaw Country 26
Outstanding 97
Pallasator 124, 139
Pallister 50
Panama Hat 139
Parish Boy 138, 140
Pathway To Honour 93
Pearl Secret 140
Pelerin 12
Penitent 56, 57
Pether's Moon 42, 140
Pinzolo 29
Pique Sous 140
Pleascach 140
Ponfeigh 103
Postponed 116, 140
Prince Bishop 28
Provenance 140-141
Puissant 13, 99
Queen Nefertiti 141
Rafaadah 106
Rainbow Pride 99
Rare Rhythm 28
Raydara 76, 141, 156
Reckless Abandon 141
Remote 141
Ribbons 141
Richard Pankhurst
 32, 38, 141-142
Risen Sun 28
Rizeena 142
Robert The Painter 56
Rocky Rider 4
Romsdal 36, 142
Royal Razalma 142
Safety Check 28
Salateen 63
Salutation 47
Sandiva 24
Scotland 6
Second Step 142-143
Secret Brief 26, 47, 52
Secret Gesture 97, 143
Sennockian Star 49
Sheikhzayedroad 143
Shifting Power 42, 143
Side Glance 5
Sir Isaac Newton
 97, 143-144, 157
Sirdaab 99
Sky Hunter 144
Smaih 41
Smuggler's Cove 144
Snow Sky 144

INDEX OF HORSES

Sole Power	77, 144-145	Telmeyd	147	Treve	68, 105, 117, 124, 153
Solow	145	Tendu	147	Tropics	153
Soluble	13	Territories	106, 147	Tullius	5, 154
Spielberg	104	Terror	87, 95	Two For Two	56-57
Spirit Of The Law	18	Teruntum Star	63-64	Vedouma	106
Star Of Seville	34, 38, 145	That Is The Spirit	54-55	Vent De Force	154
Stars And Clouds	97, 107	The Corsican	147	Vert De Grece	69, 72, 154
Stepper Point	145	The Grey Gatsby		Very Special	28
Steps	70		61, 62, 65, 67, 77, 148, 150	Wannabe Yours	36, 156
Stoked	93-94	The Wow Signal	104, 107, 150	War Dispatch	105, 106
Stomachion	145-146	Thistle Bird	84	Weld Al Emarat	64
Strath Burn	146	Tiger Jim	99	Western Hymn	36, 156
Sudden Wonder	28	Tiggy Wiggy	40, 44, 80, 81, 95,	Whiplash Willie	156
Suegioo	17		106, 110, 119, 151	Windshear	43, 156
Sympathy	94, 146-147	Tigrilla	70	Winter Thunder	156
Tac De Boistron	11, 17, 147	Toe The Line	99	Winters Moon	27, 156
Tachophobia	22	Together Forever	77, 78, 151	Words	76-77, 78, 84, 156-157
Take Cover	147	Too The Stars	75	Wrangler	94
Talawat	13-14	Toocoolforschool	152	Ya Hade Ye Delil	42
Tale Of Life	107	Toofi	70	Yuften	157
Tapestry	75	Toormore	42, 152	Zalty	99
Telescope	147	Toujours L'Amour	95	Zawraq	97, 143, 157